# Demystifying the Institutional Repository for Success

## CHANDOS
### INFORMATION PROFESSIONAL SERIES

Series Editor: Ruth Rikowski
(Email: Rikowskigr@aol.com)

Chandos' new series of books is aimed at the busy information professional. They have been specially commissioned to provide the reader with an authoritative view of current thinking. They are designed to provide easy-to-read and (most importantly) practical coverage of topics that are of interest to librarians and other information professionals. If you would like a full listing of current and forthcoming titles, please visit www.chandospublishing.com or email wp@woodheadpublishing.com or telephone +44(0) 1223 499140.

**New authors:** we are always pleased to receive ideas for new titles; if you would like to write a book for Chandos, please contact Dr Glyn Jones on gjones@chandospublishing.com or telephone +44 (0) 1993 848726.

**Bulk orders:** some organisations buy a number of copies of our books. If you are interested in doing this, we would be pleased to discuss a discount. Please email wp@woodheadpublishing.com or telephone +44 (0) 1223 499140.

# Demystifying the Institutional Repository for Success

MARIANNE A. BUEHLER

CHANDOS
PUBLISHING

Oxford  Cambridge  New Delhi

Chandos Publishing
Hexagon House
Avenue 4
Station Lane
Witney
Oxford OX28 4BN
UK
Tel: +44 (0) 1993 848726
Email: info@chandospublishing.com
www.chandospublishing.com
www.chandospublishingonline.com

Chandos Publishing is an imprint of Woodhead Publishing Limited

Woodhead Publishing Limited
80 High Street
Sawston
Cambridge CB22 3HJ
UK
Tel: +44 (0) 1223 499140
Fax: +44 (0) 1223 832819
www.woodheadpublishing.com

---

First published in 2013

ISBN: 978-1-84334-673-9 (print)
ISBN: 978-1-78063-321-3 (online)

Chandos Information Professional Series ISSN: 2052-210X (print) and ISSN: 2052-2118 (online)

© M.A. Buehler, 2013

Typeset by Domex e-Data Pvt. Ltd., India.

Transferred to Digital Printing in 2013

"The future is here. It's just not evenly distributed yet" – William Gibson

# Contents

# List of figures and tables

## Figures

## Tables

# Preface

My commitment to open access research began in 2002 as I engaged librarians, faculty, and administrators in a new mode of scholarly communication. The continuing journey embraces new technologies that allow scientists, scholars, students, and citizens to have available research. I aspire for readers to whet their appetite for findable intellectual inquiry and be able to use the materials they seek. This monograph provides multiple resources for open access opportunities and tools that enhance the research experience.

By recognizing the benefits and importance of open access to research, readers will naturally gravitate towards the scholarly works they want and need. This monograph's purpose is to convey a new direction and expanding scope with maps that will guide the reader to navigate to necessary content. Authors who seek to make their research globally available will also find guidance in how to achieve that goal.

This monograph was also written for novice and experienced librarians wanting to accelerate open access to research in their academic libraries or for their own scholarship. I hope academy librarians interested in the open milieu will find the guidance of this publication useful.

# Introduction

To create a short historical context of research availability and associated copyright issues in the past two decades, I have chronicled a few of my own experiences as a student, professional staff, academic faculty, and author to illustrate progress in how reader and researcher opportunities have evolved. As a global community, many of us are advancing open research for the greater good of its impact.

As a late bloomer undergraduate in the 1990s, it was commonplace to utilize paper indices and spend precious time perusing summaries that had a possibility of interest for a current research project – how was one to know by reading a citation and/or an abstract if the content was exactly right for an assignment? In its infancy, the Internet had few educational resources; search engines as we know them today were non-existent. On a distributed campus, scholarly articles and books had to be requested from the main library. The articles would arrive in the campus office a week to two weeks later – I unquestionably had to plan ahead and request a few extra articles for a "research cushion."

Barely two months after graduation and having resigned from my public library directorship, I started classes at the University of Arizona's (UA) School of Information Resources and Library Science. As a major research university with multiple libraries, there were few electronic research databases and a multitude of bound and current journals to be perused.

As a UA teaching assistant to the Dean of Libraries, Carla Stoffle, I was asked to create a course reserves system for journal articles to be easily accessed online by students in a particular course. At the time, this was a revolutionary concept in academia; some publishers still balk over reserve access to "their research." Publishers continue to sue academic libraries for ostensible copyright infringement to prevent students from accessing research that libraries have already paid for.

Paper journals allowed for shelf perusal, a time-consuming task. Once a student located appropriate articles, the university printing center was glad to make copies for a fee – a great time-saver. However, if there were more than two articles earmarked for copying from one journal issue, the student had to choose which two would be printed. It turns out that publisher/library copyright agreements prohibited the libraries' photocopy service to duplicate more than two articles per issue unless the reader personally photocopied the articles. Students made the time to run the copy machine, but the publisher policies did not make sense while navigating the rampant impediments to research engagement.

In the late 1990s, employed at Rochester Institute of Technology as the Library Coordinator for Online Learning, I was responsible for assisting global learners in locating necessary research. Online research databases were still in their infancy and many could only be used on campus – off-campus use and use outside of the United States was not always permitted. Following negotiations, online students eventually had equal access to research, to keep pace with their on-campus student counterparts.

Fast-forward to the early years of the twenty-first century when open access to scholarly materials was narrowly embraced in academia. A continuous increase in research periodical pricing had been brewing since the mid-1980s; libraries were serious about creating change. The University of Southampton and Massachusetts Institute of Technology were the early adopters of the "open access to research matters" concept. Each constructed open source repository software, respectively EPrints and DSpace, to archive research articles destined for global availability. Early adopters deposited articles or postprints (papers approved by peer-review) to commence filling a gap of scholarship otherwise unavailable to academic libraries, due to declining collection development funds and rising journal costs.

Three influential global research organizations and their representative stakeholders – collectively referred to here as the 3 Bs – met over a two-year period (2002–3), creating milestone statements of intent for open access to research as a common good. The Open Society Institute convened the Budapest Open Access Initiative (*http://www.soros.org/openaccess*) by launching a global campaign for all new peer-reviewed literature to be open access. It was the first approach to: articulate a public definition; suggest complementary strategies for recognizing open access as a venue; broadly define and call for open access to research in all disciplines and countries; and be the first to have the benefit of significant funding. Following the Budapest example, attendees at the Maryland-based Howard Hughes Medical Institute's meeting gathered to discuss deliverable open access actions to scholarly biomedical research, represented by the Bethesda Statement on Open Access Publishing (*http://dash.harvard.edu/handle/1/4725199*). Both the Bethesda Statement and the Berlin Declaration on Open Access to Knowledge in the Sciences and Humanities asserted that open access contributions must fulfill two stipulations: the author or other rights holder shall grant open access rights to the full version of the work and all supplemental materials, and secondly, include a statement of permission to use (*http://www.zim.mpg.de/openaccess-berlin/berlin_ declaration.pdf*).

In 2002, the Rochester Institute of Technology Libraries initially embarked on an institutional repository by conducting a faculty survey to determine their archiving needs/wants, moving forward in 2003 to create the actual tool. A few staff-led teams focused on the readers, depositors, and marketing. The idealistic possibility of creating access to the world's research with an Internet connection was an exciting proposition, worthy of pursuing.

As quickly became evident, a culture shift needed to take place by optimally garnering a faculty research deposit mandate by embracing open access concepts that would carry inherent benefits on a global scale. The initial psychological challenge for many librarians was to comprehend why the cultural acceptance of open reseach was slow on the uptake, especially when many academy library staff embraced the notion of providing a suite of repository services that included locating faculty research, checking copyright, making article deposits, and adding rich metadata for search engine findability.

The positive news is over the past two plus years while occupied with this monograph, it has been a challenge to stay apprised of and capture the nascent and evolving scholarly communication developments that include data management, discovery, social media tools, university press/library collaborations, legislation focused on open access publisher and author research content, and many other opportunities.

Inspiring new developments have emanated from publisher philanthropy. In response to the 2011 earthquake and tsunami disasters in Japan, resulting in nuclear reactor fallout, publisher Thomson Reuters pledged humanitarian aid in the form of evidence-based clinical and patient-focused research and information that encompassed the assessment and subsequent treatment of radiation exposure (*http://www.reuters.com/ article/2011/03/18/idUS234004+18-Mar-2011+HUG20110318*).

ProQuest®'s new Summon™ service supports the United Nations' Research4Life program in conjunction with the World Health Organization. Summon™, a new web scale discovery service, will assist researchers at no charge in some of the world's most disadvantaged countries by offering more than 8,100 peer-reviewed international scientific journals, books, and databases. In addition, many librarians on staff have volunteered their time to construct new Summon™ sites.

Engaging in a more recent sustainable open access model, some publishers have migrated towards the open gold journal model that requires paying an article processing charge (APC), such as Sage Open (see *http://sgo.sagepub.com/*) and Springer's BioMed Central (see *http://www.biomedcentral.com/*); the key to author and reader success is a reasonable cost factor. These articles will be published under an open access license agreement: the Creative Commons CC BY attribution license (see *http://creativecommons.org/licenses/*). New open models are directing research in new and creative venues. Conventional wisdom tells us it is likely a matter of time before open access to research is pervasive and alternative and affordable fee-based publishing models are the norm. Open actions exist in many directions and spheres; we must push back and forward, working with those who value high profits over the public good and have the impudence to undermine open access to taxpayer-funded research.

The plethora of open access scholarly materials available in the twenty-first century is impressive when considering the situation ten years ago. With too many to list, committed individuals include librarians, faculty, scientists, scholars, students, and multiple global scholarly communication organizations, focused on setting information free and unwaveringly passionate and dedicated to open research. The efforts are made – because it matters.

# Acknowledgements

As I reflect upon the research, intense writing, and editing taking close to two years plus, I think of the familiar people I know and others I have become acquainted with who have proffered support and endeavored to understand the thesis of my topic.

I offer my sincere appreciation to the University of Nevada Las Vegas Libraries for their support and gift of time to write and edit. Library colleagues and friends provided sustaining encouragement that was much appreciated. My library gratitude would not be complete without a special thank you to Chandra McKenzie at Rochester Institute of Technology, who set me firmly on the path to the notion of open access to research and all that it entails.

I am blessed to have supportive family: my parents, brother, and my two sons, and friends both near and far, who always asked when the monograph would be completed and also understood why they had not heard from me.

Writing a cohesive manuscript on a topic that evolves on a weekly basis is a challenge. In consulting source material, I have noted the validity of the information by date. At some point, the book needs to be considered complete and subsequently published. My editors agree. Sincere thanks are extended to Jonathan Davis, Chandos' Commissioning Editor (at the time) who encouraged me to submit a book proposal; George Knott, Editor (at the time), who engaged me in a number of collaborative cover design options; Peter Williams, Manuscript Editor, who finds necessary edits; Ed Gibbons, a reassuring Production Editor; and my publisher, Dr. Glyn Jones, for commissioning me to publish with Chandos.

# List of abbreviations

| | |
|---|---|
| AASHE | Association for the Advancement of Sustainability in Higher Education |
| AAU | Association of American Universities |
| ACGS | American Council of Graduate Schools |
| ACRL | Association of College and Research Libraries |
| ACS | American Chemical Society |
| ALA | American Library Association |
| ALCTS | Association for Library Collections and Technical Services |
| ANU | Australian National University |
| ARC | Australian Research Council |
| ARL | Association of Research Libraries |
| AsiaJOL | Asian Journals Online |
| AWS | Amazon Web Services |
| BDTD | Biblioteca Digital de Teses e Dissertações |
| BSC | Balanced Scorecard |
| *C&RL* | *College & Research Libraries* |
| CARL | Canadian Association of Research Libraries |
| CERN | European Organization for Nuclear Research |
| CIHR | Canadian Institutes of Health Research |
| CNI | Coalition of Networked Information |
| COAPI | Coalition of Open Access Policy Institutions |
| CRO | CSU Research Output |

| | |
|---|---|
| CSIC | Consejo Superior de Investigaciones Científicas |
| CSU | Charles Sturt University (Australia) |
| CUNY | City University of New York |
| CV | curriculum vitae |
| DASH | Digital Access to Scholarship at Harvard |
| DC | Digital Commons |
| dLIST | Digital Library of Information Sciences |
| DMP | Data Management Plan |
| DOAJ | Directory of Open Access Journals |
| DOE | Department of Energy |
| DRU | doctoral/research universities |
| EAD | encoded archival description |
| EBSCO | Academic eBook Subscriptions |
| ECS | (School of) Electronics and Computer Science (Southampton) |
| EIFL | Electronic Information for Libraries |
| E-LIS | E-prints in Library and Information Science |
| ERA | Excellence in Research for Australia |
| ERIC | Education Resources Information Center |
| ETD | electronic theses and dissertations |
| FAST | Faceted Application of Subject Terminology |
| FASTR | Fair Access to Science and Technology Research |
| FIPSE | Fund for the Improvement of Postsecondary Education |
| FRPAA | Federal Research Public Access Act |
| FTE | full-time equivalent |
| FTP | file transfer protocol |
| GSLIS | Graduate School of Library and Information Science (Simmons College) |
| GWLA | Greater Western Library Alliance |
| HEP | high-energy physics |

| | |
|---|---|
| HP | Hewlett-Packard |
| ICAR | Indian Council of Agricultural Research |
| ICOLC | International Coalition of Library Consortia |
| IES | Institute of Education Sciences |
| IET | Institution of Engineering and Technology |
| ILL | interlibrary loan |
| ILR | (School of) Industrial and Labour Relations (Cornell University) |
| IMLS | Institute of Museum and Library Services |
| INASP | International Network for the Availability of Scientific Publications |
| IR | institutional repository |
| ISI | Institute for Scientific Information |
| ISO | International Organization for Standardization |
| ITS | Institute of Transportation Studies |
| JCR | journal citation report |
| JDF | journal download factor |
| JIF | Journal Impact Factor |
| JISC | Joint Information Systems Committee |
| JUF | journal usage factor |
| KU | University of Kansas |
| LC | Library of Congress |
| LCSH | Library of Congress Subject Headings |
| LOCKSS | "lots of copies keep stuff safe" |
| MIT | Massachusetts Institute of Technology |
| NARS | National Agricultural Research System (India) |
| NCAR | National Center for Atmospheric Research |
| NCSU | North Carolina State University |
| NDLTD | Networked Digital Library of Theses and Dissertations |
| NEH | National Endowment for the Humanities |

| | |
|---|---|
| NGO | non-governmental organization |
| NIH | National Institutes of Health |
| NSF | National Science Foundation |
| OA | open access |
| OAI | Open Archives Initiative |
| OAI-PMH | Open Archives Initiative Protocol for Metadata Harvesting |
| OAPEN | Open Access Publishing in European Networks |
| *OASIS* | *Open Access Scholarly Information Sourcebook* |
| OATP | Open Access Textbook Project |
| OCLC | Online Computer Library Center |
| OCR | optical character recognition |
| OCS | Open Conference Systems |
| OERs | open educational resources |
| OJS | Open Journal Systems |
| OPAC | online public access catalog |
| OpenAIREplus | Open Access Infrastructure for Research in Europe |
| *Open*DOAR | Open Directory of Open Access Repositories |
| ORBi | Open Repository and Bibliography (University of Liège) |
| ORCID | Open Researcher and Contributor ID |
| OSI | Open Society Institute |
| OSTP | Office of Science and Technology Policy |
| OSU | Oregon State University |
| PDF | portable document format |
| PKP | Public Knowledge Project |
| PLoS | Public Library of Science |
| PMH | protocols for meta-harvesting |
| PROL | Political Research Online |
| RePEc | Research Papers in Economics |
| RIT | Rochester Institute of Technology |

| | |
|---|---|
| ROAR | Registry of Open Access Repositories |
| ROARMAP | Registry of Open Access Repositories Mandatory Archiving Policies |
| RU/H | university with high research activity |
| RU/VH | university with very high research activity |
| SCOAP[3] | Sponsoring Consortium for Open Access Publishing in Particle Physics |
| SEO | search engine optimization |
| SMU | Singapore Management University |
| SOAP | Study of Open Access Project |
| SPARC | Scholarly Publishing and Academic Resources Coalition |
| SPR | Scholarly Publications Repository |
| SSRN | Social Science Research Network |
| STARS | Sustainability Tracking Assessment and Rating System™ |
| STEM | science, technology, engineering, and mathematics |
| STM | science, technology, and medicine |
| SUNY | State University of New York |
| UA | University of Arizona |
| UCAR | University Corporation for Atmospheric Research |
| UM | University of Michigan |
| UMB | University of Maryland, Baltimore |
| UNESCO | United Nations Educational, Scientific and Cultural Organization |
| UNL | University of Nebraska – Lincoln |
| UNLV | University of Nevada, Las Vegas |
| UoM | University of Minnesota |
| UR | University of Rochester |
| URL | uniform resource locator |
| USF | University of South Florida |
| WWDL | Western Waters Digital Library |

# About the author

Marianne A. Buehler has over 25 years of diverse public and academic library expertise as a public library director on the Maine Coast, the Library Coordinator for Online Learning, and manager of the Publishing & Scholarship Support Center and the RIT Digital Media Library at Rochester Institute of Technology. Each position has offered new skills and knowledge, shaped and built upon the other. Currently at the University of Nevada Las Vegas (UNLV) Libraries, she engages in multiple aspects of scholarly communication and oversees the Digital Scholarship@UNLV as the Institutional Repository Administrator.

The author's published research, presentations, and seminars holistically have focused on fundamental contributions to the open access milieu, such as the open scholarly communication process, supporting open access journals, value-added repository services, and other topics integral to meeting the interests of campaigning for social equity to research.

Over the past eleven years, the author has given presentations and published on various aspects related to scholarly communication.

The author may be contacted via the publishers.

# Transcending traditional scholarly communication to open access publishing: why the change?

**Abstract.** Chapter 1 provides an overview of various scholarly communication motivations that interconnect with the traditional peer-review process, as unprecedented amounts of academic research development and tools have proliferated. Open peer-review is shifting the traditional paradigm towards a more engaged model that affects conventional and evolving publishing models. Simultaneously, academic libraries are migrating towards a more sustainable scholarly communication process that encompasses the benefits of utilizing institutional repositories and open access tools, highlighting the academy's scholarship. Concurrently, the recent global economic downturn and the inherent serials situation remain affected. US and UK Government legislation is also focused on open access to research as evolving publishing models continue to remain on the academic radar.

**Keywords:** academic libraries, global economic crisis, open access timeline, open peer-review, Research Councils UK, scholarly communication, serials crisis, sustainable access to research, technical services, traditional peer-review, UNESCO, UK Government legislation, US Government legislation

When a familiar and ingrained process experiences a sea change, there is an incentive to scrutinize and reconsider current practices and consider new methods that have potential for more efficiency and supportive documentation for the new model. Evolving scholarly communication practices that manifest open access (OA) to research have been on the academic radar for a full decade plus, altering publishing norms and admittance to research that typically had toll access to journal subscriptions. The classic peer-review process, a traditional component of the manuscript's review foundation, is also experiencing the tremors of transformation in multiple ways.

# Scholarly communication

Using a conventional definition, the term scholarly communication is the activity of researchers who engage in academic research by creating, disseminating, and preserving new knowledge. It encompasses the foundation of a peer-review process and uses a method that ensures information in an academic publication is verifiable and of high quality. If for any reason a research article is later found to be defective, flawed, or contains some type of fraud, the viability of all the original and future research that is built upon the findings may be brought into question.

It is useful to understand the scholarly communication process to fully grasp the carefully crafted traditional review methods that ensure research verity and value. Authors, editors, and referees associated within the review process depend on the veracity and knowledge of those involved. No system is without its failings. New technologies, such as an open access institutional or subject repository, have the ability by the nature of their findability to promote and showcase the carefully tended research and peer-review process that culminates in a scholarly product as found in the journal article. For the researchers who benefit from open access scholarly articles, it is imperative to know on which journal's review process the research was accepted and published. The accuracy and credibility of the review process is essential, especially critical in any misunderstandings that could and do circulate in higher education regarding born-digital gold journals or hybrid open access journals (with open and toll access articles) and their peer-review practices.

In the research process, a scientist or scholar completes a systematic review and investigative study of recent and retrospective research of materials that are synthesized into new hypotheses and unique connections that add value to the current scholarly literature. The creation of a new paper is a point in the process where new discoveries and research revelations may have been made and will require peer-review vetting as a next step in the verification. The work may be accepted as written, considered for publication with author revisions, or rejected. Authors may have the option to rewrite or use a copyeditor for stylistic or second-language changes to achieve the requisite academic quality.

# Peer-review

The scholarly peer-review system, also known as refereeing, is a traditional and accepted practice (since the seventeenth century) by which an author's scholarly work, new ideas, and resulting research are subjected to the critical examination of experts in equivalent fields before a paper is published and available in a journal publication or as a postprint (paper approved by peer-review) archived in an institutional repository (IR). Optimally, authors should meet the accepted standards of their discipline. Unwarranted research claims, irrelevant conclusions, objectionable interpretations, and personal viewpoints cannot and should not be included by an author in an effective peer-review system. The existing scholarly communication structure is a framework that is not perfect but can be made more efficient with competent peer-review processes in place that encompass a community of subject experts.

For each discipline in the editorial process, a variation on a theme may be used for the naming convention of the individuals managing a journal. The reader is advised to keep this in mind when considering the names of the various editorial positions used in this chapter. From an editor's point of view, it is essential for authors to pay close attention to the technical details and/or formatting requirements that are specific to each journal publication and are similar within each subject area. An author's paper version prior to peer-review is typically called a preprint, and is emailed to the managing editor. A good practice is to contact an editor in advance to confirm the synchronicity of subject area(s) in a particular journal. The journal's managing editor, sometimes paid a small fee to carry out the duties required of the editorial process, is the gatekeeper who briefly reviews the submitted paper to ascertain if it meets the goals of the journal and the quality of writing required. The managing editor strives to recruit an editorial board with subject knowledge that matches the interests and depth of the journal. Submitted papers are characteristically sent by the managing editor to at least two and up to four peer-reviewers who are experts in the field, as the paper's topic should be dependent on the particular academic disciplines covered by the journal.

The peer-reviewer or referee position is defined in guidelines related to their expertise and professional conventions. These parameters may be used for either a traditional or an open peer-review; proficiency in a specific or tangential interdisciplinary field is necessary for article reviewing knowledge. Confidentiality is essential, as referees are reviewing unpublished research. Preprint content should not be disclosed or shared unless approved by the editor. In the case of a conflict of interest, such as receiving a colleague's or an intellectual adversary's paper, the guiding sense is that it should be given to neutral reviewers. A preprint paper must be judged only by its intellectual virtues. Critical or disapproving verdicts should be supported by detailed evidence from the paper itself or other pertinent research sources. Google searches and the use of a plagiarism-detection tool such as Turnitin (*http://turnitin.com/static/index.php*) can be used if a copyright breach is suspected.

A published journal article archived in an open access venue, analogous to an institutional repository, and not properly vetted may be exposed more swiftly than a journal article that is confined behind a toll access subscription with less exposure. Costly journal subscriptions can limit a researcher's ability to read an article unless the academic library has a subscription or interlibrary loan is employed. By their inherent nature, some types of open access venues allow and encourage a global, transparent, social media peer-review system that exists because of the ease with which an article may be accessed through search engines such as Google. "Open scholarly communication is already being practiced, already making an impact, and the goal in the coming years will be to collaboratively find new ways to enhance, enrich, and implement new models of open peer-review" (Honn, 2011).

The scholarly review process may be double-blind, single-blind, or an open peer-review. Double-blind assists the reviewers in making fair judgments on the manuscript itself and can remove any personal bias, as both the reviewers' and authors' identities remain confidential. Single-blind is the peer-review procedure wherein the author is known and the peer-reviewer is not. A power shift in the peer-review process is underway to achieve a higher level of open review, encompassing internal aspects of the process, such as online technologies and ethics.

Peer-reviewers are typically not paid to analyze the content of the preprint (paper prior to peer-review) papers they review; their scrutiny counts as a valuable service contributing to their specific fields of knowledge and can be listed on their annual faculty evaluations. Reviewers normally focus on an editorial review that covers an assessment of content accuracy, whether publishing standards are met, the quality of writing, and if the paper is within the scope of the journal. The final acceptance decision rests with the publications editor(s).

The traditional peer-review process is currently confronted by a discordant and transparent open peer-review system, a safeguard against a potential abuse of secrecy that might occur. According to an *Inside Higher Ed* (Jaschik, 2011) article, some journals are revamping their scholarly communication processes, evolving into a more transparent progression of the traditional refereeing standard. The American Economic Association announced that it is ending its "double-blind" peer-review process. The Association's journals, which include the most significant findings in economics, are gravitating to a single-blind reviewing process where the author will not know who the reviewers are. The compelling reason for altering its peer-review system is to allow a reviewer or anyone else to employ a search engine to locate authors who publish specific research. Maintaining author anonymity is a facade that renders the double-blind process ineffective while journal administrative costs amplify. In addition, the economics discipline was criticized within their review process when a conflict of interest arose with referees that evaluated industries aligned with financial connections. Human nature may interfere when a choice is made to not follow set procedures that are in place to benefit all.

*Political Analysis*, a key journal in the field of political science, has also terminated its "double-blind" peer-review process. The journal did a test to determine if the authors of the twenty most recently submitted papers could be found in an online search. The majority of authors were discovered by their working papers and presentations posted on websites, including information about their respective research. With the accelerated use of the Internet for locating author scholarly content, in actual review practice there is no guaranteed double-blind (Jaschik, 2011).

# Open peer-review

The *Journal of Interactive Media in Education* (JIME) actuates an open review of its article submissions: "JIME's innovative review environment provides the opportunity to redesign the conventional journal review model to be more open, responsive and dynamic" (*http://jime.open.ac. uk/jime/about/submissions*). Reviewers' names are known and they are held accountable for their comments. Their contributions are acknowledged, giving credit to their effort and review analyses. Authors also have the right to respond to comments. Given the openness of the article evaluation, the wider research community has the opportunity to shape an article submission before its publication.

Diametrically different to the traditional peer-review process, JIME's three-part methodical procedure provides a thorough and ample opportunity for an open peer-review:

1. *Private open peer-review.* Submitted preprints are refereed by three reviewers, named and acknowledged for their review input. A private, secure site hosts the provided comments given in a conversational tone. Reviewers may post anonymously – though it is easier to

interpret their comments if one knows who the reviewers are. There is a set period of time for the three reviewers to respond.

2. *Publication as a preprint for public and open peer-review.* The preprint is made available for public open peer-review. Relevant communities are invited to participate once the editor, who has consulted with the submission reviewers, deems the submission of sufficient quality. The open review is available for one month. The editor summarizes noteworthy comments and concerns in the discussion area and stipulates necessary changes to be made by the author(s) before publication.

3. *Completing the publication process.* The most noteworthy review comments are published simultaneously with the postprint (paper approved by peer-review). Readers have the opportunity for insight into the reviewing issues, a productive building block for current and future discussions. In addition, authors may post links to their publications residing in an institutional repository, adding the value of permanent findability.

The article will be freely accessible on the JIME site, based on the open access principle that it will contribute to a "greater global exchange of knowledge" (JIME, 2011).

Integrating a determined amount of time into the initial three-person collaborative review process can alleviate the procrastination that is inherent in human nature. Editors are typically frustrated with a percentage of recalcitrant reviewers. Peer pressure to participate with a small set of colleagues may motivate timely involvement. In working collaboratively to generate and discuss a preprint's content, there is a greater opportunity for content insight, agreement, or divergent opinions.

In the second step of peer-review, the preprint undergoes global vetting that lasts a month – anyone may comment on the paper if a discussion account is created. In closing the open review, the editor summarizes and posts the significant issues on the discussion board the author is required to address for publication; it becomes public knowledge. The option for scholarly discourse is at the beginning of the review, not after the journal article is published.

At the third step, the editor continues to nurture the editorial process, compiling and revealing the list of significant issues that accompanies the postprint in its current state. Those who subscribed to the discussion will receive email alerts to new comments on the postprint's discussion forum. Papers reviewed using this examination method have a rapid publication timeline, as the editor and reviewers spend less time mired in the process.

As a sustainable process it takes less effort and time to create and open the peer-review process by utilizing an online discussion board. In the traditional review method, the journal editor emails the referees, sending multiple review reminders and communicating the results of the review, while the publishing decision is based on a small group of experts as opposed to a plethora of global subject authorities. The open review results are posted on a website and/or in a repository with no need for a print copy or being locked up behind a subscription fee or paywall.

The collaborative environment created by JIME's review procedure presents a scholarly transparency that dovetails nicely with an open access repository environment. Authors may also archive their articles in their academy's IR. The "open preprint review" progression suggests that open access principles have influenced and gained traction in scholarly publishing and the open peer-review of extended transparency in the research culture. "The fate of open peer-review cannot be left to traditional scholarly publishers, and needs to be nurtured at the grassroots level by scholars who have already embraced open scholarship" (Honn, 2011).

Successful open access to research and open source software products embodies the inherently attractive features of the scholarly enterprise, promoting a candid and direct scholarly communication process in the acceptance and dissemination of an article. Open peer-review engenders the accountability and credibility of reviewers.

The scholarly communication process is essential to promote research and publishing, allowing it to be globally discovered. A wealth of human expertise, knowledge, and time is invested in this time-honored academic research not to empower its maximum capacity by creating, sharing, disseminating, and showcasing in an open, unfettered environment for all to benefit. Open research has the capacity to be globally vetted by and accessible to all qualified researchers for their input.

Development of effective, user-centered, sustainable, and economically viable scholarly communication processes and a system that provides unrestrained access to quality intellectual content supports the mission of research institutions to access the very journal articles that researchers want for their erudite information needs.

# Academic libraries experience research cost inflation

Historically, since the mid-1980s, academic libraries have experienced escalating research subscription costs imposed by publishers, a primary impediment to libraries purchasing the scholarly content necessary for faculty and student research. Annual inflationary costs and economic downturn spikes that ensued have created a clash of interests between libraries and publishers, including the consolidation and control of the e-publishing interests of mega journal publishers, and the academic libraries' budget responses to the spiraling cost of journal and serial subscriptions. By 2003, journal prices had risen to four times more than inflation (see Figure 1.1). Libraries, at the core of purchasing scholarly

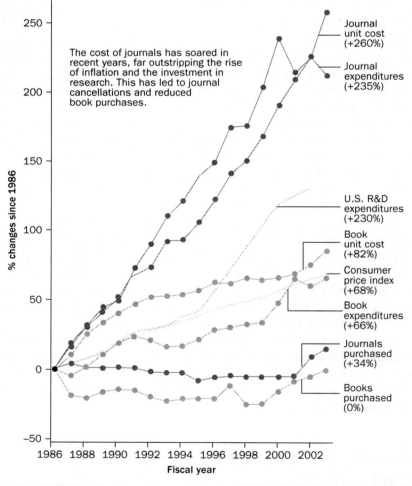

**Figure 1.1** Book and journal costs, 1986–2003 (North American research libraries)

*Source: http://www.arl.org/sparc/bm~pix/journal-price-graph~s600x600.jpg.*

and academic research primarily used by faculty and students, were at the mercy of a pricing crisis and were highly motivated to find solutions.

The average cost of chemistry and physics journals rose from $76.84 to an astounding $1,879.56 between 1975 and 2005. By spring 2008, the cost of purchasing access to scholarly journals was calculated to have multiplied 10 percent per year for the past thirty years, equaling six times the rate of inflation. An example that places journal licensing costs in perspective is to compare economic inflation to the price of a gallon of unleaded regular gasoline in that identical time period when the price escalated from $0.55 to $1.82. If that gallon of gasoline had increased at the same rate as chemistry and physics journals in the same time period, it would have cost the consumer $12.43 in 2005 and over $14.50 in 2008. Given subscription price increases, academic libraries continue to purchase scholarly content and have decreased their monograph purchasing to make up the difference (Lewis, 2008). What could libraries have done differently then and what can they do now in the face of such inflationary purchasing figures?

A more universal academic library consensus is that electronic journals are a more efficient delivery method for journal articles as opposed to the "on-the-shelf" reader access model. The ease of accessing research through personal computers and other electronic devices is far more efficient, as is using library spaces for other purposes than print journals, such as collaborative workspace. Online technologies allow libraries to continue purchasing e-journals as a more effective medium for its readers. Libraries continue to pay almost the same price for e-journals as compared with the increasingly expensive paper-publishing model (Lewis, 2008). The recent and more efficient Internet journal article access model has revolutionized information sharing, also allowing the delivery of journal articles through open access publishing models.

With the advent of the Internet's dilating scope of access in the mid–late 1990s, digital resource growth built over time and became a pervasive and practical online research presence as a ubiquitous and efficient tool for researchers using academic libraries. In the early twenty-first century, publishers realized as each year passed that producing print research was more expensive and time-consuming, as print publishing platforms in the world economy have continued to decline. Multiple publishers began the slow transformation to publishing journals in an electronic format.

Publishers' journals migrated to the online subscription format as costs continued to accelerate, as did the inflexible bundling of journals and oppressive licensing terms, resulting in a lack of access to research materials. The combined dynamics contributed to the Association of

Research Libraries' (ARL) deployment of SPARC (Scholarly Publishing and Academic Resources Coalition) in 1998. SPARC is active in creating and supporting emerging new scholarly communication models, such as institutional repositories (IRs) that are intended to increase the dissemination of scholarly research, reducing financial pressures over time.

Faced with exorbitant annual expenditures for publisher-produced research and scholarship over the past 25 years, libraries must take a stand on excessively high journal subscription pricing and efficiently manage their own institutions' research. Given the current (2008–present) critical academic financial climate that appears to be improving and the inherent complicated budgets that take in publishers' swingeing pricing models, the library community must align itself with a sustainable model that successfully serves faculty and student researchers in their quest for scholarly content.

In 2009, the ARL issued a statement appealing to journal publishers to focus their attention on the release of a public statement from the International Coalition of Library Consortia (ICOLC) to address the current global economic crisis and its effect on the library consortia that do business with publishers. The ARL used a collaborative context for encouraging publishers to recognize the economic constraints that libraries face given the pervasive economic financial downturn. These acute concerns affect not only research libraries; the greater library community also faces financial constraints to collection development.

Many public universities received far less funding in 2008 from stressed state allocations; endowment fund losses created the need to reduce staff and other operating costs, including materials' budgets that form the body of faculty and student intellectual content. Many ARL member libraries and other research institutions had to return a portion of their budget in the 2009/10 fiscal year, adding to the previous year of double-digit budget reductions. Additionally, those in charge of library budget expectations might have considered the financial cuts to be permanent. In previous years, collection development monies could be protected with special funds to increase other budget lines. The seriousness of the economic downturn from 2008 to the time of this writing, October 2013, precludes this as a trusted fiscal strategy. The current financial tenor is improving. A preference for electronic research versions over print content offers minimal decreased publishing and subscription costs (ARL, 2009).

Other areas of monetary concern to library collections include ARL members continuing to purchase "long tail" subscriptions that tend to include diverse materials from small publishers with limited circulation bases. Library subscription cancellations would reduce their cost/benefit profiles while small presses become subject to business failures. Many academic publications are published abroad and are vulnerable to high and fluctuating currency exchange rates based on global economic downturns, having potentially disproportionately higher inflationary prices (ARL, 2009).

Publishers' tiered pricing that shifts the financial burden to larger institutions to absorb escalating subscription costs is set to counterbalance vendor discounting to smaller customers while increasing larger customer costs. It has the potential to force large universities to cancel subscriptions. Ironically, research subscription vendors know that the greater share of published research content originates not from smaller-sized institutions, but the larger research universities. The ICOLC recommends publishing pricing models that are stable and discount prices are the norm for all customers. Universities and colleges of all sizes require financial equity now and into the future to have a more sustainable model of purchasing and dissemination of journal article research.

Libraries have little or no control over what five of the major publishers will propose for subscription prices to their journal databases. Elsevier, Wiley, Taylor & Francis, Springer, and Sage will continue to maintain high profit margins that squeeze the academic wallet. *Library Journal's* 2011 survey determined that nearly 50 percent of the merged ISI index content consisted of titles from these "Big Deal" publishers. The 2011 EBSCO survey revealed that 40 percent of respondents stated the likelihood of breaking up library e-journal packages and renewing only individual e-journals that are most used, as budget issues leave few alternatives (Bosch, Henderson, & Klusendorf, 2011).

According to Taylor, (2012: para. 7), if the Research Works Act (RWA) passed, it "would prohibit the NIH's public access policy and anything similar enacted by other federal agencies, locking publicly funded research behind paywalls." Both the US National Institutes for Health (NIH) policy and the UK equivalent policy document, *Innovation and Research Strategy for Growth*, state that publicly funded research is important for the progress of science; the government is committed to access that is free of charge. The Public Library of Science (PLoS) has bridged access to scholarly content with modest open access publishing article processing charges (APCs). However, open research equates to substantially diminished profits for publishers, consequently five of the major STM (science, technology, and medicine) publishers, who are accustomed to astounding profits, "have turned to the approach that uncompetitive corporations have always used in America: lobbying for legislation to protect their unsustainable model" (Taylor, 2012: para. 6).

The publisher-driven US Research Works Act (RWA) bill, introduced on December 16, 2011, would prohibit open access mandates for federally funded research and roll back the existing 2008 NIH Public Access policy that requires taxpayer-funded research to be freely accessible online, locking publicly funded research behind publisher paywalls. If enacted, the RWA would drastically restrict scientific data sharing. Global researchers and citizens would lose public access to essential health information, originally funded by taxpayers unless they paid for the articles, effectively paying twice for the research. Sponsors withdrew their support for the bill due to an overwhelming negative response from the research and education community (Taylor, 2012: para. 7).

Strong opposition to Elsevier's research article access policies included nearly 7,500 researchers who boycotted the publisher by signing a petition "vowing to stop publishing in or editing for Elsevier-published journals" (Joseph, 2012: para. 3), demonstrating a strength in research values and numbers. On February 27, 2012, Elsevier issued a statement offering broader access to their publications. The RWA bill's sponsors also acquiesced and cited "vocal feedback from stakeholders – and an apparent new belief that Open Access is the wave of the future – as rationale for backing off of the bill" (Joseph, 2012: para. 6).

Given the political and financial research access challenges, it is no surprise that academic libraries are on the frontline of supporting critical and beneficial changes to the scholarly communication milieu that integrates open access repositories into faculty and student researchers' workflows.

Considering some of the earliest journals created in the seventeenth century (1665) and since, the act of publishing academic content was controversial. The high rate of contested scholarship subsided over the centuries, as academic journal article submissions utilized the peer-review system of vetting and research. Increasingly, more scholarly society publishers have committed publishing resources towards an open access model for financial and philosophical reasons. A society journal is defined as officially adopting its publication; it additionally publishes, sponsors, or owns it (*http://www.sparc.arl.org/news-media/news/11-1205*). Society publishing studies conducted by Suber & Sutton show the 2007, 2011, and 2013 numbers of published society journals that determined how many societies were publishing full or non-hybrid open access (OA) journals. In 2007, they found 425 societies publishing 450 full or non-hybrid open access (OA) journals. The 2011 list shows 530 societies publishing 616 full open access journals. The September 2013 edition identifies 832 societies publishing 780 full or non-hybrid OA journals (*http://bit.ly/oaj-society*).

An official American Library Association (ALA) division, the Association of College and Research Libraries (ACRL), has, as of spring 2011, supported an open access publishing model in its publication, *College & Research Libraries News* (*http://www.ala.org/ala/mgrps/divs/ acrl/publications/oafaq.cfm*). It has opened its pages to the public, providing support to the evolving open access movement of establishing a precedent of globally available research articles.

Various ARL commissioned authors have written seminal reports that initially set the stage to provide support for the academy's movement towards open access research benefits. In the case of publicly supported institutional contributions of open access scholarship, the general public has reaped the rewards of access to research:

- "The research library's role in digital repository services: final report of the ARL Digital Repository Issues Task Force" (2009): *http://www. arl.org/component/content/article/6/1171*

- "SPEC Kit results of a 38-question survey of 123 ARL members in early 2006 about their institutional repositories' practices and plans" (2006): *http://www.ala.org/alcts/ano/v17/n5/nws/kit*

- "Institutional repositories: essential infrastructure for scholarship in the digital age" (Lynch, 2003): *http://scholarship.utm.edu/21/1/ Lynch,_IRs.pdf*

- "The case for institutional repositories: a SPARC position paper" (Crow, 2002): *http://scholarship.utm.edu/20/*

# Technical services: staff opportunities to support open access

Another branch of ALA that participates in and is focused on various aspects of institutional repositories is the Association for Library Collections and Technical Services (ALCTS), the premier resource for information specialists in collection development, preservation, and technical services. ALCTS members lead in the development of principles, standards, and best practices for creating, collecting, organizing, delivering, and preserving information resources in all formats. The use and constructs of cross-walking metadata from one schema to another in institutional repositories is a particularly value-added service for libraries. As fewer library resource items are purchased in a physical format, technical services staff have fewer projects and materials to process in their traditional roles. There are significant opportunities to contribute to IR content management. "Cataloging departments, with their finely honed workflows and materials cataloging procedures, can become the much-needed soldiers who volunteer for such IR-related duties as ingesting content and generating metadata" (Walters, 2007).

Staff have a productive opportunity to get involved with the repository, as one of their skill sets is the management of metadata details that provide benefit and heightened value to readers who engage search engines to find IR research. By adding Library of Congress Subject Headings (LCSH) subjects, disciplines, terms, or FAST (Faceted Application of Subject Terminology) keyword analysis that provides information about people, places and things, readers have a greater opportunity to locate research. There is a current trend for metadata specialists to adapt the LCSH to FAST, a simplified syntax that retains the rich vocabulary of LCSH and creates a schema that is less complicated to understand, control, apply, and use (OCLC, 2011). "The schema maintains upward compatibility with LCSH, and any valid set of LC subject headings can be converted to FAST headings." The brisk growth of available information demonstrated a need for a simplified indexing model that could be delegated to and used by non-professional catalogers or indexers (Bourg, Coleman, & Erway, 2009).

## Evolution of a sustainable open access movement

Libraries are finding it necessary to circumvent the financial burdens of library-purchased STM (science, technology, and medicine) serials whose publishers continue to make excessive yearly financial profits from intellectual content. Scholarly communication services are freely given by numerous professionals that possess expertise and specialized knowledge in a particular field. Editors, reviewers, and authors inherently have financial worth.

Understanding how open access has evolved helps to stimulate the future of our scholarly communications. Knowing the hurdles we have frequently overcome means we are confident in continuing to unfold new opportunities that are both beneficial and critical to scholarly communication and the availability of research. "When we shift our attention from 'save libraries' to 'save scholarship,' the imperative changes from 'preserve the current institutions' to 'do whatever works'" (Bourg, Coleman, & Erway, 2009: 1).

As open access repositories have become a sustainable opportunity for locating research by employing search engines such as Google, Yahoo, and Bing, scholarly content has become more readily available to be downloaded, read, and used. If full-text is not available, the metadata (full citation information) can be listed in the item's repository record. The IR is then used as a bibliographic citation tool. Available full-text options beyond the article or postprint download include contacting the author through a "request or contact the author button" or email and by engaging other tools. A library's link resolver tool can provide full-text article access to other university's campus search queries if they both subscribe to the journal subscription. In this context, Digital Commons® software uses a "Find in Your Library" link. A reader may request the article from another library utilizing the interlibrary loan service. Open access research materials, available through library vendor web scale discovery services (covered in Chapter 7), allow student and faculty researchers to penetrate the multitude of scholarly resources not always delivered to readers because of less effective library search tools.

# History of open access to research

Open access and the ability to use newly-created e-research platforms and tools to conduct and perform full-text searches were first conceived in the early 1990s, evolving by early 2000 into the design and creation of institutional repository and supplemental software, also enabling the creation of peer-reviewed open access journals. Major landmark contributions supported open access research discovery and the original conception and production of open access platforms facilitated by the ground-breaking standardization of the World Wide Web in 1991 by CERN, the European Organization for Nuclear Research. Tim Berners-Lee enabled those who had computers to have online scholarship available via a simple hypertext scheme, using servers already available at CERN, versus research only available through print subscriptions.

ArXiv, the first online subject repository, was created and established in 1991 as a subject-based open access portal encompassing preprints (papers prior to peer-review) and postprints (papers approved by peer-review) in physics, mathematics, computer science, and other quantitative subject areas. The mid–late 1990s brought further revolutionary open resources to the public: the Social Science Research Network (SSRN), devoted to the rapid worldwide dissemination of social science research was created; *D-Lib Magazine*, a born-digital publication focused on e-library research and development, including new technologies, applications, and associated social and economic issues, was launched; and the ground-breaking Networked Digital Library of Theses and Dissertations (NDLTD) created at Virginia Tech for archiving student electronic theses and dissertations (ETDs) on a global and efficient scale. Also of note was the creation of SPARC, the Scholarly Publishing and Academic Resources Coalition, developed by the Association of Research Libraries (ARL) to create balance in and support for new models of scholarly academic publishing (Suber, 2009b).

The end of the twentieth century heralded the Open Archives Initiative (OAI), a development of interoperability standards to facilitate the electronic dissemination of content through its protocols for meta-harvesting (PMH) that combined metadata standards and protocols for search engines to locate IR content and cause it to be obtainable to readers conducting online research. SPARC Europe (*http://www. sparceurope.org/*), created in 2001, an alliance of over 100 European research library and research members, contributed tools to support positive change in scholarly communication systems.

History professors at the University of California founded a hosted repository platform with a built-in journal system, naming it the Berkeley Electronic Press. Bepress is an electronic publishing firm established by academics who first offered its institutional repository software in 2002 for the California Digital Library's eScholarship Repository. Bepress's Digital Commons® was later introduced at the American Library Association's annual conference in June 2004. From 2004 to 2007, Digital Commons® was licensed exclusively by ProQuest Information and Learning for e-theses/dissertations. As of July 2007, Berkeley Electronic Press resumed licensing its Digital Commons® IR product directly to academic customers (Suber, 2009b).

The first decade of the twenty-first century ushered in additional open research possibilities such as PubMed, providing open access to the US National Library of Medicine's database of over 11 million citations and abstracts (*http://www.biomedcentral.com/about/faq/pubmed*), and biomedical journal literature through MEDLINE. After an initial evaluation period, BioMed Central included its full-text STM literature through PubMed

Central. The first generation of open source institutional repository software included EPrints, DSpace, and Fedora, with OAI-PMH compliant software, allowing web crawlers to harvest and update the metadata and make the citation data and full-text available to researchers employing search engines.

Additional highlighted landmark open access events in 2000–9 included:

- the creation of OAIster by the University of Michigan, the first OAI-PMH (open access initiative protocol for meta-harvesting) aggregator;
- a flexible scholarship licensing tool – Creative Commons – created by lawyer Lawrence Lessig as an alternative to standard copyright;
- the Budapest Open Access Initiative, an international effort to accelerate progress in making academic research in all fields openly available on the Internet;
- Project SHERPA/RoMEO, a collaboration of UK universities, amassed over 900 publisher permissions typically offered as part of a publisher's copyright transfer agreement, used as an open access copyright tool for researchers, institutional repository managers, and their staff;
- the Directory of Open Access Journals (DOAJ), a listing of globally peer-reviewed open access journals and their searchable content was supported by Sweden's Lund University Libraries;
- the Google Scholar search engine and its book digitization project of public domain and copyrighted books (in collaboration with five universities);
- the non-mandated National Institute of Health (NIH) Public Access Policy which requested researchers to archive all intellectual content and data within 12 months of publication (though without a solid mandate, few scientists and scholars complied with the appeal to deposit their research) (Suber, 2009b);
- the creation of the Open Directory of Open Access Repositories (*Open*DOAR) in 2006 to list IRs and engage the technology to search for research content across all repositories.

In 2007–8, Canada's Athabasca University requested faculty to self-archive their scholarship. SPARC, the Science Commons, and MIT author rights' publishing addendums were created and made available online, while the New Zealand government and the National Library of New Zealand collaboratively launched a gateway to open access research documents. Meanwhile, Harvard University's Science and Arts faculty voted on mandating open access as the default for all faculty-produced articles – a major academic precedence from a prominent research university. Concurrently, Repository 66 was shaped by Stuart Lewis (University of Aukland) from a mash-up (a webpage that combines data or functionality from two or more sources to create new data and services) of *Open*DOAR and the Registry of Open Access Repositories (ROAR). Maps were constructed to delineate which institutions in the world were using the top seven types of repository software, including a miscellaneous category (Suber, 2009b).

Most recently, in 2009 and beyond, more "open" tools and developments have added maturity to the evolution of open access institutional repositories. In 2009–10, the ROARMAP was created at the University of Southampton, indexing the world's institutional, funder, and governmental open access mandates, as well as tracking the growth rate of both mandated and non-mandated institutional repositories worldwide. Institutions may sign up and add their data.

These purposeful, strategic, useful, and disruptive, open access developments have systematically built upon each other in the creation of new repository technologies and software tools, sustainable open access publications and policies, licensing alternatives, statistical directories, standards, and mandates, leveraging new open access refinements and features. Peter Suber, a self-proclaimed independent policy strategist for open access to research (as of July 2013, Director of the Harvard Office for Scholarly Communication), is the author of multiple online open access publications and is largely responsible for purveying the ongoing "open developments" pushed out to those who follow his work. His recent monograph, *Open Access*, published in July 2012, was offered as an open publication after twelve months in July 2013.

The open access publishing momentum has built a strong foundation, offering archival venues, tools, publications, and organizational support in the past decade plus. Those committed to open access, such as the academic library community with growing faculty support for showcasing research, are using the necessary tools to make open access successful for authors and readers. Viable supporting trends persist as the evolution gains traction with new tools and available research literature. Open access publication servers continue to become available at no cost to the researcher. New institutional repositories are continually brought online. Nearly every discipline and subject area has open access resources and online venues that demonstrate scholarly communication progress.

# Academic and global open access research success

Given the effect of the current and foreseeable future's unpredictable economic climate in higher education and an unsustainable collection management model, the response from academic libraries necessitates a "call to action" to focus on maximizing institutional repository deposits by educating administrators, faculty, and students who produce scholarship about the advantages of open access, both financial and in terms of accessibility. Additionally, the US Government has recently (2011–13) mandated agencies in receipt of grant money to deposit government-funded research articles and data in an open access environment for the benefit of its researchers and citizens who have financed the scholarship.

The evolution of open access has been steady and somewhat sustainable in Europe, Asia, and North America. As of mid-2011, 80 percent of the Canadian Association of Research Libraries (CARL) had implemented an institutional repository at their universities. Since 2003, CARL has promoted the creation and use of repositories through its national program (CARL, 2012).

The Association of American Universities (AAU) also claims 80 percent of their university members now have operational institutional repositories. The AAU is a highly selective nonprofit organization of "leading public and private research universities in the United States and Canada" that are on the cutting-edge of innovation and scholarship, contributing to the nation's economy and security. The 60 AAU universities in the United States award more than one-half of all US doctoral degrees and 55 percent of those in the sciences and engineering (AAU, 2011). Included in the 80 percent figure are repositories that encompass a wide range of digital items in various subjects and types of archived materials. Tools used to identify an aggregated list of global academic repositories include the: Open Directory of Open Access Repositories (*Open*DOAR), Registry of Open Access Repositories (ROAR), Ranking Web of Institutional Repositories, and Repository66. org, a visual map delineating 2841 repositories by software platforms (as of April 21, 2013).

Globally, Europe ranks first in terms of the number of repositories and has more than twice the number of North America (ranked third) overall. Asia now ranks second. The creation and use of worldwide repositories is one indicator of the adoption of a scholarly communication tool that has value for the academic environment, such as the statistics that have been documented by *Open*DOAR. According to the global snapshot of viable repositories (August 30, 2013 by *Open*DOAR, as shown in Figure 1.2 and Table 1.1) there are 2,394 organizations worldwide that host at least one repository, and in some instances there are up to 20 repositories per university. The percentages in Table 1.1 represent organizations hosting repositories in each continent, counting only one repository per institution.

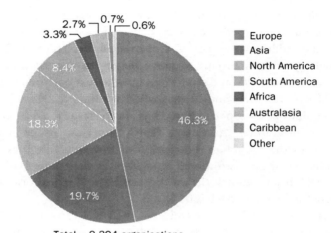

2.7% ⌐ 0.7% ⌐ 0.6%
3.3% ⌐

8.4%

18.3%          46.3%

19.7%

- Europe
- Asia
- North America
- South America
- Africa
- Australasia
- Caribbean
- Other

Total = 2,394 organisations

**Figure 1.2**  **Proportion of repository organizations by continent – worldwide**

Adding to the data profile of percentages and instances of repositories hosted by individual continent, the following information from the *Open*DOAR repository types website (*http://bit.ly/146nqs]*) illustrates what kinds of repositories are represented: 82.4 percent (1,973) are institutional repositories, 11 percent (264) focus on particular disciplines, 4 percent (95) archive aggregated research from supplementary-type repositories, and 2.6 percent (62) maintain government data.

National and international organizations realize the global enthusiasm and the need for open access, including what it promises us now and what it will offer in the future. The American Library Association's Association of College and Research Libraries' (ACRL) publication, *College & Research Libraries* (*C&RL*), announced in March 2011 that it would publish as an open access publication, endorsing the elimination

| Table 1.1 | Percentages and instances of hosted repositories by continent |
| --- | --- |

| Continent | Percentages of organizations hosting repositories | Actual instances of repositories (one per institution) in each continent |
| --- | --- | --- |
| Europe | 46.3% | 1,120 |
| Asia | 19.7% | 488 |
| North America | 18.3% | 417 |
| South America | 8.4% | 203 |
| Australasia | 3.3% | 58 |
| Africa | 2.7% | 76 |
| Caribbean | 0.7% | 16 |
| Other | 0.6% | No data available |

Information compiled by *Open*DOAR (August 30, 2013).

of a six-month embargo period. The ACRL Board of Directors chose to honor the academic library principles that espouse open access to research, consequently sustainably funding *C&RL* is a priority (Branin, 2011). It is a positive step forward, not only setting an example of professional value from library science, but also for "walking the talk" and embracing openness by the discipline that promotes it.

As academic librarians continue to promote awareness of inherent benefits and focus on a scholarly communications campaign to foster a larger body of literature in open access publications, the reality of *C&RL's* financial stability was negotiated. In the near future, ACRL will continue to evaluate options and make decisions as a result of the common academic publishing dilemma of declining paying subscribers and advertisers. If research is accessible, will a reader pay for a journal subscription when one can access it freely online? Editors, publishers, scholarly societies, and professional associations in various disciplines can face difficult financial publishing decisions when considering open access. The service and volunteer work provided by journal editorial staff and referees are a savings benefit.

Joseph Branin (2011), *C&RL* Editor, reminds readers that there is still the price of production, distribution, and administration of print and online versions of the journal. It could be debated that the print copy, the most expensive impression, could be abandoned and, as the literature shows, most researchers are online. The effect of removing the print copy option could trigger ACRL members to ask themselves what value are they receiving for their annual membership fee, even though the online publication requires some production costs and an online distribution model. A positive and fruitful advantage of *C&RL*'s open journal venue and how it evolves in print and/or online will be a useful example of how to lead the open access way, clearing the path for other scholarly societies and professional associations facing similar publishing model dilemmas. As academic librarians and library associations are at the forefront of promoting and utilizing open access models, *C&RL*'s example will be a framework for others to imitate.

## US Government open access and research policy

From a national government research posture, President George Bush signed into law the Consolidated Appropriations Act of 2007 (HR 2764), which included a provision directing the National Institutes of Health (NIH) researchers to provide the public with open access to findings in article format and data from its funded research. This is the first time the US Government requested that researchers deliver public access to research funded by a major government agency. Request is the operative word, as there was a low fulfillment.

In October 2009, the National Center for Atmospheric Research (NCAR) passed an open access policy requiring all peer-reviewed research published by its scientists and staff in scientific journals be made publicly available online through its institutional repository (*https:// www2.ucar.edu/atmosnews/news/1059/new-open-access-policy-ncar-research*). The new policy of the University Corporation for Atmospheric Research (UCAR) was constructed by the governing body that manages NCAR. A national laboratory, NCAR is sponsored by the NSF and has conducted research into the atmospheric sciences since 1960. This policy is significant because NCAR research is important: more than 30 NCAR researchers participated in the United Nations' Intergovernmental Panel on Climate Change that won the 2007 Nobel Peace Prize with Al Gore (Vice President of the US, 1993–2001). This is the closest that NSF has moved towards open access, stating in December 2008: "The adoption of open access policy for data, publications and software" is a "critical component" of the NSF vision for advanced cyber-infrastructure (Suber,

2009a; see also Suber, 2007). The data produced and the findings documented from providing US Government grant funds may impart valuable testing, analysis, and/or scrutiny to the research process, yielding an opportunity for future researchers to build upon current discoveries.

As the wheels of change in government require time for US citizen benefits to accrue, the legislative intention is to open research access. On February 9, 2012, the Federal Research Public Access Act (FRPAA) was re-introduced into both the Senate and House of Representatives. Having been introduced in two earlier sessions of Congress in May 2006 and April 2009, it has never come up for a vote.

From the SPARC website (2011a):

> FRPAA would require that the eleven U.S. Government agencies with annual extramural research expenditures over $100 million create manuscripts of journal articles stemming from research funded by that agency publicly available via the Internet. The manuscripts will be managed and preserved in a digital archive maintained by the agency or in another suitable repository that permits free public access, interoperability, and long-term preservation. Each manuscript will be freely available to users without charge within six months after it has been published in a peer-reviewed journal.

The FRPAA Bill is extremely important to the open availability of research, as each year the US Federal Government funds tens of billions of dollars in basic and applied research. The wealth of open articles would be an astonishing resource for furthering scholarly output intended for the US and, laterally, a global benefit. Primary funding is concentrated within eleven departments and agencies, such as the National Institutes of Health (NIH). The FRPAA fortifies the NIH open access mandate by reducing the maximum embargo period from twelve to six months and extends the strengthened policy to all major federal government agencies, including the National Science Foundation (NSF) and the Department of Energy (DOE) (*bit.ly/hoap-frpaa*). Research findings are typically reported in a variety of academic journal articles. It is approximated that every year, 95,000 papers are published from the NIH grant subsidies alone. It is inspiring progress to make possible the full-text of open access research for its inherent value, and significantly, only fair to US taxpayers who underwrite the research through their annual federal taxes to receive the benefit of access. Advancing science has the possibility of improving the lives and welfare of US citizens and the world's population at large. "The Internet has revolutionized information sharing and has made it possible to make the latest advances promptly available to every scientist, physician, educator, and citizen at their homes, schools, or libraries" (SPARC, 2011b).

The Research Works Act, introduced on December 16, 2011, would repeal the NIH OA policy (ensuring public access to NIH-funded research papers no later than twelve months after publication) and also block similar open access policy models at other federal agencies (*bit.ly/hoap-rwa*).

The bipartisan Fair Access to Science and Technology Research (FASTR) Act (February 14, 2013) proposal is a new, strengthened version and successor of FRPAA, which would require open access to peer-reviewed article manuscripts reporting the results of federally funded research. They have at least a dozen commonalities. FASTR (*bit. ly/hoap-fastr*) differences include coordinating agency policy procedures to gather and deposit research papers; universities will have a less burdensome responsibility to comply. Three new open licensing or reuse rights (libre OA) stipulations call for: (1) a US focus on capitalizing the impact and utility of its research funds through a wide range of peer-reviewed literature reuse; (2) a format and license provision maintaining open access and productive reuse in all formats and stated terms; (3) research papers that consist of an open license publicly accessible and allowing reuse with author or copyright owner attribution. All three licensing conditions also require an agency's annual report of the effective enabling of reuse and a computational analysis using high-end technologies.

Just days after the proposed FASTR Act, the US White House directed a number of federal agencies to develop open access policies within six months of the February 22, 2013 date. The Office of Science and Technology Policy (OSTP) Director, John Holdren, signed the order for federal agencies with more than $100 million in R&D expenditures "to develop plans to make the published results of federally funded research freely available to the public within one year of publication and requiring researchers to better account for and manage the digital data resulting from federally funded scientific research" (*http://1.usa.gov/17PSF8u*). The legislative (FASTR) and executive (White House directive) approaches complement one another and also stand on their own, each having their inherent strengths. Despite FASTR's benefits, it would have to be adopted; the White House directive took effect immediately (*http://bit.ly/17SXMcd*).

The two approaches are complementary, as FASTR does not make the White House directive unnecessary and may never be adopted. All types of research, lobbying, negotiation, and debate could hold up the FASTR Act. In contrast, the White House's OSTP directive takes effect on February 22, 2013. FASTR is still necessary to codify federal OA policies to protect the legislation from being rescinded (*http://bit.ly/17SXMcd*).

# Research Councils UK: OA research policy

The Finch Committee, chaired by Dame Janet Finch, a sociologist at the University of Manchester in the UK, was created by the Minister for Universities and Science, David Willetts, considered how UK research access could be increased. After years of deliberation and researcher controversy, the policy direction initially settled on open access or hybrid journals funded by article processing charges (APCs) as a standard. This would also be the primary medium for publishing articles, particularly, for publicly funded research. The Committee additionally recommended that the green OA model be reduced to a minor preservation role, only providing access to grey literature and research data. Finch also suggested that authors' self-archived (green OA) papers would endure an embargo period, a minimum of 12 months. If publishers did not offer an APC, the policy would be void. The UK research community vehemently protested the new publishing models, and in addition, the government stated that the universities would be responsible for funding the cost of research from their existing budgets. The yearly financial outlay was estimated to cost an additional £50–60 million a year (Poynder, (2012), translating (September 2013) to approximately US $80–95 million.

Since 2005, the Research Councils have maintained open access policies. The recently considered fall 2013 policy directed at researchers accounts for the evolving scholarly communication principles in the UK and the global backdrop. In addition, the new documentation focuses on the policy statement and publishers, targeting host institutions and publishers that disseminate peer-reviewed research. Open access to scholarship will ensure best practices in the public's barrier-free research investment as it "secures the maximum economic and societal return" for its readers.

The updated APC policy takes effect from April 1, 2013, encompassing peer-reviewed journals or conference proceedings item types and by acknowledging Research Council funding. Article processing charges are subsidized by the Council's open access block grants given to eligible research organizations. Authors of research papers are expected to publish their peer-reviewed papers, acknowledging Research Council funding in journals compliant with the RCUK open access policy. A statement of access might include where the research materials are located (see: *http://www.rcuk.ac.uk/documents/documents/RCUKOpen AccessPolicy.pdf*).

# Global open access research support

The mission of the UK's Wellcome Trust is to support the brightest minds in conducting biomedical research and the medical humanities. As of 2003, the Trust's open access policy was to ensure that their charitable mission in funding scientific work would be available and utilized by the widest possible audience, thus imbuing a richer research culture. Researchers are encouraged to retain their copyrights to provide free open access to new ideas and knowledge. Scientists' scholarly output must be published in high-quality, peer-reviewed journals, as an effective way to ensure that research can be accessed, read, and built upon (Wellcome Trust, 2011).

The Netherlands National Commission for the United Nations Educational, Scientific, and Cultural Organization (UNESCO) convened in Amsterdam, January 2011, to discuss a global-scale of open access effort as a meaningful vision for developing countries. One of UNESCO's overarching objectives is for citizens in underdeveloped countries to have the opportunity to instill lifelong learning and realize a quality education for all. UNESCO supports open access to benefit the global flow of knowledge, innovation, and equitable socio-economic development (Netherlands National Commission for UNESCO, 2011). Open access is used as a support system to enhance access to scientific knowledge for education, public health, and economic advancement. Open research is also a global public good that manifests increased visibility, usage, and impact, stimulating innovation. Access is an essential component that allows continuous analysis of data and the development of new insights through a wide range of research.

The most vigorous development is taking place in the Global South, the countries that collectively include the nations of Africa, Central and Latin America, and most of Asia; scientific research is part of their activity and progress. Research focused on international findings and data is also of mutual interest for the Global North, i.e., the developed countries that include Australia and New Zealand, as well as the Global South. There is a need everywhere to solve worldwide problems. Open access provides a common research platform to overcome obstacles to sharing and using scientific knowledge in all regions of the world.

Optimally, all global stakeholders might consider the multitude of ways to make scientific research available. Countries vary in how they conduct and organize their legal, social, and academic systems, and technological infrastructure. The amount of publicly and privately funded science varies, and the former funded research in some countries is not always available.

According to UNESCO (2011), achieving global, unhampered access to scholarly scientific knowledge has its pitfalls. International cooperation is critical to creating systems that are local as well as global, flexible, reliable, and secure, in an accessible environment. A shared North and South framework for research into the development of a reliable system with scientific quality control could be a valuable instrument of development cooperation.

Corroborative survey data from Southeastern Nigeria, a country that is part of the Global South, portrayed similar barriers to UNESCO's constrained entry to open access scholarship and effective technologies. Southeastern Nigerian Libraries surveyed 67 librarians in two federal and two state universities. According to the respondents' bio-data, 25 librarians had been in the profession for one to five years while 20 librarians had served between six and over twenty years. The purpose of the study was to determine how extensively the librarians value and make use of the open access repository culture in their scholarly communications, from the positive view that open research materials are essential and also need to address the negative aspects of the high cost of computers and Internet accessibility.

In the survey, the librarians wholeheartedly welcomed the advantages of open access and their potential roles supporting major aspects of institutional repositories. All of the survey respondents accepted the advantages listed for open access scholarly publication, such as: free and accessible journal access for all; including use of one's own research; a larger potential pool of research evidence; increased impact; a reduction in publication delays; the ability of authors to self-archive; and increased career development. The librarians also embraced their role in creating IRs in collaboration with faculty, advocating for open access, being conversant with vendor licensing and copyright in an open access environment (this excluded respondents at the agriculture university who were not familiar with these aspects), dispensing general knowledge about the repository, proposing implementation, and applying keyword and subject analysis for IR citation metadata.

The librarians all agreed in the survey that there were constraints to scholarly publishing in employing open access. Librarians may have an inadequate skill set and lack the knowledge to navigate the Internet to locate open access journals. This could be exacerbated by an unstable power supply that results in the failure of large, full-text journal articles to download, a lack of Internet facilities, the unpredictability of insecure government financial support, and also the reluctance to leave traditional and established journal publishers.

## Summary

Some journals are adopting new and sustainable models of peer-review that transcend the traditional review. Over time, these new modes of scholarly communication have opened access to research, just not as quickly as many aspire to. The worldwide-disenfranchised public and scientists/scholars are in need of the intellectual content tucked behind paywalls and the mindset that supports open access to research. Yet, the most prosperous global academic libraries "suffer serious access gaps" (Suber, 2012: 30, para. 2). As we consider the "access spectrum," it represents a diverse global experience. Libraries and researchers must continue to support state and national government level legislative measures that do not back academic publishers' exorbitant subscription fees. It is imperative for all readers to have barrier-free access to scholarly materials that meet their information needs.

# 2

# Academic shift towards open access

**Abstract.** The concept, design, and development of institutional repository (IR) software was conceived and created by academics, libraries, and software developers to create change in the scholarly communication process of making journal articles globally available. Research aggregator tools have made open access article searching a less daunting proposition by utilizing the OAI-PMH metadata harvesting technology. Talking points that engage the campus, its administration, faculty, and librarians to embrace an IR's role are critical to achieve a high percentage of buy-in to increase the rate of research article deposit, necessary without a campus mandate. Partnering with open access-amenable researchers to showcase their scholarship is a proven method of building their trust and archiving their work in an institutional repository. A content departure beyond the standard journal article has rapidly evolved into an abundance and variety of additional scholarship to archive. Social marketing strategies describe the inducement of voluntary change by selling a concept that generally benefits society, such as an IR. Faculty, administrators, and students will find a variety of value propositions in utilizing a repository for their scholarly works.

**Keywords:** academic administrators, aggregators of scholarly content, copyright addendums, ETDs, faculty talking points, grey literature, institutional repository marketing, journal article permissions, open access principles, SHERPA/RoMEO, social marketing, strategic campus partnerships, student research

Libraries are poised to support changes in scholarly communication behavior by enlightened academic librarians and faculty researchers willing to showcase their own professional intellectual content. It requires embracing change and confronting the previous quarter century of intensifying journal subscription costs. As those responsible for library and university budgets balked at the serial inflation that commenced in the mid-1980s and as journal costs spiraled out of control in the late

1990s, a worldwide economic downturn took effect in 2008. These circumstances over time gave rise to the creation and evolution of a new model of accessing research scholarship, emerging as the "institutional repository" (IR). The first IRs were launched in 2000–1; over 11 types of repositories and more than 3,479 IRs (*http://roar.eprints.org/*) have been created since the early twenty-first century by academic libraries and researchers (as of August 2013). The Cybermetrics Lab research group of the Spanish Public Research Council published its January 2013 edition (twice a year, including July) of the Ranking Web of World Universities (*http://www.webometrics.info*). Over 21,200 higher education institutions were represented. July's report included 21,451 ranked universities arranged by country (*http://www.webometrics.info/en/node/54*). "Its objective is to motivate and reinforce the role of the university as a source and distributor of high quality web contents and to promote and support open access initiatives."

# An institutional repository is launched

The initial need for a research repository was born out of the rising costs and inflexible bundling of journals that created a lack of affordable subscription access to journal articles and other scholarly content. Libraries can no longer afford many of these subscriptions. Thousands of postprints (papers approved by peer-review) and articles have been set to "open" access (OA) by authors and librarians following SHERPA/RoMEO copyright guidelines and by researchers retaining copyright through publishing contracts, postprints, and mandates. A repository can fulfill showcasing and tracking a university's overall output by highlighting research at the university and individual level. Both are essential to meet each of their administrative and research needs.

Librarians took the lead as change-agents, and once the software was created, initiated social transformation by exhibiting "creativity, courage, visibility, perseverance, and driving motivation [that] are all indispensable characteristics of people who instigate change rather than observe it" (Wireman, 1998). They collaborated with software developers and faculty who ardently researched, co-developed, and experimented, using an innovative model that provided a legal solution to allow access to the scholarship currently "locked up" behind subscriptions that held a promise to actualize an open, global research niche. Because university communities rely on their libraries to provide continued access to research and scholarship, libraries are perfectly poised to be at the forefront of open access opportunities. To be successful in creating a new and potentially controversial software implementation, there was a need for an open and sustainable mindset with the technological expertise to realize the promise of an open access ecosystem ideal for both development and implementation to evolve simultaneously.

Innovative faculty and their collaborative entrepreneurial software developers, such as those at the University of Southampton's School of Electronics and Computer Science (ECS), have been at the forefront of the open access movement. The ECS School originally had its own archive of departmental articles and its work in partnership with the library developed the institutional repository (IR) concept. In 2000–1, EPrints was designed, created, and made available to encourage self-archiving at Southampton. It was the first repository software created to enable universities to retain their scholarship for open access use. E-Prints currently has 14.8 percent (362 installations) of the IR repository software market share, as stated by *Open*DOAR (September 29, 2013). According to Leslie Carr, Technical Director of EPrints, their university library liaison joined the repository team a couple of years later and has continued since (email correspondence).

University of Southampton faculty are mandated to self-archive all of their research in their EPrints repository. As of 2010, the repository has since captured close to 100 percent of Southampton's refereed research output (see *http://eprints.soton.ac.uk/*). Not surprisingly, in 2002 it was the first academic institution in the world to adopt an open access research mandate. The EPrints software has been emulated in various iterations of worldwide repositories.

The development of the currently most downloaded and used repository software has its roots in the product, DSpace. It has 41.3 percent of the market share (988 installations according to *Open*DOAR, August 30, 2013), the original DSpace software partnership between Massachusetts Institute of Technology (MIT) Libraries and Hewlett-Packard (HP) Labs. (see *http://www.dspace.org/*).

MIT and HP commenced design and development in March 2000; DSpace was ready for faculty use in November 2002. While the software code was underway, the MIT Libraries were strategically preparing for the introduction to the revolutionary new service that was poised to transform scholarly communication library services and the road map envisioned to promote scientist and scholar research. In conversation with MIT faculty around scholarship issues, the MIT Libraries Dean observed a prevalent theme: "She began noticing a need. She quotes one faculty member as lamenting in a joking fashion that his 'entire life's work is in [his] email'" (Baudoin & Branschofsky, 2004). It is not unusual behavior for faculty to house scholarly projects on a computer hard drive. Faculty typically focus on a current writing project and as soon as the final postprint is emailed to the journal editor, the academic is on to the next research project. This is an opportune moment to have faculty email their postprints to the university's repository manager or through an IR electronic form to be deposited.

Other (IR) software products have been subsequently developed, downloaded, and employed across the world: Digital Commons®, Fedora, OPUS, Greenstone, Islandora, SimpleDL, and irplus, from the University of Rochester. Profiles of these institutional repository products are covered in Chapter 3.

# Understanding open access benefits

Most academic institutions have a strategic research statement as part of a general academic plan that aligns with goals to increase research and scholarly productivity, aspiring to national/international recognition. Integrating a venue for the very purpose of promoting and sharing intellectual content is exactly what the academic library community embarked upon when creating an IR tool in the early twenty-first century.

Once EPrints and DSpace had been created and were installed on servers, they were ready to be populated. The challenge was to begin: once the software was built, would the faculty use it? At the first SPARC (Scholarly Publishing and Academic Resources Coalition) meeting hosted at MIT in spring 2004, there were invited attendees, primarily repository managers, administrators, and developers who had been using and experimenting with the DSpace software. The major questions for the IR managers and administrators revolved around: "We have implemented the software; what strategies can be used to populate the repository; and where do we go from here to garner faculty and administrative buy-in?" (Jones & Nixon, 2004). The repositories were created and in place; the next step was to successfully populate them. Strategies that worked then continue to flourish with additional motivations that address new opportunities and faculty concerns by engaging in the evolving scholarly communication enterprise.

Faculty's basic but essential "talking points" on open access culture were uncovered at the University of Rochester Libraries while conducting a year-long anthropological study funded by the Institute of Museum and Library Services (IMLS). The IMLS grant focused on meaningful ways that academic libraries can take into consideration how scientists and scholars conduct research and what aspects of the paradigm were important to them. The study also sought to understand how an institutional repository might provide for various faculty research practices. The interview findings were based on common practices; the most important IR value for the faculty was technical security and "that *other* people find, use, and cite the work that they put into it." It makes sense that faculty are incentivized to work in that mode, as once they complete an article they move onto the next scholarly project, repeating the process of research and publishing so their peers will make use of their scholarship (Foster & Gibbons, 2005).

Once the academy's library has established an IR, there are at least two primary levels of acceptance: administration and faculty. Both are critical. A broad definition of an institutional repository emphasizes the central role of the institution, whereas a more focused definition includes the individual faculty members and their contributions. The centralized role of an IR is classically defined by Clifford A. Lynch, Executive Director of the Coalition for Networked Information, as "a set of services that a university offers to the members of its community for the management and dissemination of digital materials created by the institution and its community members" (2003). An institutional repository is a tool that supports the academy, faculty, and students. Libraries are obligated and, as would be expected, aspire to attain support for individual and collective research archiving activity, ultimately to also benefit library research collections.

Academic governance is interested in the larger picture of university community access to the institution's scholarly knowledge that it achieves through archiving research and scholarship, although that model is evolving. Administrators increasingly want a centralized location where all of the research is collected to manipulate the data for accreditation and other organizational purposes. Visibility of and access to full-text scholarship is paramount for stakeholders both internal and external, serving as tangible indicators of the extent and quality of intellectual activity. Multi-disciplinary faculty are interested in who is researching in what areas – are there opportunities for interdisciplinary subject alignment that could lead to collaboration? There is value in an institution preserving the research it produces; it has the potential to demonstrate the scientific, economic, and societal relevance of its scholarly pursuits.

The IR becomes a vital archive as additional intellectual content is contributed, effectively aggregating the inventory at an individual, department, college, and institutional level. It provides an efficient method to amass relevant academy research to maintain an annual accounting of scholarship for individual faculty members. Department chairs and the provost need to know what faculty have accomplished and published at the end of a calendar year with their annual research record.

Digital Measures, a university data management tool (*http://www. digitalmeasures.com/*), has been embraced by many universities for the fundamental reason of tracking faculty teaching, research, and service. One of the hurdles that administrators are confronted with is the inputting of the necessary faculty data. Their academic library is likely to be already engaged in the work of archiving faculty scholarly works in their IR. There is potential to collaborate and fulfill administrative and library goals utilizing an open access environment. Opportunities already exist in an institutional repository to expand the visibility, status, and value of research to both its local community and global audience. Public institutions are inherently obligated to share faculty and student research findings supported by state and federal taxpayer funding. David Shulenburger, Vice President for Academic Affairs, Association of Public and Land-Grant Universities, explains:

> The job of digital repositories is to ensure that the extremely valuable scholarly or creative products that have been paid for by the public or by donors are ultimately accessible to them, as well to students, faculty, and researchers everywhere. (SPARC closing keynote speech: *http://www.arl.org/sparc/bm~doc/shulen_trans.pdf*)

Faculty journal papers and other research materials are primary targets for archiving in the IR, with individual contributions attributed to particular work that scientists and scholars want to showcase and be of value to others in their field. Librarians endeavor to engage faculty in the culture of investing their research in an open access environment, a vital step towards ensuring journal articles and other scholarly products will be freely available to other researchers. Presenting the repository's value proposition in practice is fundamental for faculty to engage in archiving their papers and making them accessible to readers.

Theory aside, there are practical aspects to working shoulder-to-shoulder with an institution's administration and faculty researchers; each have their needs and motivations to be considered. An academic administration, as noted above, is looking after its own interests, as it must. Multiple stances can be satisfied where repositories must "serve as tangible indicators of an institution's quality, thus increasing its visibility, prestige, and public value" (Crow, 2002).

What is said or thought about an institutional repository can determine a flourishing repository or slow its intake, dependent on the library's messaging and actions. Using a strategy that takes into account the IR manager and faculty's repository goals will ensure the synchronicity of building an archive by viewing the multifaceted lens through various stakeholder needs, creating an upwardly mobile archive. The first goal of the library as initiator and IR host is to populate the repository with a variety of scholarly items so administrators and future faculty contributors are able to envision what features the repository has to offer.

# Marketing discipline-specific materials to archive in an institutional repository

An academic campus has a plethora of scholarly content, so where to begin on garnering potential repository materials? Some libraries conduct an IR pilot project, as in the case of the University of Kansas and other universities such as MIT, before creating or publicizing a repository. The Rochester Institute of Technology Library emailed faculty a preliminary questionnaire to understand and determine the needs entailed by the types of content that faculty would proffer. In considering the initial IR content, bear in mind what types of materials and from which disciplines will appeal most to the administration *and* faculty. Targeting amenable faculty to provide preliminary subject matter as an example of an archival research model may be demonstrated to other faculty to strategically garner their interest and scholarship. The Sciences have been some of the earliest adopters of repositories; the Humanities have not, although new models are evolving. Physics researchers have been open access archiving since 1991 in arXiv (*http://arxiv.org/*), initially utilized as a preprint (paper prior to peer-review) email distribution list and since, a depositing mechanism to share scholarly content. ArXiv later expanded to include mathematics, computer science, quantitative biology, and quantitative finance and statistics.

An effective marketing technique to garner IR materials is to concentrate on the disciplines that are currently amenable to open access, as it requires less effort to acquire and aggregate that content. A competitive effect might occur when scientists and scholars realize that their research could also be more globally emphasized and subsequently experience an impetus to make their work available. Historically, the Humanities have maintained their traditional subscription-only mechanisms in journals that are typically not available in an open access environment. The Humanities' open access philosophy has recently evolved to resources that include the Open Library of Humanities (*https://www.openlibhums.org/about/mission-statement/*) and the Open Humanities Press (*http://openhumanitiespress.org/*).

The hard sciences such as STEM (Science, Technology, Engineering, and Mathematics) and the Social Sciences have roots in proactively sharing their research. Martin Wachs, Director of the Institute of Transportation Studies (ITS) and Professor of Civil Engineering, is amenable to open access: "What's not to like? I welcome any technology that improves people's access to our research. By placing ITS researchers' papers in this new digital repository, we will be able to reach a larger audience" (Ober, 2002).

Zuber's 2008 study used a quantitative research design method whose sample included colleges and universities with over 15,000 enrolled students and a total of 45 repositories to "determine nationally which academic disciplines demonstrate a greater tendency to publish in academic institutional repositories." The top three academic disciplines represented in the findings were engineering, business, and education. Engineering as a discipline had a 36 percent majority of all repository holdings surveyed.

The literature suggests that a reasonable approach would be to contact physics and engineering faculty to gauge their interest in becoming early adopters of archiving their research in the IR. Explaining the unknown concept of an institutional repository would ordinarily be a slight challenge on both sides, between the institutional repository manager or library liaison and the faculty's understanding. Researchers who use arXiv and share their findings with colleagues will have a greater awareness and appreciation for an intersecting open access environment. A potential argument against IR deposits suggests they are currently depositing in arXiv; there is only an advantage to engaging in more research access points. The essential thread in this reasoning is an IR showcases the faculty scholarship at one's own institution as a collective whole, which is different than a preprint (paper prior to peer-review) and a postprint (paper approved by peer-review) in arXiv, a subject repository. An institutional repository simultaneously benefits a researcher and the academy.

Engineers and other disciplinary faculty tend to list their research and curriculum vitae on their department websites. Wherever possible, they may provide links to their articles or other scholarly materials. Common issues with websites entail a lack of timely author research updates and the fact that URLs change periodically; the reader may have to conduct further searches to locate the author's work.

Contacting a few engineering as well as physics researchers who understand the arXiv model and may already deposit their scholarship provides an amenable group to showcase what faculty work looks like in an IR. Library liaisons are typically knowledgeable about their faculty's research and have a sense of who to initially contact. Another approach is to have a dean or associate dean of research suggest prolific authors. Mentioning to a scientist or scholar a dean's recommendation is a compliment, potentially unlocking doors to open access engagement. As the repository is a new library service to some faculty, it makes practical sense to request a CV and offer to use it as a guide to locate and archive faculty scholarship in the IR.

# Article research permissions and addendums

Researchers are typically cognizant about copyright issues related to their work. To reassure faculty that publisher postprint and final article copyright permissions are reviewed, they can be verified through publisher websites or SHERPA/RoMEO (*http://www.sherpa.ac.uk/romeo/*), an online publishers' permissions compilation service provided by the University of Nottingham. At a minimum, there are six possible publisher copyrighted journal article and postprint permission outcomes from a self-archiving copyright agreement:

1. The journal publisher allows its final article copy to be archived.

2. The journal publisher permits an author's postprint copy to be deposited in the IR.

3. The journal publisher grants an author's preprint copy to be deposited in the IR.

4. There may be specific permissions ranging from joint authorship, research grant terms to be added to the item record, and adding publisher-required information.

5. The journal publisher may have set an embargo for a specific time period, such as six months or longer.

6. There is no publisher agreement in SHERPA/RoMEO or on a publisher's website. Repository staff needs to email/call and request permission directly from the publication editor. Email is optimum to retain a record of the interchange. This text can be standardized and used repeatedly for efficiency. Editor responses should be maintained in an e-folder and/or printed out and filed in a hard copy folder for future referrals and in case journal permissions change.

According to the Sherpa RoMEO website (*http://www.sherpa.ac.uk/romeo/statistics.php?scope=provisional*), in the last year and a half (since January 2012) there has been a 5 percent increase in publishers allowing some form of self-archiving.

As of August 31, 2013, 70 percent of the 1,000 publishers listed in the SHERPA/RoMEO copyright database (see *http://www.sherpa.ac.uk/romeo/statistics.php*) authorize some form of open access self-archiving in repositories (see Table 2.1). The database includes a majority of the principal journals in most fields that allow OA to an author's final peer-reviewed manuscript (postprint) or the version prior to peer-review (preprint) (*http://www.sherpa.ac.uk/romeo/PDFandIR.php?la=en*).

The publisher's version of an article may be located and obtained from a research database, Google Scholar, the author, a search engine query, the library's shelf collection by scanning and printing or through inter-library loan. Pre and postprints can only be acquired from authors.

If there is no approval to use the publisher's final article copy and an author's postprint is not obtainable, the bibliographic citation metadata (all of the item record details: author(s)/editor(s), article title, abstract, journal title, publisher, publication date, page range, document type, volume number, funding sources, and citation) can be made accessible at the very least. Full-text scholarship may be procured for readers by

| Table 2.1 | Summary: 70% of publishers on this list formally allow some form of self-archiving |
|-----------|-----------------------------------------------------------------------------------|

| RoMEO colour | Archiving policy | Publishers | % |
|--------------|------------------|------------|---|
| Green | Can archive preprint and postprint | 388 | 30 |
| Blue | Can archive postprint (i.e. final draft post-refereeing) | 418 | 32 |
| Yellow | Can archive preprint (i.e. pre-refereeing) | 100 | 8 |
| White | Archiving not formally supported | 388 | 30 |

*Source*: SHERPA/RoMEO, Centre for Research Communication, University of Nottingham.

engaging a link resolver (a vendor service that provides links between a search query and a customizable list of resources to find a full-text article). An academic library has the ability to set up a link resolver within a digital library, such as an IR, that enables a reader to seamlessly navigate from a citation to the full-text (if available). In addition, when the researcher clicks on a *Download* button (as an example) there will be a list of options to choose from that a library can customize (Barner & Tal, 2012):

- the actual item record and full-text article;
- a page that provides library service options to locate the article, such as interlibrary loan, a choice to communicate with a library subject liaison or chat service;
- an annotated metadata field to alert the reader that the item's full-text is unavailable due to copyright constraints.

An OpenURL, in the context of an IR, is a standard URL formatted to enable off-campus repository readers to more easily find an article copy they are allowed to access by logging in to their respective university institutional repository. Open access scholarly materials available through library vendor web scale discovery services are covered in greater detail in Chapter 7.

Alternatively, when a researcher arrives at an IR impasse where only metadata is available, many repositories offer an email, "Tell a Colleague" or "Request a Copy" option that sends the reader's message to the author requesting a postprint. The author can reply to the email with an attached file.

Two copyright addendum options sponsored by Creative Commons and the Scholarly Publishing and Academic Resources Coalition (SPARC) are available to support an author's quest to ensure open access to postprints or articles. Each addendum provides non-exclusive author rights to create derivative works and the ability to reproduce, distribute, publicly perform, and display the author's article in conjunction with teaching, presentations/lectures, and other scholarly and professional activities. Creative Commons Scholar's Copyright Addendum Engine can be used to generate and subsequently attach a Science Commons addendum (*http://scholars.sciencecommons.org/*) to publication agreements requesting a publisher to:

- provide immediate access to retain sufficient rights to deposit a copy of the author's postprint or the published article version immediately online to a site without a paywall;

- honor a "delayed access right" by immediately archiving a postprint to a non-paywall website or an IR. The postprint must be embargoed for six months after the official publication date or by author notification of postprint acceptance-check publisher policies.

After the author fills in the form's specific information, a PDF document is produced to attach to the postprint.

The Science Commons' and SPARC's collaborative license (Addendum to Publication Agreement) are legal instruments that focus on the Creative Commons Attribution Non Commercial license or a similar authorization permitting the public to re-use or re-post an article. It also stipulates the reader's use of an article is non-commercial and acknowledges the author (*http://www.arl.org/sparc/bm~doc/Access-Reuse_Addendum.pdf*).

An efficient and expeditious option to acquire deposit permission is to encourage faculty to simultaneously convey their postprint to the IR and retain their rights to archive by using the green open access "self-archiving through repositories method" to "supplement the subscription access to the publisher's proprietary version of their research with free online access (OA) to their peer-reviewed drafts by depositing them in their institutional repositories immediately upon acceptance for publication" (Harnad, 2011). Faculty who acquire the habit of directly archiving their postprints, where approved by the publisher, as the final step in the scholarly communication process will benefit from an accelerated use of the research and subsequent impact.

This is a potential point in the faculty–librarian conversation where faculty may not be universally familiar with the principles of open access and copyright; there are multiple copyright qualifications and archiving options. As researchers respect copyright, they want to ascertain their actions are within the law. Documentation listed above explicates the multi-layered IR copyright permission process as a useful resource faculty can refer to for allaying concerns.

As a follow-up to depositing faculty scholarship, emailing them with a link to their newly archived research affords them an opportunity to view their scholarly "record" and visually comprehend what an IR is and the probability of potential reader and citation impact. Depending on institutional repository software features in use, researchers may anticipate an item download count found in a range of repository types and formats, such as:

- located in irplus (University of Rochester repository) a department page with a list of file names and number of downloads (*https://*

*urresearch.rochester.edu/institutionalPublicationPublicView.action?in stitutionalItemId=13591*);

- monthly emails providing the number of item downloads for the previous month and the total downloads since the article was ingested in Digital Commons® (bepress, a hosted IR product) (*http://www. bepress.com/download_counts.html*);

- T-Space (University of Toronto): A DSpace statistics webpage for the university community. Public users must request a login account to view statistics (*https://tspace.library.utoronto.ca/policies/policies.jsp*).

# Additional types of high-value research

In addition to journal articles, there are other "high-value" original scholarly research materials to cultivate with faculty that deserve open access visibility, some of which have been historically stored on computer hard drives given a previous lack of an archival mechanism. Much of this intellectual content is considered grey literature, a body of research that librarians typically and selectively collect to maintain and manage that is not easily found through conventional publishing channels. The advent of institutional repository software has granted these materials a new life and a secure future, as the nature of the repository and its archival options lend themselves to embracing grey resources. This literature may be comprised of materials underserved by traditional publishing: original research such as primary source materials, technical reports, government research (may include notes, observations, data), student theses and dissertations, conferences, presentations, lectures, publicly funded research and datasets, and educational course materials are prime candidates for the IR.

Librarians, with their discerning collection development skills, are poised to evaluate grey literature for its validity, including incorporating metadata and providing persistence of access, such as archiving in an open access environment to increase its accessibility. Librarians might collaborate with faculty or an archivist on a project that entails worthwhile grey literature typically unavailable to readers. This valuable content is normally hidden in: file cabinets; special collections and university archives; on computer hard drives; or in other storage spaces. Dependent on value or restrictions, research and special collections' actors may suggest archiving these materials.

Metadata fields in a repository record assist in the spectrum of authority control. Institutional repositories that include an *Item Type* or a *Comments* field, as an example, enable IR staff to complete metadata fields to discern grey literature for researchers. Thorough metadata is necessary to easily locate this literature in all of its manifestations and to identify an item's findability and validity. "Libraries need to continue to be involved in identifying it and defining its value and should play a role in providing persistence for valid grey literature" (Huffine, 2010).

Table 2.2 shows examples of grey literature and conventional research item types that are prime materials for the scientist, scholar, or student to engage with. Grey literature tends to be informally published, fugitive, and ephemeral. Since IRs have been in existence, this content has become more easily accessible, as much of it has enduring value and is targeted to be archived in perpetuity.

The Grey Literature Network Service (GreyNet), based in Amsterdam, the Netherlands, was founded in 1992 to "facilitate dialog, research, and communication between persons and organizations in the field of grey literature" (*http://www.greynet.org/*). More recently, GreyNet has evolved into an in-house grey literature archive of PowerPoint conference presentations that also include the first page of the conference proceedings.

**Table 2.2** Grey literature and conventional research item types for ingesting in an institutional repository

| University materials | Faculty research and course materials | Student IR materials |
|---|---|---|
| University publications, patents, white papers | Preprints, postprints, journal articles | E-theses/dissertations (ETDS) |
| Audio/visual presentations, transcripts | Conference papers, posters, PowerPoints | Professional papers and capstones |
| Special collections and archival content | Publicly funded research and datasets Open access journals | Journal articles |
| Hosted conferences, PowerPoints, events | Technical reports | Conference papers, posters, PowerPoints |
| Governance meeting minutes: academic senate, institute and staff council, student government | Working papers Audio/visual presentations, transcripts Monographs, books, open textbook content Educational course materials, syllabi | Undergraduate honors research Audio/visual presentations |

In May 2011, the Institutional Repository Search Tool (IRST), an organization of experts that support the advancement of knowledge and influence world-class research and teaching, data-mined GreyNet's entire collection of conference papers (*http://irs.mimas.ac.uk/demonstrator/*). Based at the University of Manchester and in conjunction with the UK's Joint Information Systems Committee (JISC), the IRST has completed the inclusion of GreyNet's entire collection of grey literature conference papers from 1993 forward to be searched and downloaded.

Grey literature and other value-added item types are prime content to archive in a repository, providing additional research materials to researchers. The Grey Net International website maintains a comprehensive list of document types (*http://www.greynet.org/greysourceindex/document types.html*).

Another option for valued and high-profile IR research may include monographs where the copyright agreement has expired and the authors are free to republish in an open access repository. The textbook, *Introduction to Compiler Construction with UNIX*, by Schreiner and Friedman, transferred into the public domain twenty years after the publishing contract was signed in 1985. Professor Schreiner contacted Rochester Institute of Technology's IR manager to request the scanning and archiving of the monograph (personal correspondence). While the technical validity of a 20-year-old UNIX book should be questioned to justify the effort involved in scanning and archiving as well as using server space, it turned out the book specializes in Java and other programming techniques that maintain their value to master and better utilize current programming systems.

Because books are typically written for financial gain and contracts involve royalties on sales, they differ from journal articles where no author royalties exist. It does not make financial sense for book or monograph authors to give away their personal profits by archiving their work in an IR. Publisher copyrights tend to be closely guarded, although there are exceptions, such as Allen Hatcher's *Algebraic Topology*, first published by Cambridge University Press in 2002. The publisher markets and sells the hard copy and is amenable to researchers freely downloading the open access version. Minor errors are continually edited and updated on site. Out-of-copyright books may acquire rejuvenation in academic interest and be easily findable if archived in an institutional repository. Regardless of copyright constraints, there is value in making the metadata available for readers to locate research and be accounted for in an institution's annual academic assessment. Internet search engines will discover the books and potential readers will find them. Faculty talking points for open access books are growing – here are a few:

- The Internet-First University Press (Cornell): *http://ecommons.library. cornell.edu/handle/1813/62*. Readers may download monographs for free or purchase print-on-demand.

- The John D. and Catherine T. MacArthur Foundation Series on Living and Learning with New Media from the MIT Press: *https://mitpress. mit.edu/books/living-and-learning-new-media*. This report summarizes the results of a three-year ethnographic study, funded by the Foundation Series, on how young people are living and learning with new media in varied settings – at home, in after-school programs, and in online spaces.

- AU Press (Athabasca University, Canada): *http://www.aupress.ca/ index.php/*. Readers may download books for free; the press publishes nearly all of its books (and journals) in an open access context. Monographs may also be purchased.

- Open Access Publishing in European Networks: *http://www.oapen. org/xtf/home?brand=oapen*. Interested readers may download OAPEN social sciences and humanities monographs, utilize Google Books, or purchase from Amazon.com. This is a collaborative European initiative to implement an open access publication model that is sustainable and "aims to improve the visibility and usability of high quality academic research by aggregating peer-reviewed Open Access publications from across Europe."

Journal article authors who published in the mid-1980s are discovering that some of their retrospective research is enjoying a renaissance now that the articles are open access and easily found. Anecdotal evidence from faculty at the University of Nevada, Las Vegas and statistics on article downloads demonstrate that scholarship from the 1980s is indeed being rediscovered. Bernard Rentier, Rector of the University of Liège (Belgium), commented in an interview:

> Many people, including myself, have noticed that our old papers have begun to live a new life. For instance, one of my articles dating back to 1985, and which had been completely forgotten, has begun a new career, and is now being downloaded frequently! (Poynder, 2011b).

# Talking points that engage the campus: visibility and accessibility tools

A primary talking point for an IR already laden with positive aspects is the global visibility of research. As institutional repositories adhere to an internationally agreed upon array of technical standards, all of the metadata (citation information, keywords, and other identifiers) is revealed in basically the same way. The OAI-PMH protocol (Open Archives Initiative Protocol for Metadata Harvesting) exposes metadata for findability and search engines facilitate information retrieval through interoperability of indexing the contents of IRs. These back-end online processes engage in the discovery of open access scholarship and research repositories that comprise publicly available global research. External search engines index the content and therefore are the primary means by which a researcher finds open access scholarship (Carr, 2006).

Google, Yahoo Search, Lycos, MSN Search, Teoma, and Gigablast search engines use OAI-PMH for metadata harvesting. The OAI-PMH defines a mechanism for harvesting records containing metadata from repositories that support scholarly communication (*http://www.oaforum. org/tutorial/english/page1.htm*). According to the *Ranking Web of World Repositories* website, an initiative of the Cybermetrics Lab, a research group belonging to the Consejo Superior de Investigaciones Científicas (CSIC), the largest public research body in Spain, these search engines explore a repository's index and return matches to researchers. On their website, it states that these six search engines listed above are the only ones that quantitatively search and analyze an index returning matches (see *http://repositories.webometrics.info/about.html*).

Resource discovery using the OAI-PMH is not limited to search engines. International aggregators, such as OAIster, the Directory of Open Access Repositories (*Open*DOAR), the Registry of Open Access Repositories (ROAR), and the Directory of Open Access Journals (DOAJ) use the OAI-PMH protocol for amassing metadata on scholarly items within their respective websites. Researchers can conduct queries from these aggregator sites to maximize their scholarly query potential.

## *OAIster*

Originally created by the University of Michigan, OAIster is a free, OAI-PMH compliant and accessible citation-only research database discovery tool currently owned and managed by the Online Computer Library Center, Inc. (OCLC) for searching scholarship in open access repositories (*http://oaister.worldcat.org/*). Institutional repository managers and metadata librarians/specialists may use the WorldCat Gateway (*http://www.oclc.org/gateway/gettingstarted/default.htm*) to upload their repository content metadata to OAIster and WorldCat. The metadata can be customized by how it is displayed and associated with specific digital collections. The schedule for metadata harvesting is customizable by month, by quarter, semi-annually, and annually.

## *Open*DOAR

The Directory of Open Access Repositories is an authoritative directory that supports academic and research activities in open access repositories (*http://www.opendoar.org/*). Each *Open*DOAR repository listing has its recorded information checked by staff, a thorough review approach subsequently providing a list of quality-controlled repositories. As of August 2013, the database lists over 2,394 IR listings and allows for repository content searching. Unlike OAIster, *Open*DOAR links the reader directly to the full-text IR record (if available). It is maintained by SHERPA Services, based at the University of Nottingham's Centre for Research Communications.

## *ROAR*

The Registry of Open Access Repositories is hosted at the University of Southampton, UK and is made possible by funding from the Joint Information Systems Committee (JISC), "inspiring UK colleges and universities in the innovative use of digital technologies, helping to maintain the UK's position as a global leader in education." ROAR is part of the EPrints.org network and promotes the progress of open access by imparting timely information about the development and status of repositories throughout the world. Researchers may search for full-text scholarly materials at: *http://roar.eprints.org/*.

## *DOAJ*

The Directory of Open Access Journals was conceived in 2002 (*http://www.doaj.org/doaj?func=home&uiLanguage=en*). In response to recent growth and increased demands for new developments, a new library community-based solution has assumed operations in 2013. The DOAJ's goal has been to increase the visibility and ease of open access scientific and scholarly journals' use by stimulating increased usage and impact. The Directory's objective is to showcase all open access scientific and scholarly journals that use a peer-review quality control system. All content is freely available. As of August 2013, there were over 9,901 journals and 1,201,052 articles in all subjects and multiple languages, from 120 countries.

# Faculty

In addition to searching or browsing these scholarly tools, the faculty researcher's work will be aggregated either as a citation for resource discovery, as publisher full-text if copyright permits, or where there is green access (postprint). A one-time deposit in an open access repository has a ripple effect of manifold opportunities to be automatically integrated into other exploratory tools, such as search engines. Maximizing a research article's visibility and accessibility are key tactics to potentially increase impact.

Journal article impact inquiries have been conducted with positive results for articles that reside in an open access environment. Studies reveal that the more obtainable an article, the further potential to be frequently cited, garnering greater impact. Open access is affecting citation count metrics. According to the 1999–2002 report from the Open Citation Project (which includes Southampton University, Cornell University, and arXiv.org), the goal was to measure the speed of scientific communication and user activity in mature eprint archives of research papers, such as arXiv. Among the aspects considered were the rate at which findings affected other researchers' ideas found to be increasing dramatically. Driving this impact factor was free, unrestricted access to research papers. High-impact papers were retrieved more often and over a longer sustained period; the peak of citations occurred sooner and was higher for papers deposited in each succeeding year. The research implied that the speed of scientific communication and the rate at which ideas affected other researchers was increasing dramatically as a ripple effect (Hitchcock et al., 2002).

Taking into consideration the number of new faculty over the previous ten years who archived in open access repositories since this study was completed, their influence has more than likely expanded exponentially, especially for the high-impact journal articles. Open access is affecting alternative metrics (altmetrics), such as citation counts from the scholarly literature. In repositories that track file downloads it is possible to also include these metrics. Some journal publishers allow referenced blog observations and other social media commentary tools for readers to write critical public remarks that may enhance (or not) an article's review, while also providing an opportunity for others to respond to existing observations. Repository software commenting tools are increasingly more popular with readers. As an example, Digital Commons® uses Intense Debate (*http://digitalscholarship.unlv.edu/ nursing_fac_articles/1/*). There are numerous social media tools included in the tool package. Twitter, one of the tools, has shown amazing results in promoting OA research, culminating in greater readership and potential impact. Comprehensive information regarding a variety of impact factors are covered in Chapter 6.

Access to the various open assessment tools functions to determine how and where research is being used and cited. In conjunction with discussing IR intersecting talking points with faculty who aspire to continually maximize their citation impact, it is useful for them to know that studies show an open access advantage is actually a quality advantage. Readers are freed from the constraints of merely possessing access to articles only available by means of a journal subscription. "If scholarly output is locked away behind fire walls, or on hard drives, or in print only, it risks becoming invisible to the automated Web crawlers, indexers, and authority-interpreters that are being developed. Scholarly invisibility is rarely the path to scholarly authority" (Jensen, 2007). As open access to intellectual content expands, researchers will have a larger pool of superior quality articles to choose from.

The remaining talking points for faculty are concerned with an IR's sustainable features. Repositories are technically secure systems and provide URIs that are not subject to change. Readers may request IR scholarship to be "pushed out" by subject-based email alerts and RSS feeds. By furnishing a mechanism for open access research, repositories are a constructive response to inflationary journal subscription and interlibrary loan request costs, and photocopying, while article publishing lag time may be diminished. The repository remains a sustainable tool provided the library ensures continuous researcher buy-in and recurring use, as an IR's success is built on the quality of its content and the number of items. It is a responsibility of the "unofficial repository marketing team," i.e., library staff, to ensure that faculty, students, and administrators are continuously presented with the ideals of the IR and its benefits. A university department, college, or academy mandate is advantageous for a campus and the global research community to maintain the trajectory of scholarship flowing in and openly procurable. Mandates are detailed in Chapter 4.

# Administrators' IR point of view and documenting academy research

The scholarly communication engagement of academic administrators is critical to a successful repository enterprise in a different but equally essential way to faculty scholarship. Articulating the advantages of an IR requires an approach that is typically initiated by the library dean or repository manager with a presentation to the university's academic or deans' executive council, characteristically composed of a variety of administrators. Management may consist of the president, provost/vice provosts, academic deans, and vice presidents of finance and business, university advancement, student affairs, diversity and inclusion, research, and potentially other members and invitees. Other stakeholders may include a senior advisor to the president and a student government president, for obvious reasons of their positions. It is not unusual to have a repository manager to co-present or be available to field IR questions.

Academic administrators are characteristically not at the forefront of the open access milieu, although there are solid exceptions. Bernard Rentier, Rector of the University of Liège, envisions not just a change, but seeks "a global revolution" in scholarly communication to demonstrate to the world the quality of research Liège university's scientists and scholars are achieving and facilitate making their papers available to increase both their impact and visibility within the global research community (Poynder, 2011b). Administrators against open access publication as a result of a conjecture that faculty are using an IR to publish journal articles without the conventional peer-review process needs a clarification of terminology. Whether an article is made available by journal subscription or through an open access journal, it is incumbent on the editors to be transparent and address the peer-review issue. Conversing on the notion of showcasing the Directory of Open Access Journals (DOAJ) as an aggregator of peer-reviewed articles may eliminate possible ambiguity.

These same administrators typically create biannual strategic documents for education planning purposes and to inform external communities where their tax dollars are being spent. It is not unusual to have a reference to research activity embedded in an academic document that states a central goal to increase scholarly productivity to become or remain nationally recognized. Using the documented research goals as an opening and continuous thread throughout a presentation reinforces the importance of the university's research objectives the library and the IR can play an integral part in fulfilling.

As a general principle, university stakeholders should be aware of the IR tool and consider embracing the value of "access to research as a public good." It can be achieved by the university actively promoting the stakeholder economy to off-campus donors, state and local citizens, businesses, and other entities that would appreciate access to intellectual content. This is an opportunity to take notice and confirm the institution's repository that promulgates their research and exponentially raises the visibility of the academy.

To enable university administrators to blend the IR concept with the library's messaging without the benefit or knowledge of their own institution's repository, a useful approach is to show them examples of external repositories to get a sense of what advantages might accrue. Libraries encourage internal stakeholders, including faculty to visualize the tool's benefits and the value proposition it provides on multiple levels, including individual, department, and college research activity.

A library dean can affirm the library's principle as the nexus of campus research and the sharing of knowledge by making the case for faculty and sudent scholarly endeavor support, also providing high visibility for the institution's scientist and scholar strategic research. The dean will also be aware of the potential negativity and be knowledgeable at some level about new modes of scholarly communication to introduce and sustain the repository message with the assistance of the IR manager or scholarly communication librarian, to garner campus research and archival content.

The primary focus is best served by concentrating on the benefits of open access for higher education materials. These might include the aggregation of the academy's scholarship in a centralized location, extending the visibility of the academy's research, and supporting collaborations with potential to expand. By browsing or exploring an IR's scholarly assets using search engines, the attendees will have a visual understanding of the concepts.

Invariably, during a library's IR presentation, academic administrators and faculty will also want to know how faculty and student research will be archived in the repository. How will the scholarship be garnered and what is the process for faculty and student research and other academic materials to be acquired and accessed by the local and global online community? As scholarly communication demands necessitate depositing new types of materials press forward, an evaluation of needs and new processes will be necessary. The notion of managing and curating data in an IR (small to medium datasets) is an ideal example of what academic libraries are currently encountering.

A repository sustainably links faculty and student scholarly materials in perpetuity (using uniform resource identifiers), aggregating intellectual property in one location. There is less paper to be handled and the opportunity to accumulate research is gradually assuaging the effect of subscription cuts and journal price inflation over time.

Administrators want an optimal system that tracks and highlights faculty and student scholarship. Further talking points based on academic management need also center on archiving mandated/non-mandated grant research output and accompanying datasets. Deans and other administrators are naturally interested in the various metrics collected from IR content and usage. Repository statistics may be harvested in various ways, dependent on the particular IR software. Metric and analytic tools are covered in Chapter 6.

## Graduate and undergraduate student opportunities to showcase their research

Academic administrations have recognized that undergraduate and graduate student research is valuable and has a profound presence in an open access repository environment, particularly graduate work. Repository statistics show a high rate of document downloads as proof of the research worth in e-theses/dissertations (ETDs). "Theses and dissertations are the most useful kinds of invisible scholarship and the most invisible kinds of useful scholarship. Because of their high quality and low visibility, the access problem is worth solving, and nothing solves the access problem better than open access (OA)" (Suber, 2011). Student scholarship has historically been exposed only in print format that requires a visit "in person" to university archives or an interlibrary loan.

Most academic libraries aspire to digitally archive graduate student ETDs and enter respective metadata, having already engaged the graduate schools in the benefits of open access theses and dissertations. ETDs have gained research traction, subsequently benefiting the graduate student, the university, and the local and global research communities. Many universities have policies mandating ETDs in an IR. Typically saturated with original research, ETDs have a solid record of receiving a plethora of researcher downloads.

The evidence for download impact and for the success of an ETD mandate is shown in the high rate of "hits" at Brunel University, host of the University College London's IR. Each of Brunel's e-theses is transferred on average more times than other types of research output in their repository. As of fall 2009, the University of Glasgow, Scotland's ETD collection had one of many highly downloaded theses – in excess of 37,000 times, a figure that underscores the potential reach of a successful ETD (Brown & Sadler, 2010).

Another advantage of ETDs that has benefits now and in the future is students previously in the research process will have archived a thesis or dissertation for other students to use and review as an example for their own work. Graduate students can easily share their ETDs with a current or prospective employer or, if applying to another graduate school program, refer an academic admissions officer to the student's ETD.

Graduate students also co-research and collaborate with their colleagues and faculty to create posters and write articles, becoming competent in completing a literature review and penetrating the depths of discourse and data analysis. An IR offers the graduate student novice various prospects to become skilled at using essential research tools and become proficient in the scholarly communication process for current and future publication submissions. Librarians have an opportunity to play a role in engaging students in the open access philosophy and publishing opportunities.

Dedicated associate deans and graduate coordinators at the University of Nevada, Las Vegas (UNLV) aspire to support their students by partnering with faculty to peer-review their posters. The Greenspun College of Urban Affairs conducts an annual graduate research symposium where faculty peer-review student work. This provides an occasion for students to present and archive their findings in the IR (*http://digitalcommons.library.unlv.edu/grad_symposium/*). UNLV's Howard R. Hughes College of Engineering hosts an event "that recognizes the scholarly work of our engineering and computer science graduate students within the college." "The objective of the event is to promote and publicize the research activities of the College of Engineering and to inform our stakeholders of our students' achievements" (*http://digitalscholarship.unlv.edu/celebration/2012/april27/25/*).

University of Rhode Island (US) and the Technical University of Braunschweig (Germany) graduate students collaborated on an international partnership for research and education with a grant to investigate micro-fluidic technology and its applications. The initial outcome of the research was a poster. It is not unusual for a poster to

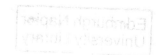

develop and evolve into a future journal article. By documenting their scholarship in an OA repository, the students have recorded their findings and may further solidify the intellectual content by expanding on the poster's subject matter (*http://digitalcommons.uri.edu/discovery/2011/posters/2/*).

Another instance of graduate scholarship showcased in an IR is a Harvard Law School student's award-winning research paper, "Providing a corrective subsidy to insurers for success in reducing traffic accidents," archived in DASH (Digital Access to Scholarship at Harvard) (*http://dash.harvard.edu/handle/1/4889453*). Working with the faculty of graduate and undergraduate research programs who explicate the benefits of open access can be a successful talking point for encouraging students to aspire to conduct research, and subsequently impart those studies by depositing them in their affiliated institutional repository.

Honors' theses, posters, articles, and conference presentations can be contributed to an IR. This is a positive OA trend for students and the academy to highlight undergraduate scholarship and engage the students in the value of open research. At Mt Holyoke College, Massachusetts, Liberal Arts' students have the prospect of archiving their honors' theses in the college's repository (*https://ida.mtholyoke.edu/jspui/handle/10166/141*).

The UNLV University Libraries' Lance and Elena Calvert Award for Undergraduate Research has endowed funds to sponsor its annual research competition. The honor and prize recognize "excellence in undergraduate research projects that incorporate the use of University Libraries' collections and demonstrate sophisticated information literacy skills on the part of the undergraduate researcher" (*http://digitalcommons.library.unlv.edu/award/*).

As graduate and undergraduate students commit at a deeper level of open access to research, institutional repository managers and liaisons will continue to inform instructors and motivated students to actively contribute their scholarship to the global effort.

# A social marketing approach to garnering content and populating the IR

There is a plethora of institutional repository talking points to attract faculty and their students to adopt a variant means of scholarly communication to showcase the output of their research activities. The open access concept supports a simple solution that may seem obvious, but for those faculty members entrenched in subscription access only, open scholarship can be a leap in understanding the intellectual value in archiving journal articles or postprints in an IR.

To be successful in garnering faculty scholarship, it is critical to understand their specific set of needs and innate scholarly goals. Their research is a personal enterprise where ownership of content and the ability to communicate results to peers is paramount. The term *institutional repository* may have a low attraction to faculty, implying "the system is designed to support and achieve the needs and goals of the institution, and not necessarily those of the individual" (Blythe & Chachra, 2005). Unless the value of individual faculty members' scholarship is identified and taken into consideration, there may not be perceived benefits for these faculty. For the institutional repository to prosper, multiple user requirements and viewpoints should be taken into consideration, especially when engaged in marketing.

Once the peer-review process was established in the mid-seventeenth century, scholars have published without personal reward for the sake of knowledge itself. Peer recognition and social value was and is currently their recompense and of foremost importance. Tangentially, libraries are strategically repositioning themselves beyond their traditional role as custodians of research resources to manifest a dynamic engagement with a scholarly communication paradigm that directly involves scientists and scholars and their published works. Librarians endemically "have a democratic vision of universal learning and education" (Rausing, 2010) and are leveraging their expertise in organizing, maintaining, and providing access to digital intellectual content, authority control (organization of bibliographic information), and metadata tagging. Coupled with library expertise and continuing to work closely with faculty, IR managers and library "ambassadors" are marketing and growing institutional repositories that afford extraordinary visibility beyond the physical academic environment. Over time, the library's scholarly communication efforts can become a "hook" to the university and its stakeholders as the community realizes the value propositions that engage and attract an administrator's strategic goals.

Faculty scholarly communication behaviors in research publishing activities may be contradictory to the academic libraries' vision of open research benefits. A successful repository is dependent on whether or not researchers are willing to deposit their articles. At varying levels, libraries are focused on the scholarly communication exchange to: cost less; publish more quickly; and be more effective in garnering a range of existing research availability. As this monograph is in progress, faculty everywhere are engaging at a higher level of OA to research by their own volition and by university and federal mandates. The need to take action is fundamental to social marketing, as a basic and systematic application of marketing to achieve a change in a specific audience's behavior for a societal good, such as education, health programs, or other aspects of social awareness that affect a population segment.

# Social marketing theory

The theory underlying the discipline of social marketing is to induce voluntary change by selling ideas or lifestyle changes that benefit a target audience or society in general. In basic marketing, to promote a product there are four initial Ps to consider – Product, Price, Promotion, and Place. These Ps represent a blend of basic concepts that provide the background theory. Social marketing subsequently appends four additional Ps: Public, Partnership, Policy, and Purse-string, enabling the marketing program to operate effectively (Kar, 2011).

In promoting an IR and employing social marketing theory, all eight Ps have an intrinsic place in the marketing design of the repository system:

- *Product*: an IR with all of its features.
- *Price*: inclusive of staff time and effort in archiving materials – the smaller or leaner the effort, the greater the benefit.
- *Promotion*: communication activity to promote the IR and garner attention by explicating the model to inspire use by archiving journal articles and other scholarly content.
- *Place*: ease of access to the repository and clarity of navigating documentation.
- *Public*: responsiveness to each stakeholder group that has its own needs: faculty, administrators, students, library staff.
- *Partnership*: IR collaborative efforts among library staff and with stakeholders, such as faculty, administrators, and students.
- *Policy*: open access mandates, IR and university policies.
- *Purse-string*: IR outcomes that match administration, faculty, or libraries' funding interest.

According to an advertising consultant, "In marketing terms, a service qualifies as an intangible product. And successful products either bring in money or generate usage and provide benefits" (Gierveld, 2006). An institutional repository meets the criteria as a product that needs to attract its own market through its services to garner scholarly materials and provide the benefit of global access to research.

An institutional repository qualifies for this definition of a successful product, particularly in generating the use of research and providing benefits to readers and authors. In marketing theory, Kotler, Armstrong, Saunders, & Wong (1999) state that every product has three levels: the *core level*, the *actual level*, and the *augmented level*. These are discussed below with examples of what each marketing level offers an institutional repository in terms of universal usage and deliverable benefits. Repository managers, liaisons, and additional library staff may find these useful in advertising and promoting the academy's IR (Gierveld, 2006).

- *The core level product represents primary benefits, describes the item, and solves problems.* The IR showcases archived scholarship at faculty, department, college, and university levels; increases visibility and accessibility; provides local and global dissemination of research typically locked up behind journal subscriptions or the levy of an article processing charge (APC); promotes university intellectual content; utilizes a platform for scholarly work that is under-served by traditional publishing; aggregates research in a centralized location; and allows graduate students to point to their ETDs for current and prospective employers' use as a career tool.

- *At the actual level, product features, quality, design, and packaging is described by: user perceptions, the object for use, a set of characteristics, and gives an identity.* Institutional repositories provide: open access; enriched and accurate metadata; a search feature to locate and view an author's intellectual content; item findability utilizing a search engine or easy browsing by author or department; a sustainable value that includes perpetual URIs and is digital rather than paper; an archive with relevant scholarship; opportunities for higher citation impact; prospects for interdisciplinary research collaborations; and is an engaging academic tool.

- *The augmented level includes features that make a product easy to use and ensures customer satisfaction.* Repository staff use a process of examining CVs to check article copyright (SHERPA/RoMEO); staff request publisher permissions; supply media migration services for faculty; and endorse the use of email alerts and social media applications that include RSS feeds. Some repository software tools are configured for monthly download metrics of archived articles and additional scholarship, have sustainable work flows, and maintain "about the IR" documentation for users. Digital Commons® (DC) created a Discipline Commons Network™ featuring repositories by discipline, institutions, keywords, and publication information. Only full-text scholarly items are included in the network (*http://network. bepress.com/explore/?q=library*).

Modifications to scholarly communication behavior are necessary for researchers to add an institutional repository to their already hectic research and article dissemination activity. Academic libraries are poised to comprehend researchers' work patterns and fulfill their needs to design and create a new generation of ongoing versatile services to support the research process. An academic library's efforts towards establishing a useful and quality-perceived repository will encourage the rate of interest and deposit.

A strategic marketing plan has the ability to endorse a library's scholarly archive. Borrowing a social marketing communications strategy used for a project that persuaded people to increase their recycling habits, the approach offers a practical contextual framework of four elements that can be applied to develop and deliver a communications methodology to influence faculty to engage in showcasing their intellectual property in an open access repository (Gierveld, 2006).

According to Mee, Clewes, & Read (2004), four strategic communication elements were employed on a recycling project where citizens needed support to be convinced to alter their behaviors and embrace an increased level of sustainable activity. The successful project strategies can be extrapolated to encourage scientists and scholars to deposit their research in an institutional repository:

1. A *profiling strategy* helps brand the item and raises awareness of why repositories were created and how they are useful. It also encourages an understanding of the IR's scholarly communication value and benefits to the faculty and administration. The creation of marketing collateral, such as factsheets, newsletters, articles, presentations, and university-wide emails, facilitates faculty and administrator awareness to globally showcase and deposit their work; subsequently they assume a more positive attitude towards open access.

2. A *pull tactic* is about the features that attract faculty, administrators, and students to the IR with incentives that offer direct rewards, such as timely proxy archiving or self-archiving, media migration services, download counts, and worldwide exposure – all scholarly communication services they have not previously received. Make it

easy for authors by checking copyright and email requests for faculty postprints to activate and maintain their repository presence.

3. A *push strategy* entails continuing to promote the IR's attractive features and involves the intended audience utilizing a collaborative, two-way dialog approach. Capture scientists' and scholars' attention with informal conversations, presentations, collaborations, knowledge of discipline-specific and scholarly communication opportunities. Follow up on faculty referral endorsements and enquiries in archiving upcoming conferences, migrating existing paper journals, and other scholarly activity.

4. The *consultation approach* focuses on attracting scientists and scholars to new modes of disseminating scholarship and engaging their colleagues, including graduate students. The repository manager and liaisons are some of the influencers that create initial opportunities to purvey repository benefits by giving presentations, setting up informal meetings, and making individual connections.

Marketing an institutional repository is all about the benefits of adding an essential scholarly communication tool to publishing toolboxes, sustaining researchers' intellectual content. The business of promoting an IR across multiple disciplines requires an understanding of diverse research styles and needs to be taken into consideration, while continuing to develop and convey an enduring marketing plan. Institutional repository tools are in constant evolution and implementation phases; there will always be a demand for product development and a flexible, but solid, communications strategy to engage librarians, faculty, students, and academic administrators. Repository managers will want to consider focusing on the IR's expectations of depositors and readers to ensure that the product and the attendant services meet their needs. Institutional mandates remove the necessity of marketing to garner recently published faculty articles. Engaging a campus in social marketing theory has the potential for migration towards a research mandate, the garnering of retrospective articles, and a variety of additional types of scholarship.

# Successful marketing strategies and best practices for garnering IR content

The broader model of a marketing approach to garnering content and populating the institutional repository encompasses the eight Ps of social marketing and provides a framework and a breadth of details, especially the two Ps, Product and Promotion. They are the focal points for the IR message: communication activities are carried out to garner interest, explain the open access concept, and motivate faculty to archive intellectual materials in the academy's repository. "Academic libraries must move beyond this limited perception of our utility and expand our role to become partners in a broader range of scholarly activities at our institutions" (Gilman & Kunkel, 2010). By proactively being involved in the research process, the academic library has an opportunity to play a vital role as a scholarly communication collaborator. This is an opportune point in time to continue advocating for change in scientific and scholarly practices that benefits faculty, students, the academy, and promotes the IR.

Marketing activities provide day-to-day opportunities for the library's IR manager and liaisons to interact with faculty and administrators. Once a repository is created, it will continue to require basic scholarly content such as journal articles, presentations, conference materials, and university records that illustrate the broad concept of the IR to initially engage academics and maintain their interest. The concept of open access benefits underlies this essential scholarship tool.

An institutional repository manager will be most successful in garnering content if there is a continuous stream of IR marketing points ready to call on at any time and in any appropriate situation. Focusing on strategic scholarship deposits by campus colleagues creates movement in the IR, giving it a greater potential to be viral. There will be faculty who spread the word to their colleagues and additional scientists and scholars will communicate their enthusiasm towards the open access advantages.

Academic campuses tend to have a research dean or provost who has a wealth of faculty publishing knowledge and research across all disciplines. An appointment with these valuable administrative resources is sure to yield a list of faculty to approach for garnering scholarly materials. Contacting faculty and mentioning that a research dean recommended their intellectual content for the IR has the positive potential to elicit a curriculum vitae (CV) subsequently emailed as a guide to locate full-text articles and additional scholarship, or to add bibliographic records where copyright prohibits deposits.

Campus associate deans are key people to engage and discuss the value of scholarly assets in an open access context. Library liaisons may secure a meeting with their college's associate dean to discuss which faculty are the prolific research producers in the college. In the same conversation, associate deans may be amenable to an IR presentation given at a monthly executive meeting or will defer to department chairs to set up faculty presentations. The department head's referral is a positive introduction to the repository: "The dean suggested I contact you about a *high-impact* scholarship tool that is beneficial to faculty and student research." This top-down approach is an effective tactic to engage the interest of academic administrators in the benefits of open access to research.

Focusing on garnering strategic campus faculty and student scholarship creates movement in the IR. The notion of a static repository will discourage use – retrospective material has value, as does current content. The top-down approach in conjunction with the bottom-up tactic of attracting faculty and student scholarly materials produces a holistic means of capturing repository content from all academic sectors. Scholarship may include articles, chapters, monographs, working papers, technical reports, conference papers/posters, theses/dissertations, capstones/professional papers, honors theses, datasets, audio/visual presentations, white papers, and publicly funded research.

Staff and administrators may also be attracted to the IR and use it for archiving a variety of multi-organizational minutes. An example from Rochester Institute of Technology (RIT) is their Advisors Council Minutes (*https://ritdml.rit.edu/handle/1850/3312*). Collaborating with the university's archives to deposit meeting minutes in the repository is an efficient method for the committee and the academic community to access the minutes and presentations from meetings. Staff interested in senate minutes can search across one or multiple collections for keyword phrases to link threads of information together to acquire related subject matter. The repository's capability for keyword searching across a collection returns all relevant documents in a list. The virtual IR file cabinet model saves time and potential frustration for its reader. RIT's meeting minutes are deposited in the IR (*https://ritdml.rit.edu/handle/1850/2432*). The academic senate and council proceedings are emailed to the RIT community with a persistent link to the repository; it is efficient and effective as a workable archive. Most importantly, it is a way to illustrate the IR's significance and capabilities that encourages faculty, staff, and students to peruse the repository.

The more current and varied the scholarly content, the greater the prospect of repository buy-in. Other campus entities, centers, conferences, labs, research partnerships, interdisciplinary programs/projects, special collections and university archives are always considering ways to promote their research and archival materials to remain visible and viable. Contacting the office that sends campus-wide emails with references to a recently developed department's newsletter, a unique program of speakers, or a campus-sponsored conference, shows genuine interest on the part of the library to collaborate on showcasing academic activities. Series of competitions, student poster sessions, award-winning research datasets, and academic-affiliated presentations are part of the research and grey literature that tends to vanish after its initial debut.

To capture the elusive research activities, it is essential for the IR manager and liaisons to reach out and build relationships within the campus. Those who hesitate to be creative in marketing and garnering scholarly materials may encounter a loss of faculty interest if they pause too long. A first contact may not bring in immediate content, but with sustained effort and sincere interest a researcher may alter an attitude about the benefits and importance of open access.

The ongoing promotion of the repository is successful and faculty have agreed to archive their scholarly output in the institutional repository. Some academic libraries prefer to upload faculty research while others allow researchers to self-archive their work. There are a number of valid reasons why IR staff proxy-archive the deposit of materials for faculty as part of a suite of services, encompassing most repository software:

- The process is easy and efficient – would faculty take the time to self-archive without a mandate?

- It becomes part of the researchers' scholarly communication workflow to email completed articles or postprints to the IR manager or use a library-created electronic submission form.

- It provides version control by ensuring that related documents link to one another.

- A style guide may be produced and consulted to ensure all entries have complete and uniform metadata, such as capitalization, naming conventions, authority-controlled vocabularies, and other essential information.

- It serves the needs of internal/external stakeholders by making intellectual materials available.

- An author's scholarly content can be showcased by offering a "Researcher Page." As an example, see the University of Rochester web page at *https://urresearch.rochester.edu/viewResearcherPage.action? researcherId=153*. In addition, Digital Commons® offers SelectedWorks pages for their researchers (*http://digitalcommons.bepress.com/ repository-software/faculty/*). Authors are featured by linking faculty research to a brief biography, photograph, and subject expertise.

- It represents a private document management system that safely stores and manages files.
- It supports a collaborative working area for faculty-to-faculty and faculty-to-student use.

## Summary

With or without university or system-wide academic mandates primarily focused on articles and postprints, there is an overabundance of research that is locked up behind paywalls, on computers, and in file cabinets. Periodically reviewing our approaches to targeted content and best practices can yield scholarly materials from the least likely people and places. Engaging with multiple campus constituencies that contribute research engenders collaboration and has the potential to build unique collections.

# 3

# The successful institutional repository

**Abstract.** A number of factors and features indicate institutional repository success, although the implementation of a faculty senate mandate, such as Harvard University's model and the University of California's ten campus system example, is unsurpassed for building and accelerating the pace of scholarly research. This chapter discusses a recent study that focuses on the number of existing journal articles exemplifying how few articles readers have at their collective disposal and the potential for further discovery. In addition to the touchstone article, this chapter discusses a wide range of scholarly material types of which some items are grouped in the grey literature category and, with permission, academic content can be deposited, dependent on local collection development policies. Difficult-to-locate erudite material is especially of value to readers who require a range of knowledge for their research.

**Keywords:** administrative documents, COAPI, collection development, CONTENTdm®, grey literature, content types, journal article study, open access mandates, repository annual reports, success factors

## Institutional repositories' internal and external success factors

Faculty, administrators, students, and libraries all view key institutional repository (IR) success factors through a diverse lens to satisfy each of their academic needs. From an IR manager's point of view, optimal and successful repositories showcase the breadth of current and retrospective archived research across the academy including other campus materials, such as from Special Collections. The academic library selects and provides the software, supports its physical maintenance and/or financially, and offers a suite of services that enhances the value of the scholarly content and its authors. These are *internal factors* to the IR.

*Externally* there is the potential research impact factor (see Chapter 5), local and global use of scholarship, and a sense of success from "how well the IR fulfills or brings the library closer to achieving its long-term goals in terms of service to the academic community" (Yakel et al., 2009). The notion of an IR's acceptance is most likely the major achievement that all other factors, such as content recruitment and deposit success, contribute to and determines what builds the repository community. Faculty, administration, staff, and students who acknowledge the value of open access (OA) and want to partake of its worth on an individual, department, college, and university level will contribute their work. Libraries, as leaders of the external innovative IR role, employ their scholarly communication expertise to participate in an integral campus role, serving various constituencies.

The heart of librarianship emphasizes linking researchers to needed information. Research becomes more valuable when it can be located, shared, and utilized. Consequently, librarians and faculty are leaders in this pedagogical vision and have been advocating for worldwide access to knowledge since the advent of the Internet. More specifically and pervasively, the creation and use of open access repositories has accelerated since the initial design creation and early twenty-first century deployment.

## Specific factors/features that constitute IR success

The primary scholarly communication motivation of scientists and scholars is to publish their research findings, make them visible, be further applied, and built upon by academics in their respective fields. Their careers are contingent upon research progress and impact. As described in Chapter 1, the peer-review process is a freely given service conducted by qualified editors and reviewers. Historically, as standard practice, authors typically assigned the accepted article copyright to the publishing journal; that model is evolving as authors are retaining their rights through exercising addenda, licensing, and requesting to retain copyrights. The research article has been freely given to publishers to sell library and individual journal subscriptions; savvy authors consider their own research and open access needs for the present and future. The open archiving model occurs when an author requests to retain the postprint (paper approved by peer-review) and/or other rights by using a recognized publisher addendum, such as the SPARC Author Addendum (see *http:// www.arl.org/sparc/author/addendum.shtml*). The Addendum's credibility is based on a team of lawyers who created the legal document.

At this juncture, there is another opportunity where an author could ideally deposit a publisher's green OA postprint in the institutional repository (IR), another milestone in archiving research for open access use. If academics developed the habit of immediately depositing their scholarly content, copyright permitting, IRs would be acutely successful, as would the authors' research visibility. The *internal factor* of repository wealth is primarily based on deposited intellectual materials that populates an IR, relying on obtainable academic research.

An author's survey results chart, created by Alma Swan (2006: 53), portrays researchers' motives for publishing their work. The uppermost motivation that scholars chose for publishing the outcomes of their work was to communicate results to peers and make an impact in the literature, closely followed by advancing a career and enjoying personal prestige. Less than 10 percent of the survey participants chose financial reward as a reason for issuing their research results, as in reality it typically does not apply. The *internal factors* of archiving scholarship have to occur first before acquiring the optimum *external advantages* of elevated impact and status.

Interestingly, there is a paradox within the researchers who value sharing their findings; they are not necessarily archiving their journal articles or postprints in an IR where the citation impact advantage would benefit them and the distribution of scholarly content would be more pervasive. Many authors are not aware of the institutional repository research dissemination model and the inherent access value proposition. Authors may exhibit deposit inertia with regard to these associations. When faculty researchers lack cognizance concerning the principle of open access, the primary issue for the academic library is to build awareness, help shape the perception of open scholarship and its inherent possibilities, such as enhancing research dissemination to maximize the potential impact of their own work (Swan, 2006). The IR as a scholarly communication tool embraces social media features, including altmetrics (alternative article metrics), such as download counts, commenting, following, cited, saved, or recommended, as ways to substantiate or criticize an author's work.

Researcher deposit inertia may be overcome either by proactively supplying a current curriculum vitae and continual updates to the IR staff or by archiving their own intellectual content, dependent on local deposit practices. There is an obvious challenge to garner scholarly materials, as a mere 15–30 percent of research papers are being deposited in repositories that do not have mandates. Author incentives, positive feedback from readers, download statistics, and colleague encouragement may boost the numbers to the 30 percent mark (Harnad, 2011; Sale, 2006).

In the last year and a half (since January 2012) and according to the Sherpa RoMEO website (*http://www.sherpa.ac.uk/romeo/statistics.php?scope=provisional*) there has been a 5 percent increase in publishers allowing some form of self-archiving. As of August 31, 2013 (*http://www.sherpa.ac.uk/romeo/PDFandIR.php?la=en*), the database includes a majority of the principal journals in most fields that allows OA to an author's final peer-reviewed manuscript (postprint) or the version prior to peer-review (preprint). There is also a multitude of business, government, industry researchers, and taxpayers who are not affiliated with academia, as well as academics from underdeveloped countries that have an appetite for research that has been historically beyond their reach.

Widespread misconceptions of what open access entails, a lack of value awareness, and archiving inertia are the main contributors to the paltry number of journal articles posted in a repository in comparison to the quantity published each year. Despite educating scientists and scholars to create an awareness and culture of openness and encouraging the habit of depositing scholarly materials, the research community falls short of the 100 percent mark of archiving all research. Repositories are unsuccessful in realizing a fully populated IR with potential content where there are no department or institutional mandates to deposit scholarly articles. Conversely, IRs are growing exponentially where there are academic and funder mandates.

# Institutional repository mandates, their rewards, and deposit methods

In 2008, the Harvard University Faculty of Arts and Sciences adopted a policy that requires faculty to deposit their works in *DASH*, their open access repository. It also provides for the university's nonexclusive copyright license to archive and publicly distribute all faculty-produced scholarly articles. As of June 2013, faculty have deposited over 16,000 journal articles (see *http://dash.harvard.edu/*). Harvard's archiving mandate has precipitated further university and statewide deposit requirements. According to the ROARMAP, there are 176 institutional mandates as of August 30, 2013 (see *http://roarmap.eprints.org/*).

An IR mandate is the most effective method of populating a repository with scholarly articles and postprints. Once an article deposit "habit" is in place, the next archiving frontier can include a variety of scholarship types that may incorporate conference proceedings, presentations and other intellectual materials. The primary success of a repository is based on a high level of academic faculty content that is deposited and made globally available. It is a researcher's best academic interest to archive and share scholarship for greater visibility and subsequent impact. It is also in the vested interests of an institution's responsibilities as a whole to showcase the scientific and scholarly inquiry that can be found within the academy. By mandating faculty research in an IR, the administration's value proposition of fully tracking scholarship for accreditation and other requisite record management purposes efficiently serves multiple goals.

As documented in the literature, overcoming the inertia of depositing an author's postprint or publisher's article copy, dependent on copyright, is a direct path to fulfilling the promise of an IR – voluntary practices are ineffective. Two surveys conducted by Swan (2006) reveal how researchers would react to the creation of a new obligation from their institution or grant funder to deposit their published journal articles in an OA repository: "with a vast majority (81%) [saying] they would comply with such a requirement willingly. Fourteen percent said they would do so reluctantly and only 5% said they would not comply at all" (Swan, 2006).

Three years later, the ITHAKA S+R 2009 Faculty Study found similar survey results with reference to a significant positive interest in open access deposits, but relatively mediocre researcher deposit numbers. Fewer than 30 percent of faculty archived any scholarship in an IR (Schonfeld & Housewright, 2010). Sale's (2007: para. 6) research confirms the global experience of the "already converted and practicing self-archivers" where "voluntary deposit policies are known to achieve no greater deposit rate of current research than 30% and more usually around 15%." If we combine the studies' results with the previous years and a greater awareness of open access benefits and deposit campaigns, we would have expected faculty to fulfill an IR mandate – not so.

Approximately 2.5 million papers are issued every year in the world's 25,000 peer-reviewed research journals, representing all scientific and scholarly disciplines. It is in a researcher's best interest to minimally archive articles and conference proceedings in an OA repository for readers' use and to supplement with a productive means of evaluation through research impact, download counts, usage/citation figures, and optional social media comments and tags (Harnad, 2011).

At this point in time, green archiving mandates and gold open access through journals are the primary means to garner the majority of the academy's scholarship. Green and gold open access models should be pursued concurrently, "as green and gold access is complementary and synergistic" (Suber, 2013: 58). The gold model represents open access through journals, either born-digital or a publisher's gold journal that exercises article processing charges (APCs) paid by either a grant, university department, or libraries, allowing the article to be globally available. According to the ROARMAP (March 2013)) (*http://roarmap.eprints.org/*), there are 179 institutional mandates, 40 sub-institutional mandates, 8 multi-institutional mandates, 82 funder mandates, and 106 thesis mandates across the global repository community. Nineteen mandates have been proposed. Obligatory archiving has made the point that it grows an IR. Yearly increases of four types of mandate are portrayed in Figure 3.1

The ORBi (Open Repository and Bibliography) (*http://orbi.ulg.ac.be/*) at the University of Liège (Belgium) (*http://www.ulg.ac.be/cms/c_5000/home*) has an optimal mandate where the Rector (Vice-Chancellor/Chairman of the Board) has decreed all scientific papers and their accompanying metadata (since 2002) must be submitted to the IR for annual faculty performance reviews – no other method is accepted. An

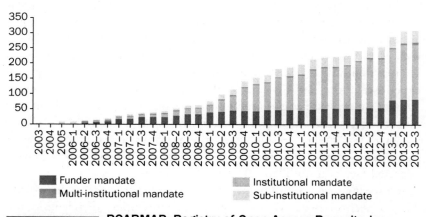

| Funder mandate | Institutional mandate |
| Multi-institutional mandate | Sub-institutional mandate |

**Figure 3.1** **ROARMAP: Registry of Open Access Repositories Mandatory Archiving Policies**

Source: *http://roarmap.eprints.org/*. This work is licensed under a Creative Commons Attribution 2.0 UK: England & Wales License.

annual curriculum vitae is also required as is a list of repository-archived references. The processes and documentation provide an incentivized "carrot" approach for all university faculty evaluation procedures to be eligible for scholarly opportunities that encompass promotion, grant applications, and professional designation (Poynder, 2011b). Every subject area at the University of Liège has attained some form of full-text representation or access (philosophy, law, politics, science, medicine, veterinary medicine, psychology, education, management, biotechnology, and architecture) in the repository. By transforming the current culture and method of pedagogical evaluation, the university can expect a dramatic shift in gaining open access traction.

Another high-minded institution, Charles Sturt University (CSU) (*http://www.csu.edu.au/*) in Australia, also required their faculty (in 2008), to submit peer-reviewed author postprints from 2007 onward to the CRO (CSU Research Output) (*http://digitool.unilinc.edu.au/ R?func=search&local_base=GEN01-CSU01*). University specializations include agriculture, veterinary sciences, business, communication, environmental science, humanities, social sciences (including library science), medical science, psychology, religious studies, and teaching/education. CRO statistics will be used to determine research funding for universities and to also provide data to their Promotions Committee.

The National Institute of Technology, Rourkela, India (*http://www. nitrkl.sac.in/*) is the premier national institution for technical education in India, funded by the government. Their mission is "to advance and spread knowledge in the area of science & technology leading to the creation of wealth and the welfare of humanity." The Institute established a 2006 resolution: all faculty and student research papers, including theses and dissertations, were expected to be self-archived or submitted to a librarian for deposit in their IR (*http://roarmap.eprints.org/20/*). The administration reserved the right to analyze and refer to this archive for the assessment of faculty performance when necessary (*http://www. nitrkl.ac.in/research.html*).

In March 2009, the Oregon State University's (OSU) library faculty were the first in the world to unanimously vote to pass an open access library policy (*http://roarmap.eprints.org/120/*). The faculty's Scholarly Communication Working Group members wisely provided background details and ensured there was understanding of the IR issues before faculty saw the proposed policy. Their guiding principle stated that faculty must archive the final published version of their articles, conference proceedings, book chapters, presentations, and internal reports authored by library faculty that were of interest to others *no later than the date of publication or distribution.* If a publisher disallowed their final copy, OSU library faculty were encouraged to negotiate for an acceptable version of the final paper for deposit, such as a postprint or preprint (Wirth, 2010) (see *http://ir.library.oregonstate.edu/*).

The OSU Libraries' open access college mandate is what Arthur Sale (2007) refers to as a "patchwork mandate," a three-part approach to an archiving commitment:

1. The institution as a whole has not yet adopted a mandate, but a department or college commits.

2. A strategy should be pursued to achieve an institutional mandate in the long term.

3. The effort goes towards garnering college/department/school/center mandates one by one, eventually to cover the academy's entire faculty.

Decrees from a department head or votes at a democratic faculty meeting with a positive outcome will solidify commitment to a mandate or policy for archiving scholarship in a repository. In addition, a postprint may be archived with publisher permission at the time of article acceptance. Given varied publisher copyright policies, the preprint, postprint, or the publisher's final formatted article copy may be the legal version to deposit. Preprints are usually a legitimate impression and can be deposited.

Another essential aspect of a mandate or faculty vote policy is the "immediate deposit/optional access" (Harnad, 2006: 4.31) strategy that includes the full metadata and the manuscript version approved by peer-review, the postprint:

- is immediately deposited upon acceptance for publication;
- is deposited in the university's institutional repository;
- may require an embargo for a set period of time.

This tactic effectively overcomes archiving inertia and necessitates an immediate deposit of both the postprint version and its respective metadata. Publisher embargoes or a funder deadline to archive permit the metadata to be available to researchers; the full-text can be released after the embargo period ends. This tactic does not threaten publishers concerned with the effects of immediately releasing the intellectual content (Suber, 2006). The instant release of OA metadata makes the article searchable and findable by Google Scholar and other search engines. An author can be contacted for a postprint while the article is temporarily embargoed. Most IR software products allow for setting an embargo date to automatically end and subsequently open the dark file on a specific date.

The "recurring permissions" theme of these four organizations – the University of Liège, Charles Sturt University, the National Institute of Technology, Rourkela, and Oregon State University Libraries – may also be found in other institutions of higher education recorded in the ROARMAP list of IR mandates (*http://roarmap.eprints.org/*). They recognize the high intellectual value an institutional repository innately provides for access and the benefits that faculty and the academy reap from mandated open access postprints or scholarly articles. In addition, the university administrations recognize the mandate as imperative to ensure the inertia that is part of human nature is overcome to populate repositories.

Academic institutions that have not enacted mandates have a "limited circle of like minds" to support campus-wide open access policies and suffer a lack of a collective voice to create change. The University of Kansas (KU) Dean of Libraries altered the status quo by initiating the formation of a coalition in response to hearing scientists, scholars, and librarians discuss the challenges of complying with an open access mandate, as some publishers disallowed faculty to archive their journal articles in the institutional repository. KU was the first US public university to adopt an OA policy for faculty research published in peer-reviewed journals. Their policy "asserts the rights of KU faculty to provide broad, free access to their journal publications to colleagues around the world" (Smith, 2011).

Subsequently, the Coalition of Open Access Policy Institutions (COAPI) was launched by the KU Librarians in July 2010 to initially include 21 North American universities and colleges, now expanded to 46 institutions, as of August 30, 2013 (*http://www.arl.org/sparc/about/COAPI/*). The Coalition is considering a gold APC model – library collection purchasing funds would pay for the article to be published in return for lower subscription fees. Exercising an expanding collective voice is a distinct advantage in leveraging policies and bargaining with publishers. The Coalition has launched as a formal membership organization, inviting other academic institutions to join (Howard, 2011). COAPI members also participate in a one-stop resource, Open Access Now, by sorting, nominating, and publishing the most relevant open access news from a variety of sources (*http://oanow.org/*).

# There are millions of articles

Who would have imagined the notion of research journal articles obtainable in an open access environment could cause a publishing furor? With the advent of the Internet, the article itself can be considered fundamentally representative of the scholarly communication process, including its fixed characteristics that make it a unique artifact. A 2010 study (Jinha) depicting the multitudes of recent and retrospective scholarship has been shown to exceed 50 million scholarly journal articles and a count of 26,406 active academic journals at the end of 2009, the first documented article originating from 1665. Based on a 2006 figure of approximately 23,750 journals, there is a direct association among the numbers of researchers, journals, and articles that were used as a foundation for this study. This type of enquiry is not precise science, but presents an overall concept of journal article history. The year 1726 was chosen for the first year of calculations, as it corresponds to the beginnings of steady journal development that documented increased numbers of journal articles for nearly three centuries.

Ulrich's Serials Analysis System™ (*http://www.ulrichsweb.com/ulrichsweb/usasfaq.asp* and *http://www.istl.org/03-summer/databases.html*) was the primary metric (using the resource title) successfully employed with the most comprehensive and advanced classification system for determining pragmatic estimates of periodical totals (Jinha, 2010). It utilizes essential filtering in global, peer-reviewed publications that are currently publishing refereed journal articles. Any library with a subscription allows its readers to login with an institutional username and password.

With this time-consuming and labor-intensive study currently at academia's disposal to determine the approximate number of articles available for scientists' and scholars' use worldwide, by what means can academics envision and approach the magnitude of all scholarly content potentially obtainable and compiled to benefit the global research community? Currently, there are possibly thousands of archived resources considered a massive collection of current and backdated research materials. The perception of availability through using Google Scholar or other search engines is not as effective as using a subject index. Subject indexing is a skill typically used by a proficient library cataloger who employs a controlled vocabulary, keywords, or more informal tags to portray or summarize what an item consists of.

It is possible to overcome obstacles to collecting and systematizing the 50 million plus articles, especially with a united effort, possibly in the form of grants that cover multiple institutions and non-profit research bodies. Academic faculty and librarians, institutional repository managers, and independent researchers who have a dynamic stake in open research, possess the skill set and knowledge to locate, capture, preserve, and make available peer-reviewed scholarly content. Information scientists who conduct research in areas such as archival science, library science, computer science, public policy, and other social sciences would likely have an interest in such a project.

The legacy size of some 50 million research articles is almost unthinkable, yet at the same time it is inspiring to imagine the possibility of establishing and managing a globally sustainable resource with the potential to transform and achieve a new level of reachable intellectual content. Success elements of such a mission would be to increase scholarly impact, lower the high cost of peer-reviewed journal articles, make the research openly available and easily accessible, and remove the inequitable barriers in the technological infrastructure that developing countries face. Even in the Global North, most scholarship is not readily obtainable. Now that researchers and librarians know there is an estimated 50 million articles or more in existence, a shift has occurred in the academic spectrum to contemplate overcoming the challenges to corralling the research and outline a dissemination plan.

While the worldwide scholarly community considers how to direct the advancement of peer-reviewed research inventory using current practices for greater access, indexing, and preservation, additional investigation is necessary to learn more about the infrastructure of existing scholarship and what is needed to move obtainable research forward to being open, such as:

- overcoming barriers to access including financial obstacles, navigation and retrieval, availability of technology, and the disparate locations of networks/libraries;
- calculating the global aggregate online (open access) and/or in paper format in libraries;
- locating articles in the public domain;
- access to exploiting existing journal subscriptions;
- alternatively using interlibrary loan to locate an eprint or a reprint.

In reviewing the history of scholarship, "we can look backwards to understand how the mountain [of literature] was constructed; consider what it means today; and how it can best be constructed to expand the benefits of research and the opportunities to engage in it in the future"

(Jinha, 2010: 8). As the need and aspiration for all peer-reviewed journal articles to be accessible is realized and as the obstructions in technology are transcended, our scholarly future holds a promise for a less complex access to open research.

## Content in a successful IR

Institutional repositories were originally conceived and created to counteract the "serials crisis" that commenced in the mid-1980s and had not substantially abated by 2011 (see Figure 3.2). Academic libraries

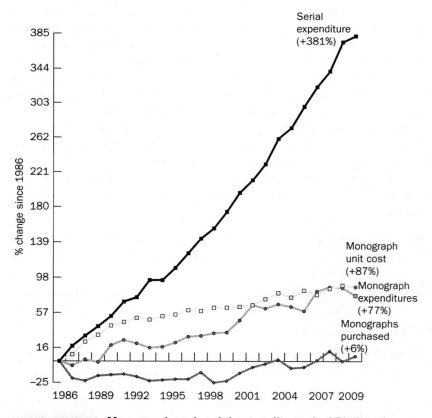

**Figure 3.2**    **Monograph and serial expenditures in ARL libraries, 1986–2009**

*Source: ARL Statistics 2008–2009*, Association of Research Libraries, Washington, DC.

were not renewing all of their journal subscriptions and have unbundled some of their contracted "Big Deal" serial packages. The high cost of research and of doing business – especially with five of the major publishers, Elsevier, Springer, Wiley, Taylor & Francis, and Sage – escalates every year through inflation, if not through actual price increases. According to Suber (2010), journal prices have risen four times faster than inflation since 1986.

Academic libraries are investing in repositories to provide journal articles and an array of additional, original research materials to bypass the high cost of delivering publisher-compiled scholarship. Formidable journal cost increases present an access issue for students, scientists, and scholars, aspiring not only to locate and read full-text scholarship for their own work, but also to build upon others' articles, accelerating both the research process and the subsequent openly available scholarship.

# Primary types of IR materials

An institutional repository is a sustainable means to archive global, open access scholarship. Repository software typically is easy for researchers to navigate and academic libraries maintain and optimize its features. The initial focus on archiving peer-reviewed journal articles, the core currency of research, was the result of a concentrated impulse to enable journal articles or postprints to be freely accessible with no accompanying price tag. When IR managers discovered faculty were only 15–30 percent invested unless mandated to expand the scholarly communication process by depositing articles, they sought out other erudite research to showcase and populate repositories with additional worthy content. Targeted collection development may be integral to the mission of an IR advisory committee and is covered in more detail in Chapter 5.

Complementing the journal article research are other original and peer-reviewed intellectual materials that will engage readers and be a compelling value proposition for the academic library that collects and deposits conference proceedings, posters, monographs, book chapters, open access journals, publicly funded research, technical reports, working papers, datasets, audio/visual presentations, podcasts, department/institution publications, e-theses and e-dissertations (ETDs), graduate capstone projects, professional papers, and honors theses, to name multiple possibilities. Highlighting the breadth of an academy's intellectual wealth is an advantage while showcasing faculty and student scholarship;

administrators are also obligated to a state's public research funding and other academy stakeholders. Prospective students are fortunate to have an opportunity in advance to view the level, scope, and type of research that faculty engage in and what research will be expected of them by viewing existing student theses and dissertations archived in an IR.

## Conferences

Conferences archived in an IR after the fact enable repeated access to the original content, allowing those who could not attend or missed a presentation session entry to the research. By collaborating in advance with the organizers to ensure that the presentations, audio-visuals, posters, and information about the symposium are saved and all open access scholarship author permissions secured, presenters and participants will benefit from the archived content. Hosted and open source conference software is available to enrich the online visuals and details of a symposium, including archiving and making presentations and transcripts available. The Public Knowledge Project (PKP), DSpace, and Digital Commons® software host academic conferences, although faculty organizers may be independent in the peer-review and request assistance with the maintenance of the OA conference content. Additional open source conference software options are located at *http://www.arl.org/sparc/publisher/journal_management.shtml*.

Open Conference Systems (OCS), part of the PKP (*http://pkp.sfu.ca/ocs-conferences*), provides a listing of conferences on their website primarily supplying symposium information and occasionally presenter names/affiliations and abstracts, although the PKP has provided full text for their 2009 conference (see *http://pkp.sfu.ca/ocs/pkp/*). Examples of how the software presents the materials may be found at:

- Imaginative Education: Provoking Excellence Across the Curriculum – see *http://www.ierg.net/confs/index.php?cf=2*
- Workshop of Physical Agents 2012 – see *http://www.jopha.net/waf/index.php/waf/waf12*
- The International Society for Human Ethology – see *http://media.anthro.univie.ac.at/ishe_conferences/index.php/isi/isi_2011/schedConf/presentations*

Digital Commons®, a hosted institutional repository product, requires an annual fee for managing content on their server that includes setting up a repository shell with a customer's preferred features. Overall, symposiums tend to provide the full-text or abstracts of sessions, posters, and audio-visual presentations. Online conference materials focus on faculty, graduate, and undergraduate students showcasing their research. The examples below depict varied possibilities for the design and substance of symposiums to be archived in an IR.

- Sustainability is a pervasive topical area of scholarship for faculty and students that several academic institutions are pursuing. The University of Nevada, Las Vegas has an Urban Sustainability Initiative, for which yearly conferences play a profound research role: see Annual Nevada NSF EPSCoR Climate Change Conference (*http://digitalcommons. library.unlv.edu/epscor/*).

- Syracuse University's 2011 graduate student conference's theme was the *Articulations of Power*. The Future Professoriate Program residing in the Department of History hosted the symposium (see *http:// surface.syr.edu/hst_fpp/*). The program's goal was to assist graduate students to develop and polish professional skills related to teaching, research, and professional identity.

- The University of South Florida (USF) Office of Undergraduate Research holds an annual university-wide Undergraduate Research Symposium and Celebration (see *http://scholarcommons.usf.edu/ur_ symposium/*). The symposium serves to highlight the substantial research accomplished by USF undergraduate students with faculty mentorship and to encourage their peers to become actively engaged in scholarship.

- DSpace software also has the capacity to host conferences. The 56th Indian (East) 2011 Library Conference, held at Jindal Global University, focused on the public library of the future, covering its opportunities and challenges. Full text is available at *http://dspace.jgu. edu.in:8080/dspace/handle/123456789/106/browse-title*.

## Monographs, books, and journals

The Directory of Open Access Journals (DOAJ) with its current number of 9,903 journals (as of August 30, 2013), is a testament to the economical and viable nature of these peer-reviewed online publications. This open journal model has proved successful and valuable over time; some academic university presses have applied OA journal model features to monograph and book publishing.

The University of Illinois, Urbana-Champaign Library website defines the distinction between a monograph and a book. The *monograph* typically is a "one-volume work, gives in-depth treatment to a specialized subject, is written by a scholar in the field, and is formulated primarily for an academic audience" (*http://www.library.illinois.edu/learn/tutorials/monograph.html*). A *book* is defined by Merriam-Webster "as a set of written, printed, or blank sheets bound together into a volume *or* a long written or printed literary composition" (*http://www.merriam-webster.com/dictionary/book?show=0&t=1314564859*).

Full-text of monographs and books has historically not been part of an IR's purview. They are prime candidates to be sold for profit by publishers and authors. Monograph publishing contracts that expire offer the advantage of depositing them in a repository, particularly if the topic remains relevant. Creating an IR monograph item record with rich metadata will, at a minimum, alert readers to a book's existence and potential worth, such as the Utah State faculty monograph example at *http://digitalcommons.usu.edu/usufaculty_monographs/25/*.

The traditional trend of not archiving a monograph or book in a repository is fading with multiple OA options to download or an option to print a copy (see additional references below to *Buy or Download* books). To offer free monograph downloads, Digital Commons® created a repository Book Gallery alternative to showcase academic books that reflect an academy's published research. Monographs or books may also be offered for a reasonable price:

- A Professor Emeritus of Biological Sciences at the University of Nebraska – Lincoln (UNL) is the author of *A Nebraska Bird-Finding Guide*. As a top expert in his field, he has written more than 50 books and 150 articles on birds and other wildlife. According to Amazon.com, this book is out of print. The open access publishing model is a viable choice as the book is currently offered for sale or for free download, including the covers and full-text, through UNL's IR: *http://digitalcommons.unl.edu/zeabook/5/*.

- Purdue University Press is publishing a series of e-books to download at no charge – *http://docs.lib.purdue.edu/purduepress_ebooks/*. The variety of e-book topics include anamorphosis in the literature of the Spanish Golden Age, and the history of organizing Purdue's new Home Economics Extension Service in 1914: the art and science of program management, women succeeding in the sciences, contemporary agriculture controversies, and more.

- Since 1969, personnel from the South Carolina Institute of Archaeology and Anthropology at the University of South Carolina, and with additional collaborators, have encapsulated archaeological projects that explain the results of multiple excavations, utilizing artifact analyses, and conducting ethno-historical research. There are over 100 technical monographs available to make use of – see *http://scholarcommons.sc.edu/archanth_books/*.

- The Australian National University's (ANU) E-Press, in operation since 2003, publishes peer-reviewed, full-text monographs available in paper/PDF format for purchase and HTML formats for open access reading online, printing, and for mobile devices. The motives for finding an effective mechanism for disseminating high-quality ANU scholarship centered on eliminating barriers inherent in existing models of scholarly communication. It acknowledges the conventional academic press overhead is no longer affordable and recognizes "emergent electronic press technologies offer a feasible alternative to the conventional academic press in terms of cost and available infrastructure." The press provides topical monographs in the Social Sciences and Humanities – see *http://epress.anu.edu.au/titles/index.html*.

Publishers are discovering that open access monographs are promoting the purchase of hard copies, a winning opportunity for publishers and for readers who prefer a copy-in-hand and those satisfied with viewing the online version. "Breaking down price barriers of research monographs aligns university presses once more with the core values of the academy and, more prosaically, hugely increases usage" (*OASIS*, website).

Open scholarship, in all of its manifestations, is essential if researchers are to share, use, and build with ease upon original and subsequent work. The monograph already has potential to be the next frontier of intellectual content to be freed in an open access context.

The first OAPEN (Open Access Publishing in European Networks) conference, sponsored by SPARC Europe, convened in February 2011 (*http://project.oapen.org/index.php/news/41-results-1st-oapen-conference-berlin*). Its primary focus was to promote and support open access monograph publishing models. The conference's message was to raise a background awareness of OA monograph and book possibilities. In attendance were over 70 experts, representing publishers, universities, libraries, practitioners, funders, and authors, "to explore specific means to promote open access publishing for the humanities, social sciences, and other areas."

The Conference emphasized minimizing the barriers to open access monographs as book printing has: become increasingly more expensive; reduced marketing undertaken by publishers; and libraries with budget and purchasing experience are purchasing fewer books in order to pay for serials acquisitions. Low awareness and skepticism of quality monographs and books is mirroring the open access journal model when it was first introduced and that currently still exists at some level (van Wesenbeeck, 2011).

Other monograph topics included raising the awareness of an OA model and the question of publication funding. The concept of creating a Directory of Open Access Books that models the DOAJ was introduced. Also recommended for consideration was the notion to qualify as an OA academic publisher, requiring some type of certification and application procedure. By increasing the awareness of open books as an "effective form of publishing and dissemination," funds may be available to support and solidify OA monographs as an "accepted publication model" (van Wesenbeeck, 2011). Open access book lists are extensive over the Internet, each representing their own sponsoring body. The Graduate School of Library and Information Science (GSLIS) at Simmons College maintains an example of a non-proprietary open access book resource listing – see *http://oad.simmons.edu/oadwiki/Publishers_of_OA_books*.

In 2009, Bloomsbury Academic (*http://www.bloomsburyacademic.com/*) launched an OA book and monograph imprint under the model, the "thesis is simple; you may lose a few sales because you are publishing free online, but then you gain sales because more people have heard of the book as they can read the content online" and decided to purchase a print-on-demand monograph. Free downloads are integrated with the Creative Commons non-commercial license (see *http://creativecommons.org/*). To finance Bloomsbury Academic's business model framework it garnered revenue from student course packs, actual book sales, and commercial royalties. The expensive inventory of a full print run will not be sitting in a warehouse awaiting monograph sales (Murphy, 2008/9).

University of Michigan's (UM) philosophical approach to the open access monograph publishing method (Bonn, 2010) takes into consideration the idea that "the crudest form in OA book publishing" is saving money by entrusting that free downloads and print-on-demand will lower the cost of publishing open access monographs.

Endorsement of OA monographs could be more forthcoming if scientists and scholars were encouraged to focus on the dissemination of ideas, author visibility, increased sales of print publications, and the likelihood of an online first publication that diverges from the traditional.

Ostensibly, publishers are centering their attention on incurring a less expensive workflow for future monograph production. In practice, there are currently few alternative options for monograph and book publishing and their subsequent dissemination.

The open monograph is fundamentally challenged by centuries of traditional publishing history. While some authors and their colleagues are not yet keen to offer credence and adopt their use, recent scholarly communication models, both in theory and in practice, can be more beneficial to researchers by accommodating new technologies promising practical advantages.

Currently, the majority of the monograph and book holdings of the HathiTrust (*http://www.hathitrust.org/home*) are in-copyright works; the largest numbers are estimated to be orphan works, i.e. books whose owners have not been identified or located. The Universities of California, Michigan, Florida, and Wisconsin are collaborating to locate orphan works to provide an opportunity for rights' holders to assert ownership and have their books archived in the HathiTrust, if they choose. Digitized books will provide open access to HathiTrust partners if the orphan works do not find their "parents" and if a library has a copy in their print collection (Farley, 2011). Approved orphan work's plans will "bring a larger percentage of our digitized works directly to our students and faculty in support of their work" (*http://www.universityofcalifornia. edu/news/article/26172*).

In fall 2011, the Authors Guild and other stakeholders filed a lawsuit that indicted the universities and the Trust over the mass (millions of books) digitization and alleged copyright infringement. The HathiTrust digital repository and the five universities filed a response that pleaded the First Amendment and some copyright protection (*Chronicle of Higher Education*, 2011).

The case was retried in October 2012. The federal judge who oversaw the major copyright infringement lawsuit brought in 2011 by the Authors Guild against the HathiTrust digital repository and its university partners ruled that the libraries' indexing of digitized works counted as fair use (*http://chronicle.com/blogs/ticker/judge-hands-hathitrust-a-win-in-fair-use-case/50462*).

The University of Michigan Press has deposited the majority of its monograph content in the HathiTrust, a collaborative repository for the cultural digital collections of the 50 partner research libraries. To achieve access to these collections, the HathiTrust monographs were scanned by the Google Books Library Project, the Internet Archive, and in-house library initiatives (*http://www.google.com/googlebooks/library.html*). All of the UM Press's most recently published books were uploaded to the HathiTrust repository immediately or within a year of publication. The software offers searching and viewing, and each page can be downloaded one at a time for use. Books for sale may be purchased through the viewing application or by utilizing traditional distribution options.

Digitalculturebooks (*http://www.digitalculture.org/*) has a unique business model where the imprint is co-produced by the UM Press and the Scholarly Publishing Office; rights are held by the UM Library. Engaging the concept of merging new media studies and new scholarly practices in the humanities, digitalculturebooks incorporates hyperlinks and multimedia formats. The traditional, scholarly peer-review process is maintained for these books that are conveniently online, free to read, and may be purchased in print or in an e-book format. Creative Commons licenses are typically applied to the digitalculturebooks publications, an additional worthy feature (Bonn, 2010).

## *Book chapters*

Authors who contribute to a monograph or book by writing a chapter may be able to secure an open access option through the publisher. As mentioned in the previous section on monographs and books, publishers are experimenting with new and creative modes of dissemination; open access may be one of the options. If OA is not an obvious alternative, an author can request a preference for the chapter to be globally available.

It is a fundamental process to request permission for a journal article to be openly accessible. Authors can employ the Scholars' Copyright Addendum (*http://scholars.sciencecommons.org/*) for journal articles; it can also be exploited for chapters by completing the online form. Authors may copy and paste the PDF form into a Word document; it can be edited to reflect a chapter in place of a modified article request. An addendum conversation in advance of emailing the book editor may prove fruitful, as some editors have never considered the benefits of open access for their publications. Requesting to publish a chapter through open access has potential for inculcating a need for publisher awareness. One deliberate action may lead to another positive method of research availability.

Macalester College's IR has an archived book chapter of little known original historical content, deposited by a Professor Emeritus. The chapter depicts the ease of embedding a repository record with Web 2.0 features, including applications that facilitate information sharing in an OA environment, interoperability, and a user-centered design with full-text files, exemplifying an option for social media comment (*http://digitalcommons.macalester.edu/thdabooks/1/*). Other features incorporated in the IR record are the book cover (even though the book will not be published until 2013), an image gallery with artwork from World War II, external links of interest, an audio file, and a video interview with the author. The book tells the story of how prisoners of war (POWs) survived their ordeal using music and theater as an essential part of society life. Digital Commons® technology and software applications support these features.

"Justice Carter's Dissent in People v. Gonzales: Protecting Against the 'Tyranny of Totalitarianism'" is the title of a book chapter (*http://digitalcommons.law.ggu.edu/pubs/172/*) focused on a controversial issue on how to best "protect individuals from law enforcement conduct that violates constitutional protections" where illegally obtained evidence in a criminal case often results in the alleged criminal going free.

The Complutense University of Madrid's IR also features a chapter, "Aggression in Terrorism" from one of its faculty as a particularly timely global topic that is of immediate value. This chapter pinpoints behavioral scientists' explanations and the authors' contradiction of their research model using various supporting theories (*http://eprints.ucm.es/9995/2/353_CSP-Chapter_02.pdf*).

## Open access journals

The creation and support of peer-reviewed open access journals offer a three-pronged approach to: fill a gap in traditional journal content, ensure that the research will be openly available, and publish more effectively and sustainably. These are basic motivations to start up an open peer-reviewed journal publication. In some "academic circles," open access journals still conjure up a sense of a lack of peer-review and infer an absence of quality. The truth is that the majority of OA journal articles (excluding predatory journals: *http://scholarlyoa.com/publishers/*) follow a traditional scholarly communication peer-review process and showcase their publications side-by-side with their traditional publishing colleagues. The Directory of Open Access Journals (DOAJ) (*http://www.doaj.org/doaj?func=home&uiLanguage=en*) has a peer-review policy for a journal's inclusion in the Directory: "The journal must exercise peer-review or editorial quality control to be included."

Traditionally published paper or e-format journals may have editors who choose to take advantage of the open access model for editorial efficiency and to exercise an open access vantage point. Retrospective journal issues can also be scanned and deposited in an IR. Out-of-print journals may be resurrected and enjoy a productive presence in a fresh venue. Repositories have the innate ability to showcase research to its best advantage and remove access barriers to global readers.

- The University of Massachusetts Amherst Libraries hosts the journal, *Landscapes of Violence* (*http://scholarworks.umass.edu/lov/*), an interdisciplinary publication devoted to the study of violence, conflict, and trauma. The primary goals of the journal include the creation of an inclusive platform designed to reach a broad audience ecompassing scientists, academics, policy-makers, and the public.

- Published by graduate students, the *Coyote Papers* are a publication of the Linguistics Circle, part of the Graduate Student Organization of the Department of Linguistics at the University of Arizona (UA). Journal material types include working papers and proceedings. The students have seven full-text issues dating from 2001 to 2013 in the UA Campus Repository (*http://arizona.openrepository.com/arizona/handle/10150/107274*).

- Boise State's *McNair Scholars Research Journal*, created in 2005, delivers a unique opportunity for McNair Scholars to experience the scholarly communication process and to develop essential writing and revision skills. It also serves under-represented student groups in graduate education and first-generation college students from low-income backgrounds, providing scholarly enrichment, exposure to conducting research, and additional academic experiences (*http://scholarworks.boisestate.edu/mcnair_journal/*).

## Self-publishing and printing options

The advent of libraries embracing self-publishing has gained traction to fill a sustainable niche in publishing service options. Lulu.com and other companies offer a print on demand (POD) service that includes transforming an OA journal, monograph, or conference proceedings into a relatively inexpensive and high-quality print version. Academic libraries and bookstores are purchasing Expresso Book Machines to self-publish and simultaneously print special collection materials, theses and dissertations, and open textbook content. Traditional publishers, such as HarperCollins and Penguin (*http://ondemandbooks.com/news.php*), are using this model to curb overhead publishing costs. This disruptive technology bears watching for the academy's future publishing applications.

# Additional types of original research items

An IR can capture a wide range of original materials and information of value. Rare and unique research or local collections of interest as well as academic publications in the public domain may pique the interest of those who are fortunate to become aware of them online. Non-digitized collections force researchers to travel in order to view and utilize these exceptional items that in the past have only been collected in physical locations, such as university libraries' Special Collections.

## *Newsletters*

Newsletters have the advantage of being easily deposited in an open access venue for global consumption. As a result, institutional repository managers have been garnering and staff depositing them in IRs as part of the academy's historical record to reach their audience. Thomas Jefferson University's *Health Policy Newsletter* has archived issues from 1994 to summer 2013 (*http://jdc.jefferson.edu/hpn/*): "The School of Health Policy and Population Health's mission is to foster health policies that contribute to the delivery of high quality and cost-effective care by conducting research and educating healthcare providers, policy makers and consumers."

Another academic newsletter, *Scholarship@RIT*, was conceived and published by the Rochester Institute of Technology (RIT) Libraries Publishing and Scholarship Support Center. The focal point rested on aspects of cutting-edge faculty and student scholarship. The scholarship/ copyright column spotlighted topics that comprised promoting Open Access Week activities, why self-archive, and navigating copyright while engaging open access (*https://ritdml.rit.edu/handle/1850/49*).

To focus a campus' scholarly communication lens, an academic library may choose to create its own newsletter (electronic, paper, or both), emphasizing research and scholarly topics, or offer a column in an existing campus publication. The periodical can be brief or expanded to highlight other aspects of campus scholarship and research information. This is an opportunity to collaborate with academy stakeholders immersed in the open scholarly communication milieu. Being creatively engaged in highlighting faculty research and its output may further connect an IR manager and liaisons to their academy's scientists and scholars.

## Audio/visual presentations

### Podcasts

Podcasts (MP3) created from presentations represent an efficient technology, as attendees can listen to the recording again and those not present have the option to hear it later at their convenience. A few examples:

- UNLV's Black Mountain Institute luminaries authors T.C. Boyle, Junot Diaz, Paul Theroux, Alissa Nutting, Joyce Carol Oates, and many more – see *http://digitalcommons.library.unlv.edu/ blackmountain_lectures_events/*.
- The University of Cambridge archives its Arcadia Lectures and Seminars – see *http://www.dspace.cam.ac.uk/handle/1810/226647*.
- Australia's Moore College has over 3,000 sermons and ecumenical talks available on their repository website – see *http://myrrh.library. moore.edu.au/*.

### Presentations

Audio/visual presentations (MP4) created from various venues and deposited in an IR provide a benefit similar to that of an archived podcast but with the added impact of visuals. Many academies capture speaking events as mp4s; the rights to publicly archive are potentially worth pursuing for public use.

- From the University of Maryland Law School, this presentation focuses on their 2011 IR Day (*http://digitalcommons.law.umaryland. edu/ir/2011/may24/6/*): "The presentation addresses outreach to content creators, the establishment of workflows, and the expansion of a repository beyond the limits of the traditional IR mandate."
- Graduate research projects and ETDs may enlist audio/visual aspects to complement their text. One student-created animation "follows the stories of various community members as they make their way through a society on the brink of destruction." At McMasters University, Canada, the mp4 complements a major research project paper (*http://digitalcommons.mcmaster.ca/cmst_grad_research/3/*).
- Brookings Mountain West sponsors a public lecture series delivered by Brookings Scholars who visit UNLV to engage with "faculty and students on collaborative research, and meet local, regional, and state

leaders in business, government, and social services." This lecture is one of many Brookings Mountain West events, entitled "Booms and busts: Russia and its oil, 1970 to 2011 and beyond" (*http:// digitalcommons.library.unlv.edu/brookings_lectures_events/28/*).

## Government documents

In library circles, locating government-sponsored research is widely known as a challenge. These documents and other materials generated tend to be dispersed and sizeable in volume. Over time, libraries have collected government reports and used a variety of cataloging and shelving identification, and recently have documented them online. Institutional repository managers have begun locating and archiving past and present government reports in academic repositories to enable preservation, complement tangential research, and increase access and electronic longevity, employing stable and permanent identifiers to locate the reports in perpetuity.

Libraries, as primary collectors and archivers of intellectual content, have foreseen the concerns over the collection and preservation of "electronic government documents that vanish rapidly from web sites with governments seemingly giving little thought to longevity, reliability, and authenticity" (Devakos & Toth-Waddell, 2007: 1).

- As libraries grapple with long-term permanence issues and access to government documents, the literature is disappearing both online and in paper as the research has the potential to be deascensioned in both formats.

- In 2005, Canada's Ontario Legislative Library collaborated with the Ontario Council of University Libraries to provide enduring global access to their provincial government documents ascensioned to their DSpace repository (*https://ozone.scholarsportal.info/about/comm-and-coll.jsp*). Committed to long-term preservation, a library team archives approximately 4,500 born-digital documents per year that require timely, retrospective, and continual availability (Devakos & Toth-Waddell, 2007).

- The London School of Economics and Political Science archives a variety of government documents that concur with their academic subject mission in communities and local government, e.g., the manual: *Multi-Criteria Analysis* (*http://eprints.lse.ac.uk/12761/1/ Multi-criteria_Analysis.pdf*).

Due to accelerated research on the topic of sustainability, academia is focused on local and regional "environmental aspects" to entice students who are committed to accelerate the sustainability performance of the academy's campus and beyond (Galayda & Yudelson, 2010). One method of increasing the visibility of sustainability research is to archive government documents and reports in an IR that reflect topics such as conservation, energy, development, transportation, and water resources.

- The University of Nevada, Las Vegas Libraries IR staff deposit scholarly government research documents on initiative-focused urban sustainability to benefit faculty, students, and the greater context of need (see *http://digitalcommons.library.unlv.edu/govdocs/*).

- From agriculture to wildlife conservation and management, Utah State University, as a Utah regional depository, has commenced archiving government documents in their institutional repository (see *http://digitalcommons.usu.edu/govdocsregional/*).

## *Reports*

### Technical reports

Technical reports are characteristically considered part of the array of grey literature as they typically are not published and can be frequently found on personal computers and in file cabinets. (*http://www.library.gatech.edu/search_locate/techres/techrepdef.html*). They are a source of scientific and technical information in document format written by researchers and submitted to the sponsoring organization for review. The report may be a precursor of research that is later published in a journal article. Institutional respositories have become an online venue for technical reports that characteristically are in high demand, hence the high number of downloads.

- Research content at Florida's Mote Marine Laboratory is primarily technical reports that are deposited in their repository (see *https://dspace.mote.org/dspace/*). In addition to text, the reports may include illustrations, charts, and maps.

- Technical reports in taxonomy and aerospace engineering are archived at the University of Glasgow (see *https://dspace.gla.ac.uk/simple-search?query=technical+reports&submit=Go*).

- The School of Computing at the National University of Singapore is prolific in highlighting their technical reports' research (see *http://dl.comp.nus.edu.sg/dspace/handle/1900.100/12*).

- At the University of Maryland, the Virtual Technical Reports Center archives eprints, preprints, and technical reports (see *http://www.lib. umd.edu/ENGIN/TechReports/Virtual-TechReports.html*.

## Additional report types

Before the introduction of the IR concept, reports in general were characteristically stored on an individual's computer with no permanent means to share them publicly. The advent of repositories has enabled a range of report types that the academy and readers may find useful to be deposited in their respective institutional repository.

- The Association for the Advancement of Sustainability in Higher Education's (AASHE) Sustainability Tracking Assessment and Rating System™ (STARS) self-reporting documentation is an academic asset to complement an academy's sustainability record. Faculty, staff, current and prospective students, and other interested parties have the necessary and expedient access to sustainability reports, benchmarking for change. UNLV showcases their STARS reports (see *http://digitalcommons.library.unlv.edu/reports/*).
- Cornell University's School of Industrial and Labor Relations (ILR) archives a variety of journal articles, grey literature, born-digital research reports, and ILR publications that support its mission (see *http://digitalcommons.ilr.cornell.edu/reports/*).
- Supported by Denmark's International Centre for Research in Organic Food Systems, the Organic Eprints repository is an international open access subject archive that retains papers and projects related to research in organic food and farming. The Country Reports range alphabetically from Africa to the United States (see *http://orgprints.org/view/subjects/*).

## *Assorted research and creative works*

A multitude of academic research and creative works continue to provide open access value to the global scholarly community. A variety of item types are worth the consideration of archiving in an IR:

- Committee proceedings may appear dull and uninteresting. However, the Birdstrike Committee Proceedings (see *http://digitalcommons.unl. edu/birdstrike/*), archived and spanning the years 1999 to 2011, are creatively facilitating the exchange of information, specifically to "promote the collection and analysis of accurate wildlife strike data, promote the development of new technologies for reducing wildlife hazards, and promote professionalism in wildlife management programs in airports through training and advocacy of high standards of conduct for airport biologists and bird patrol personnel." This is serious and essential research for bird and aircraft safety.

- The University of Rochester (UR) has archived over 21,619 original music scores and books (as of September 2013) that are in the public domain (see *https://urresearch.rochester.edu/viewInstitutionalCollection. action?collection Id=63*). Many of these scores are unique to the UR's Sibley Music Library collection and originate from the nineteenth and twentieth centuries.

- "The Report of the Secretaries of State: Bipartisan Advice to the Next Administration" is a politically high-powered symposium report authored by former Secretaries of State Henry Kissinger, James Baker III, Warren Christopher, Madeleine Albright, and Colin Powell where they gathered "to discuss current U.S. foreign policy with the goal of providing advice and counsel to the next presidential administration." The University of Georgia Law School has made the audio/visual presentation and additional text files available (see *http:// digitalcommons.law.uga.edu/conf_coll_symp_symposia/48/*).

## *Images*

### Image collections

Photograph collections have been resurrected from various university special collections, scanned, and archived for use in repositories. DSpace and Digital Commons® developers have designed and built image displays for their academic customers that creatively and effectively display individual photographs.

- The University of Cambridge holds over 100,000 global images, dating from the late nineteenth century to the mid-1980s (see *http://www. dspace.cam.ac.uk/handle/1810/752*). The broad subject matter of the Royal Commonwealth Society Photograph Project includes: royal tours; trade, industry and agriculture; immigration; education and health; family life; and recreation. The original titles of some gallery photos are no longer politically correct, but have been preserved to convey the historical colonial consciousness and attitudes of the time.

Snake charmers, rickshaw travel, brewing banana beer, and sowing rubber tree seeds are representative of these provocative photographs.

- DePaul University's "Asian American Art Oral History Project" features the image gallery works of 122 artists that have participated in this endeavor (see *http://via.library.depaul.edu/oral_his_gallery/#b. mon.tag*). Click on "View Slideshow" to observe the images.

- Regional libraries' special collections and archives have created consortiums to partner and coordinate the transition from individual library image collections in their respective academies to a collective union of catalog images, retaining their historical context. In addition to the advantage of combining institutional efforts, analogous research materials are searchable at one website location.

A successful consortium of 29 participating university libraries from 16 US states (as of September 2013) have collaborated on the Western Waters Digital Library (WWDL) (see *http://www.westernwater.org/*) under the auspices of the Greater Western Library Alliance (GWLA). Funding comes from the National Endowment for the Humanities (NEH) and the Institute of Museum and Library Services (IMLS). The WWDL offers open access to a wide range of significant water resources in the Western United States. "Finding aids" describe a collection's content, significance, and relevance to a particular research topic. These archival collections encompass classic water literature, legal transcripts, maps, reports, personal papers, water project records, photographs, audio recordings, videos, and other water-related material.

## CONTENTdm® projects linked to repository documents

CONTENTdm® software (see *http://www.contentdm.org/*) is being used ubiquitously for library special collections and archival materials. Its function is to showcase visual content that incorporates finding aids and the written context. Descriptions, explanations, and accompanying research that tells an authentic story enhance the images. Research is based on and revolves around the images and additional documentation. Featured CONTENTdm® library and cultural heritage collections may be found online (see *http://collections.contentdm.oclc.org/*).

A symbiotic relationship can exist between a repository and CONTENTdm® management software. A case in point, at UNLV the IR administrator collaborated with the Digital Collections Librarian on an LSTA (Library Services and Technology Act grant) project that combined the unique attributes of both the IR and Digital Collections. "The Historic Landscape of Nevada: Development, Water, and the Natural Environment" project (see *http://digital.library.unlv.edu/collections/ historic-landscape*) includes maps and photographs in multiple instances that are associated with the water research and raw datasets archived in Digital Scholarship@UNLV.

As an example, archival and local research content from the "Historic Landscape of Nevada" (see *http://digital.library.unlv.edu/objects/hln/ 773*) is linked to a 1973 water conditions report at Lake Mead to the UNLV IR (see *http://digitalcommons.library.unlv.edu/water_pubs/117/*). The repository also links back to the Digital Collections' project instances of water documentation. Researchers utilizing either of the UNLV's digital collections or IR will have reciprocating opportunities to seek further enriching intellectual materials.

## Yearbooks, magazines, newspapers, and administrative documents

In addition to maintaining a record of scholarship and academy activity, open access is essentially about linking research and reader, vital to promote, inform, and accelerate academic enquiry. Peripheral, but nonetheless significant, is an academy's policies, procedures, and practices that relate to alumni, current students, and college or university administration. Academic programs and curricula are generally influenced and directed by faculty, deans, university adminstrators, and staff. The daily life of students and after graduation can be important at the time and thereafter. Yearbooks, alumni and student magazines/newspapers, undergraduate and graduate course catalogs, and other archival documents have intrinsic value for the needs of the graduated student. There is also the likelihood that researchers' work will be showcased or discussed in these periodicals and administrative venues. Repository software enables publications and documents to be systematized and deposited for future use.

### Yearbooks

As a worthwhile service, archiving university publications online is of potential need and interest to its students' alum and faculty, such as a yearbook. University and college content, managed by library archivists, receive repeat appeals from student alumni and researchers related to finding people, athletic activities, and other information contained in a yearbook. The time-consuming process to find answers is particularly challenging, especially when the requestor may not have all of the necessary details to fulfill the query. Scanned yearbooks archived in an IR suggest a use for specific academy research, such as locating classmates.

- As a prototype, the Associated Students published California Polytechnic State University – San Luis Obispo's *El Rodeo Yearbook* on an annual schedule with many of the volumes featuring a theme. At present, the digitized collection contains volumes 1927 to 1990 – see *http://digitalcommons.calpoly.edu/elrodeo/*.
- Babson College yearbooks – see *http://digitalknowledge.babson.edu/ybks/index.html*.
- Eastern Kentucky University yearbooks – see *http://encompass.eku.edu/yearbooks/index.2.html*.

## Alumni magazines and oral histories

Through alumni publications, graduates are historically kept informed about the current tenor of their academy, athletics, and the whereabouts of their classmates, providing a mechanism to continue fostering interest in their alma mater. Using these principal means of communication among alumni and the academic community encourages a continuing sense of belonging by purveying intellectual and educational topics of value to graduates.

- As is often the case in many academy publications, Cornell University's alumni association magazine has multiple names that have evolved over time (see *http://ecommons.library.cornell.edu/handle/1813/3157*). The IR is an effective means to clarify the name changes by listing all magazine titles and archiving the associated issues in one location. Cornell plans to complete the scanning and deposit of the publications in their IR from 1899 forward.
- The Kalamazoo College alumni magazine spans 1906 to the present (see *https://cache.kzoo.edu/handle/10920/4060*). The College publication's title has undergone a metamorphosis of eleven names. The delineation of the naming convention and year in the repository is helpful to the researcher.

- *JD*, the alumni magazine of the University of Maryland School of Law, is published to provide law school news. In addition, "*JD* engages its readers in substantive assessments of pressing contemporary issues in legal education and the practice of law" (see *http://digitalcommons. law.umaryland.edu/jd/*).

- Oral histories that chronicle the life and culture of the Illinois Wesleyan University from the 1930s, such as interviews and recorded events, are enduring aspects of the alumni experience (see *http:// digitalcommons.iwu.edu/oral_hist/*).

## Student magazines and newspapers

Academic-sponsored student magazines and newspapers are an organizational mechanism to chronicle students' present life and activities on campus. Article topics may range from opinions, concerns, student activities, politics, sports, art, and other college-life related non-fiction literary composition or creative works. Alumni and other interested parties may contact current publication editors to request a variety of information deemed important. This can be a challenge for editorial staff that cannot answer the query and have to consult back issues that may be stacked in an office closet. Student-managed publications also serve as a campus memory, especially effective if the full-text is openly available online in an IR for readers to conduct their own keyword inquiries. Back issues may be continually scanned into PDFs and archived online as ongoing projects.

- *The Flat Hat* is a student-run publication at the College of William & Mary (see *https://digitalarchive.wm.edu/handle/10288/20*). It is a rich source of information, announcing events taking place on campus as well as reflecting student opinion. Publication commenced in 1911.

- *The Reporter Magazine* has been a student-managed publication since 1951 (see *https://ritdml.rit.edu/handle/1850/3581*). To assist in answering inquiries, the archived magazine item records cover detailed metadata, including various editors, photographers, managers, and article authors. It boasts a 32-page, four-color magazine published weekly during the academic year by Rochester Institute of Technology students.

- Providence College's student-run weekly newspaper, *The COWL*, has been published since 1935 and is archived in the College's institutional repository (see *http://digitalcommons.providence.edu/cowl/*).

## Administrative documents

Enduring characteristics of an academy's online administrative documents is its systematic and openness to organizational materials essential to the governance, its staff, and students to gain access. Academy papers are typically organized in file cabinets and on personal computers. Using online tools, electronic documents can be openly archived, sequestered, and if necessary only available to a specific group of individuals. Few IRs have these documents listed in their repositories. Depositing these often-needed and frequently consulted minutes, executive/organizational papers, and meeting presentations, is an efficient means for timely access by knowing where the records are and having the ability to retrieve them. A repository's virtual file cabinet is available anytime and from any location. Within each of the institutional repository organizational collections, a repository manager/administrator can set reader permissions.

A time-efficient and frustration-saving feature of a repository collection is that the documents are searchable within each hierarchy. All reports within a particular topic can be retrieved by using a keyword or phrase search. Repository software offers search box mechanisms to penetrate academic documentation and archived governance materials. The need to locate documents to prepare for a meeting or to refer to a preceding vote in an IR requires less effort than leafing through a paper file cabinet or email. Some collections may require a login and other files are open, dependent on the proprietary nature of the content. As an example, RIT archives a large number (approximately 5,000) of its organizational documents and presentation materials (see *https://ritdml.rit.edu/search? query=academic%20senate%20minutes*):

- Academic Senate minutes, meeting presentations, documents and agendas;
- Institute Council minutes;
- Staff Council minutes;
- Student Government minutes;
- Academic Affairs;
- Curriculum Committee minutes; and
- College of Liberal Arts Faculty Meeting minutes (see *https://ritdml.rit. edu/handle/1850/3233*).

Secretaries for the Academic Senate and Institute Council deposit and then email their respective minutes to the RIT community, from the president to the students. There is potential for large numbers of the collective staff and students to access the IR and read the documents therein, leading to a greater curiosity and use, also building an open access consciousness. Once in the repository, readers may also peruse colleague scholarship and decide to archive their own work.

## Institutional repository annual reports

Academic stakeholders, such as the provost, vice provost, vice president of research, academic deans, and the library dean, represent the views of their respective constituencies and appreciate/expect to be apprised of an IR's annual activities and accomplishments, especially as they relate to the faculty and administration. As an organizational document, the report is central to illustrate the university's role in campus scholarly communication activity, while also providing an opportunity to highlight the academy's research output. Employing Google Analytics adds an in-depth unique snapshot of reader and browser activity to contribute to the report.

- Repository reporting from the Oregon State University's Libraries includes an IR overview, measures of success, growth opportunities, and challenges. (see *http://ir.library.oregonstate.edu/xmlui/handle/1957/12962?show=full*).

- California Polytechnic University incorporated secondary IR annual reporting items such as quantitative measures of success, first-year pilot phase documentation, and additional opportunities (see *http://www.arl.org/sparc/bm~doc/digitalcommonsirreport.pdf*).

- Butler University supplemented their 2011 annual report with two-year highlights and statistics, listed the staff and student IR teams, and provided a number of Google Analytics including the: top 10 downloaded items; top 10 collection downloads; leading 20 full-text downloads sorted by faculty contributor/department; and the highest 20 full-text downloads sorted by title (see *http://digitalcommons.butler.edu/reports/4/*).

- Pacific University's IR annual account has an efficient chart that simultaneously delineates monthly submissions and download counts (see *http://commons.pacificu.edu/libfac/16/*).

# Summary

Part of the personal and organizational reward for an academic repository is the satisfaction of research dividends that participants have acquired by embracing a scholarly tool that benefits scientists, scholars, administrators, staff, students, and community. The visibility of the academy's scholarship in all its manifestations, including unique and local collection items, has an established role and function in an institutional repository. Research and creative output establishes credibility, especially when the global community has access to view, use, and build upon the university's productivity.

## Summary

# 4

# Institutional repository collaborations and building campus relationships

**Abstract.** Library liaisons are the formal contacts between the libraries and a specified academic unit to foster communication channels. Due to declining funds that once supported a more robust traditional collection development program, liaisons have an opportunity to embrace a necessary point of service in the scholarly communication arena through aspects of collection development in an institutional repository (IR). By engaging a mindset shift to collect scholarship from faculty to deposit in an IR, academic libraries and global researchers will continually benefit from the accumulated research. Mandating the deposit of an academy's research ensures that faculty scholarly endeavors are openly available to be used and built upon. Academic subject disciplines have typically varied in their open access to research uptake. With the transformation in open publishing models and mindsets, a range of subject area options is emerging.

**Keywords:** aggregator databases, article processing charges, campus relationships, collection development, IR disciplines, IR reports, library liaisons, mandates, research strategic plans, S.R. Ranganathan, studies, surveys

## Acquiring institutional repository content

An institutional repository (IR) manager may initially or always acquire the majority of scholarly content on a campus by building relationships that assume various models. A more formal but effective option is to present the basic theory and practice of open access (OA) and its direct benefits. Meetings or presentations may address scholarly communication needs from the perspective of an individual, executive council, a center, college, library liaisons, editors that manage a journal, or an administrator with organizational documents to archive. An efficient and effective way to communicate the abstract context of what a repository offers, is to meet in a presentation-equipped room or, if meeting informally, an iPad can provide the means to a "show and tell." Showcasing the research at an individual, department, college, or university level is compelling, as it not only considers the single academic but the full hierarchy the individual faculty is also engaged in. Statistical evidence provided by altmetrics (alternative article publishing metrics) include download counts and social media interactions. Google Analytics reports are welcomed by academics wanting to know immediately not what readers think about their scholarship, but a variety of statistics focused on usage. (For more details, see pages 156–7.)

When encountering campus faculty in meetings, at events, and in general conversation, it is productive to know their subject areas and where they spend their research efforts. Faculty characteristically have a diverse portfolio of scholarly assets that would be globally advanced if highlighted in an IR. Within the context of intellectual content, initiating a dialog about a faculty's research and subsequently referencing the benefits of an IR has potential to create interest. Following up with an email that includes repository links and rearticulating the advantages fuses the verbal with the visual description.

Office staff may be entrusted with publishing a department's newsletter, a college's journal, an alumni publication, or they have knowledge of grants and awards achieved by their unit's research activity. Conversing with personnel reiterates the prospect of locating a variety of scholarly content.

An academy's standard means of communication is the conventional daily email that chronicles current and upcoming events of interest. These emails routinely contain information about scholarly activities, such as talks or presentations, new publications, campus poster sessions, and locally sponsored conferences – all potential opportunities to garner IR content.

# Staff, collaborations, who contributes, and why

Some of the barriers to populating an institutional repository with faculty research are not related to technological challenges; they are the result of a library's distribution of tasks. With the onset of open access (OA) responsibilities, the IR manager encourages faculty, administrators, and students to consider depositing journal articles, presentations, conference proceedings, undergraduate and graduate e-theses and e-dissertations (ETDs), and other scholarship. Garnering content can be a slow process, as the IR manager is also tasked with administering the repository and many of the inherent duties, as well as canvassing the campus for intellectual matter. It is economical to hire students to deposit scholarly materials in the IR; they are typically enthusiastic about their new skill set and the global benefits of depositing research. Institutional repository staff must carefully train and monitor student repository work activity to ensure accurate metadata and deposit decisions based on publisher copyright guidelines.

The daily reference, instruction, and collection development interactions with faculty occurs with the library liaisons. It is part of their overall job description to offer their subject expertise, have knowledge of their faculty's research interests and publications, grant activity, and understand the prime concerns of their academic departments in relation to the liaison's support.

# Engagement of liaisons with campus constituencies

Traditional library collection development has been at odds with flat library budgets. Collection management librarians are generally trying to save their most valued and affordable research resources by cancelling, unbundling, and recommending that liaisons create efficient approval plans. With fewer but more critical library budget decisions to be made, the academic librarian is less vested in the traditional collection development process of the past. The University of Minnesota (U of M) Libraries have streamlined their ordering processes and have freed up liaison time by a significant expansion in the use of approval plans (Williams, 2009). Consequently, liaisons are doing far less or are not as previously engaged in the collection building process. There are also fewer dollars to purchase monographs and books.

To manage the Washington State University Libraries' monograph and book requests more effectively due to sparse acquisition budgets, the library has eliminated interlibrary loan (ILL) fees. Library readers have been obliged to use ILL services to fill their primary research needs and beyond. The dean of libraries believes "that spending money to fulfill an expressed need is money well spent" (Starratt, 2010). Libraries are in the tenuous position of simultaneously choosing between not charging borrowing fees for a specific title that is not immediately available or purchasing a monograph or book that may or may not suffice for a pressing research demand.

Due to shifting and new services, academic libraries have experienced consistent staff reorganizations in the past ten or so years. Library liaisons have fewer hours at reference support points; staff and mature students may take on some part of that role. Virtual reference services replace some traditional assistance. At the U of M Libraries, reference lines are being drawn and distinctions made "between what patrons can expect from on-demand reference services (walk-in desks) and expert help services, available by appointment" (Williams, 2009). In addition, some service points are being merged and librarians are spending less time at reference desks.

As libraries in the US and abroad are altering their collection purchasing and reference assistance models, the academic library liaison experience in sub-Saharan Africa has its own challenges. Libraries in this part of the world have built partnerships with publishers for access to high-quality peer-reviewed research subscriptions. Scientists and scholars frequently emphasize the lack of access to journals as an obstruction to their scholarship. In reality, the journal content is obtainable; the disconnect is the awareness and demand for library instruction and marketing of where and how to access research in specific subject areas (Harle, 2011). The need for education in information literacy skills is vital and intersects with the awareness of locating open access intellectual content.

Academic libraries worldwide, not only in Africa, face the demand for effective training in locating resources in research databases. Proprietary databases vary from one interface model to another and are not necessarily intuitive. Busy faculty who cannot or are reluctant to attend an instruction session obviously do not reap the benefits. Purchasing costly research not employed for a variety of reasons is a misuse of a library's monetary and staff resources. Researchers who make use of Google Scholar or *OpenDOAR* will discover open access scholarly resources, dependent on discipline and publisher copyright policies.

Patchwork and institutional mandates require faculty to archive research articles with the potential to become the mechanism to build and populate an IR, greatly contributing to the local and global aggregate. The OAI-PMH harvesting, archiving, and search tool, *OpenDOAR* (*http://www.opendoar.org/index.html*), has the ability to amass metadata across all its repositories, the vast majority of which use software with built-in protocols. While conducting a subject or author search, results are returned in a composite list from institutions that match the search query. Clicking on the link will take the researcher to the home repository of the scholarly item. The reader will either find the full-text or may engage the IR's built-in email option or employ the *Request Article* button to solicit the author's postprint.

# Groundwork for patchwork and institutional repository mandates

At a minimum, a teaching faculty, an institutional repository manager, a department head, dean, provost, or rector may instigate the consideration of a patchwork or institutional mandate by virtue of a perceived need or urge to know more about what it means to exercise a directive for open access to research. Once there is one or more academy patchwork mandates, it is more likely that additional IR campus sanctions will occur in the future (Buehler, 2011). Deans and department heads may pursue and compete to some degree for the distinction of a scholarly communication status quo. They may also ambitiously plan for the future while remaining connected to present academic needs. An IR manager, who continually markets the benefits of OA, might reference another department's or college's success in terms of visibility through a variety of altmetrics, providing an impetus for faculty and administrators to consider the open access advantage.

The timing of implementing a college's repository community or a mandate is relevant to whether a project is executed or suspended. Interim deans do not make major decisions, particularly when a significant shift in a research culture is suggested. "Organizations who experience a vacancy in a senior leadership position such as the CEO of a corporation or the dean of a college will often decide to appoint an interim professional who takes over in a caretaker capacity" (Diab, 2011).

The optimistic news is that a college department head, dean, or advocate for academic OA can alter the existing research landscape when there is a change in leadership. As an administrator leaves an institution, someone new will be hired to take the place with staff expectations for the new hire to exhibit a progressive perspective.

In 2006, Rochester Institute of Technology's (RIT) Manager of Publishing and Scholarship Support Services and the Library Director presented a proposal to the Graduate Council to retrospectively scan all university theses and dissertations. The ancillary impetus to digitize the theses and dissertations was ETD visibility and a lack of shelf space in the RIT Archives for more pressing archival purposes. The Provost was consulted by the Library Director to garner funding from the nine colleges, including the Graduate College, for the project. The proposal temporarily failed to make any progress.

A new provost was hired in 2007, generating general optimism for showcasing faculty and student scholarship and the ETD scanning and archiving IR project. He embraced the idea of showcasing RIT's graduate research on a global scale. The Library Director and Provost marketed the idea to the colleges who agreed to pay a share of the theses and dissertations scanning cost, contributing funds to ensure a sense of collaboration and completion, and to encourage project traction.

The IR manager oversaw the work of the Kirtas (*http://www.kirtas.com/*) scanning machine operators, staff, students, and the myriad of other logistics to make the project a success. The 2008–9 nine-month enterprise to scan approximately 6,000 theses and dissertations was a major achievement; the ETDs continue to be proactively deposited in RIT's Digital Media Library (Buehler, 2010). The movement of an academy's staff is fluid; administrators leave an institution and new ones are hired, yielding motivation for change.

An open access directive to archive faculty research articles provides an academic thrust that also engages university administrators. The basic setting of the deposit mandate groundwork entails an in-depth analysis and consideration of purpose and a faculty senate review process committee, at a minimum. The undertaking can take years to navigate and come to a resolution. The investigative process and information is shared for consideration and democratically voted upon.

Individual dean mandates, resulting in conferring with the IR manager, usually do not have the "teeth" that the faculty senate authorized decree experiences. The dean mandate model may consist of multiple conversations between the IR manager and deans or associate deans, the latter charged with the task of aspiring to 100 percent open access scholarship deposit. In response to an actual dean's question related to how the process works, "How does one mandate the deposit of scholarship in an IR?" the reply stated "the act of requiring all scholarship (or, at a minimum, metadata) to be deposited in the IR, dependent on publisher copyright." More than likely, any faculty objections will not deter administrators determined to see their college's article research accumulating visibility, highlighting the academic unit's intellectual content (Buehler, 2010).

The typical executive query may progress from the positing of a mandate to the dean wanting to understand the next steps, asking "How do we physically move our scholarship to the IR?" Many academic libraries proxy-archive faculty research by delegating the scholarly deposits to recruited library staff and using students to also archive scholarship. A positive statement of purpose might include a sense of flexibility: "It is whatever method that works best for your college." There are several choices and policy variations across repositories. Depositing alternatives may include faculty and administrative staff involving the IR manager (or equivalent personnel) by:

- emailing CVs, harvesting personal website content to garner additional materials, creating a department research bibliography from a library's journal database to assist in locating articles or metadata;
- emailing individual items or utilizing FTP options for large file transfers;
- directly harvesting from arXiv and other OA subject repositories;
- delivering CDs or a USB flash drive with various large file content, such as PowerPoint presentations and MP3s/MP4s).

After reviewing a CV or other bibliographic sources, institutional repository staff can send a final request list of postprints (papers approved by peer-review) to an IR manager or directly to faculty after publishers have been contacted by email or phone to secure permissions or to clarify a copyright if not available on the SHERPA/RoMEO website (*http://www. sherpa.ac.uk/romeo/*). Staff may also directly email authors to collect postprints, preprints, conference proceedings, or presentations to complete a researcher's repository profile (Buehler, 2010).

Proxy-archiving academic content is a "time-saving benefit" to faculty and may be a tipping point of convenience to enact a mandate. Framing the conversation as a scholarly communication collaboration increases the value proposition of working with administrators and faculty. Once there is at least one patchwork IR mandate, it has the potential to be a gateway to further campus traction for other deans and department heads to consider requiring the deposit of scholarship in the local repository. There is potential for a viral effect, as competition for downloads and a presence that showcases research is what many faculty and administrators hope for and aim towards. "One of UNLV's central goals is to increase research and scholarly productivity and become a nationally recognized research university," and, in addition, to "enhance awareness of the value of research in the community and state" (University of Nevada, Las Vegas, 2010).

Another reason to focus on the IR's mandate advantages utilizing postprints is the ease of researcher scholarship findability and the "no fee" model of searching OA aggregator databases, such as *Open*DOAR. Open access to scholarly works removes the challenge of searching individual, library-purchased subject databases (if your library subscribes) by alternately providing options, such as Google to employ a search to locate OA interdisciplinary scholarship. The Directory of Open Access Repositories (*OpenDOAR: http://www.opendoar.org/*) yields a plethora of available research or a metadata record an email away from the author who has a postprint or copy of the article. The larger academic community has not yet reached a critical mass of IR mandates or devised a means to corral the 50 million published articles (see Chapter 3) that have the promise to restructure our scholarly research avenues (see Figure 4.1).

In February 2010, the University of Virginia faculty voted on an open access resolution to exercise any or all copyrights on their articles in any medium. As an alternative to mediated deposits by library staff and hired students, researchers would utilize the IR framework and deposit their own scholarship in Libra (*http://libra.virginia.edu/*) (Meloni, 2011). The "build it and they will come" strategy without a mandate allows scientists and scholars to procrastinate and make arbitrary and uninformed decisions on archiving their work.

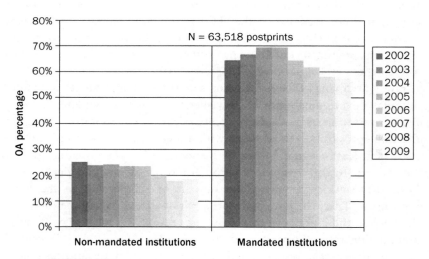

**Figure 4.1**  **Mandates triple the percentage of green open access (self-archiving)**

Percentage of green OA self-archiving averaged for the sampled four institutions with the earliest mandates, compared to the percentage of control articles from other institutions published in the same journals (for years 2002–2009, measured in 2011). Respective totals are derived from Thompson-Reuters-ISI Index (Poynder, 2011a).

Introduced to the strategic benefits of OA by a science librarian at the University of Liège, Rector Bernard Rentier announced to the faculty: "depositing papers in the repository was henceforth the sole mechanism for submitting them to be considered when researchers underwent performance review and the ability to receive grant monies" (Poynder, 2011a). Fourteen months after the Open Repository and Bibliography (ORBi) was launched, it had accumulated 30,000 bibliographic references and more than 20,000 full-text documents.

# Academic strategic research plans

Most academic institutions include research components in their strategic plans to ensure that faculty and students aspire to benchmarked goals. Repository capacity has the potential to fulfill many of these objectives that could contribute to increased content and potentially support a mandate. Below are excerpts from three university strategic plans that encompass likely scholarly communication opportunities within an IR.

- *University of Louisville (2007)*. Among the expected results of increasing appreciation for research and all types of intellectual output by students and faculty alike, are to amplify quality scholarship and research, improve nationally important metrics, and elevate the reputation of the institution, as well as to devise new and use established ways of measuring research and scholarly productivity (*http://louisville.edu/research/strategic-plan/research-strategic-plan. html*).

- *Simon Fraser, British Columbia (2010–15)*. "Many of [the Simon Fraser] Centres and Institutes play an important role in disseminating the results of university-based research to the public sphere and contribute significantly to public policy decisions" (*http://www.sfu. ca/vpresearch/docs/SRP2010_15.pdf*).

- *University of Illinois, Urbana-Champaign (UIUC) (2005–6)*. Two out of the four strategic priorities that emerged from the planning process were to develop UIUC into an urban research university and the nation's preeminent public research institution (*http://www.uillinois. edu/strategicplan/*).

Universities have strategic research plans with the potential to capitalize on repositories to further their research agenda. It is of benefit for administrators to be aware of IRs' existence and vast potential as a sustainable and scholarly tool that inherently has a multitude of benefits and a range of beneficiaries. "The effort to develop policy and strategies will undoubtedly cause greater appreciation of the value of university research within the university community and enhanced distribution will increase research value externally" (bepress, 2009b).

By collaborating closely with a campus department, such as UNLV's Research and Graduate Studies division, the Digital Scholarship@UNLV IR has an opportunity to be better understood, exploited, and promoted. The strategic document "Focus 50–100: Research and Graduate Education Implementation Team Progress on Action Plan Items" (2010) concentrates on defining UNLV research programs as stated by the document and aims to develop mechanisms to promote research collaborations, to establish a culture of research excellence, and to advance the research infrastructure. The IR is mentioned in UNLV's strategic plan: "An institutional electronic repository/archive was established by the Lied Libraries, and it holds great promise for promotion of UNLV scholarly activity, both nationally and internationally" (University of Nevada, Las Vegas, 2010: 6). An IR is the ideal tool to promote and support the university's stated research goals. UNLV's repository administrator works in partnership with the Research and Graduate Studies' officials by building an IR presence that supports faculty and graduate student research.

# Engaging with campus constituencies

Liaisons are at the forefront of connecting with their colleges' faculty and students in a variety of ways that increasingly encompasses scholarly communications, specifically the academy's repository.

## Library liaison roles in scholarly communication

The academic library's improving financial affairs coupled with the subsequent shrinking of liaisons' traditional collection development and reference roles, offer an opportunity to learn and accumulate new skills that contribute unique expertise within the campus. With the advent of IRs, college and research libraries' strategic advantages have acquired an awareness and comprehension of the shifting scholarly communication landscape and integrated tools. It is reasonable to incorporate librarians into this arena where they spend much of their time working with a college's faculty and students who would benefit from this knowledge. Librarians have expressed being uncomfortable with entering into a scholarly dialog where there is a sense the academic faculty may be more acquainted with or have greater expertise on the topic. An essential aspect of this shifting paradigm is library support to "reinvent the liaison model" (Williams, 2009). Librarian liaisons are becoming more knowledgeable, competent, and comfortable in the metamorphosis of the scholarly communication culture that includes:

- a willingness to engage in a new form of relationship building;
- a commitment to a full spectrum training approach;
- building expertise in value-added collaborative services; and
- embedding a systems thinking approach (participation at all levels, united through a common understanding of a system) (Senge, 1994).

This method "recognizes the innate networks, the interconnectedness, interdependency, and collaboration among people in organizations" (Malenfant, 2010) where liaisons would be marketing their libraries' expertise in an innovative way as a vital contribution to the academy.

In the past ten or so years, academic libraries in an environment of persistent change have: reorganized multiple times to accommodate faculty and student needs; become more efficient by integrating new online services and tools; and constructed a robust scholarly communication infrastructure for research within the intrinsic academic culture. The erudite framework that encompasses an IR is a microcosm of the library and academic organization, operating as a complex organism within itself.

The systems thinking approach utilized by liaison librarians provides an opening for the creation of a new mental model that embraces making decisions in novel circumstances, yields feedback on results, and allows an ongoing evaluation of the action and the consequences. It is also subject to change, which has the potential for flexibility. In addition, a person must be able to psychologically rehearse intended actions to achieve a goal (Davidson, Dove, & Weltz, 1999) that dovetails into the new liaison/subject librarian prototype of participation in a sustainable scholarly communication service ideal. The mental model is an analog for re-tooling, reaching out, and partnering with college constituencies. Committed liaison librarians are redirecting their time and focus to have a perspicuous:

- mindset that faculty are academic colleagues;
- investment in a new and crucial library role;
- support of the transformation in the scholarly communication system;
- opportunity for college liaison leadership.

Those who are willing to take risks will flourish in their new role and translate opportunities into practice by focusing more on services than library collections.

Academic librarians, at the early stages of managing and administering IRs, in partnership with faculty, administrators, and students, had much to offer the evolving liaison model. Currently, there is a greater baseline understanding of scholarly communication among faculty and library staff, less prevalent five to ten years ago. Institutional repository managers/administrators welcome liaison librarian collaborations to construct new repository relationships that establish and foster IR communities and collections. Meanwhile, "moving from a facility-based [library] operation to an expansive campus-wide enterprise potentially enables anyone in the university community to participate in sharing scholarship through the IR" (Buehler & Boateng, 2005). Library liaisons that use influence in their roles as education partners are of strategic importance to understanding and populating a repository.

Transforming scholarly communication practices within all disciplines provides an opportunity for liaisons to "acquire new skills and leverage more specialized expertise among their library colleagues in service of their clients" (Hahn, 2009). Liaisons invested in their library's repository and scholarly communication services might consider articulating and developing at a minimum a basic mastery of knowledge concerning:

- assisting with or creating tools to facilitate the scholarly communication process;
- navigating and understanding author rights' tools, such as addendums;
- article publisher copyrights, consulting SHERPA/RoMEO, or contacting publishers;
- the benefits of an IR to an individual faculty, a department, a college, and university;
- talking points for faculty, administrators, and students;

- IR collection building, and knowing what types of scholarly materials can be deposited;
- research recruiting processes and garnering appropriate IR materials.

To engage the campus, be knowledgeable, and feel comfortable with new concepts or added responsibility involves a necessary learning curve. It takes time to assimilate the scholarly communication system and understand how all facets correspond to one another. Workshops, presentations, documentation, pairing up with the IR manager for individual, department, or college conversations and related activities are meaningful to and supportive of the process. Knowing that staff are accountable to the repository, are available and enthusiastic to collaboratively assist with a presentation, an email, or a conversation, is beneficial.

Once liaisons feel more confident in their knowledge of open access and an IR, they can apply the scholarly communication context to users' needs while interacting with them in reference consultations or instruction situations. Integrating scholarly communication details that include practical institutional repository knowledge into general or discipline-specific research guides/LibGuides (*http://www.springshare.com/libguides/*) also conveys the sustainable concept of open access research to faculty and students. Mainstreaming an IR can be accomplished by explaining the benefits and value where appropriate, as "facilitators in getting the content into the repository and content out to users" (Jenkins, Breakstone, & Hixson, 2005: 11).

## Campus repository connections

Liaisons can merge their traditional administrator, faculty, and student connections with new scholarly communication contributions by engaging organizations, institutes, centers, and special programs that address a broad range of research interests. These entities continually persist in showcasing their efforts and outcomes to remain viable, appreciating the attention that highlights their work. Campus units that establish a new or strengthened relationship with the library that revolves around a scholarly communication framework of depositing research is a compelling reason for liaisons to embrace the institutional repository.

Liaisons are a valued resource for an IR manager to confer with while also engaging them to approach their college and associate deans, department heads, and faculty in promoting the IR. They have a pulse on the faculty and colleges they support. An added value proposition of involving a liaison in the IR is the benefit of familiarity and understanding of how an individual college operates and the awareness of any obstacle or potential advocacy that may exist.

The new frontier of collection development has a future within the IR. Hypothetically, if liaison librarians were able to amass all their faculty's scholarly content and readers contacted authors to garner their full-text research, libraries would not be as dependent upon research database subscriptions as is currently the case. Authors might consider retaining· their article copyrights where possible and not rely on the journal publisher to maintain their postprint copy by immediately depositing it upon acceptance in an IR for perpetual use, with publisher permission. "To help shape this new digital world of scholarship, it is crucial for scholars to be proactive managers of their copyrights" (McMillen & Tucker, 2010). Liaisons have symbiotic relationships to inform and support faculty to capitalize on retaining postprints and their copyrights where possible.

Some readers do request postprints and research clarifications from authors, although it is unlikely to become a pervasive habit unless researchers consider engaging more heavily in that practice. By liaisons maximizing their current faculty and student relationships to establish new or deepen seasoned scholarly communication roles, augmenting repository collections by these means holds a plausible promise for archiving a sizable amount of intellectual assets.

Library administrators, in concert with liaisons, are encouraging and supporting a paradigm shift away from "a collection-centered model to an engagement-centered one" (Williams, 2009). Academic libraries' liaison job responsibilities and position descriptions are evolving to include scholarly communication knowledge and outreach activity. The evolution of the current method scientists and scholars use to communicate and disseminate their research has motivated academic libraries to grasp and subsequently support current and evolving erudite processes.

At the University of Minnesota Libraries (U of M), their recently altered liaison model has matured over the previous five years by engaging in a collaborative process using a "Position Description Framework." This document is the basis for librarian position descriptions that delineate any directional modifications in a liaison's goals. It is comprised of ten elements that integrate ten roles within each element (Williams, 2009). The scholarly communication component is likely to affect several distinct aspects of the roles to some degree. In addition, accountability to the initiative incorporates a self-assessment, job description updates, and a performance goal requirement of author rights (Malenfant, 2010). Rights management expertise is an essential strategy in the transformation of the disseminated scholarly communication process directed to guide scientists and scholars to retain their article copyrights for future research use, simultaneously for both the author and global researchers.

In response to the scholarly communication initiative at the University of British Columbia (UBC) in 2007–9, the UBC Libraries created a steering committee that identified campus stakeholders (Kirchner, 2009). Library liaisons, as key staff in the program, worked with their faculty by garnering discipline-based research to contribute to the initiative. A scholarly communication training program was established with input from liaisons and the steering committee, who attended a workshop based on their new and expanded roles given by the Library's IR Coordinator.

Librarians were additionally asked to take advantage of Lee Van Orsdel's "Faculty Activism in Scholarly Communications Opportunity Assessment" (*http://www.arl.org/bm~doc/opp.pdf*), a subject area information-gathering instrument created for the ARL/ACRL Institute on Scholarly Communication (*http://www.arl.org/sc/institute/index.shtml*). By sharing the accumulated faculty assessment form details that included a thorough examination of publishing practices: grant activities, data curation, open access journal queries, documented citation impact factors, OA "activist behaviors," existing librarian relationships, and an exercise to discern what faculty might have read or heard about OA from their peers, the liaisons adopted a holistic view of what faculty were aware of and their scholarly behaviors (Van Orsdel, 2007). The completed forms most likely illustrated some potential for transforming current relationships to encouraging new ways of interacting that revolve around scholarly communications.

One of the marketing outcomes of the UBC Library's scholarly communication campus efforts was the appointment of grant managers interested in author rights and the management of copyright transfer agreement workshops taught by liaisons. With Canada's current climate of aligning its three national research grant funding agencies to "include a commitment to developing a shared approach for improving access to publicly funded research in keeping with internationally recognized best practices, standards and policies for funding and conducting research" (*http://www.science.gc.ca/default.asp?Lang=En& n=1E7A5F18-1*), there is an extensive and ongoing opportunity for UBC's and other Canadian IRs to benefit from these library-supported workshops that confirm the impulse of open access to research matters.

York University's Science Librarians have developed a diverse strategy to assist faculty in complying with one of the grant agency's policies, the Canadian Institutes of Health Research (CIHR), to provide open access to their scholarship. The CIHR content is research-intensive, encompassing intellectual materials from university faculty, teaching hospitals, and Canada's research institutes. Librarians focused on supporting faculty by communicating open access concepts, cultivating CIHR compliance, and being present at grant funding informational meetings, was an opportune time to liaise with faculty researchers (Fernandez, Nariani, & Salmon, 2010).

Open access researcher resources were comprehensively developed by the science librarians, such as:

- a webpage for faculty to stay apprised of CHIR policy (*http://www. arl.org/bm~doc/spec-311-web.pdf*);
- in collaboration with research officers to arrange faculty workshops in the interpretation of copyright policies, how to post research in the IR, open access publication options, author rights; and
- including a scholarly communications website that detailed York University Libraries article processing charges (APCs) subsidized for specific OA publishers (*http://scholcom.yorku.ca/*) such as BioMed Central, the Public Library of Science (PLoS), and the Hindawi Publishing Corporation.

A faculty author survey was administered by librarians to assess their satisfaction with the Library's financial support of OA journal article publications. Survey results proved that faculty are appreciative of the monetary support towards APCs and, overall, open access is accepted by the departments' Tenure and Promotion Committees, a source of significant satisfaction. While researchers tend to be mindful of tenure and promotion accountability, "their primary consideration is impact" (Fernandez, Nariani, & Salmon, 2010: 13).

# What and how subject areas play a role in the IR

All disciplines have a role in an IR. Some subject area publishers tend towards more liberal and supportive open access policies than other publishers, and there are authors who may be more resistant to depositing scholarly content in a repository. The studies and surveys listed below provide an overview of recent OA practices and what future opportunities may be possible.

## Multi-disciplinary studies and surveys

A multidisciplinary and quantitative study conducted by Mukherjee & Nazim (2011) explicated subject area coverage in IRs from 2005 to 2010 by utilizing Hitchcock et al.'s (2007) Digital Preservation Service Provider Models for Institutional Repositories study (*http://www.dlib.org/dlib/may07/hitchcock/05hitchcock.html*), and *Open*DOAR statistics ranging from the years 2007 to 2010 (see Table 4.1). The directory was created in 2006, consequently the Hitchcock analysis was useful to combine and extend the years including the numbers of subjects, item records, and archives for an expanded view of IR disciplines. A total of 1,766 institutional repositories were accounted for in the study. Repository content types listed in the order of prevalence were: journal articles, conference/workshop papers, working papers, books/chapters, multimedia, learning objects, ETDs, bibliographic references, datasets, software, patents, and other item categories. Subject reporting covered 29 disciplines. The multidisciplinary subject category was the leading classification comprising an amalgam not separated out into individual disciplines. Of the subjects listed in order by the number of archives and records, the top five disciplines were health/medicine, history/archaeology, geography/regional studies, computer/information technology, and business/economics. The bottom five subject areas with the lowest number of archives and records in the study were civil engineering, architecture, electrical/electronic engineering, psychology, and management/planning (*http://eprints.rclis.org/16849/*).

## Chemistry and economics

An analysis commissioned by the Joint Information Systems Committee (JISC) Research Communication Strategy Project at the Centre for Research Communications, the University of Nottingham, was conducted with chemists and economists who support open access, but not consistently. Overall, the academics were unaware that their institutions had OA mandates. There was a similar low awareness among faculty regarding funder mandates. Regardless of lacking knowledge of the OA directive, the majority of survey participants were not affected by the

**Table 4.1**  Subject coverage of institutional archives (IAs)

| Subjects | Number of records | Number of archives |
|---|---|---|
| Multidisciplinary | 3,075,515 | 1,098 |
| Health and Medicine | 1,717,651 | 128 |
| Chemistry and Chemical Technology | 1,272,043 | 36 |
| Biology and Biochemistry | 1,018,408 | 63 |
| Physics and Astronomy | 843,155 | 48 |
| Computer and IT | 784,791 | 85 |
| Mathematics and Statistics | 685,545 | 45 |
| History and Archaeology | 574,051 | 105 |
| Geography and Regional Studies | 560,312 | 105 |
| Fine and Performing Arts | 520,411 | 49 |
| Business and Economics | 434,451 | 78 |
| Technology (General) | 356,504 | 92 |
| Ecology and Environment | 270,445 | 54 |
| Law and Politics | 202,143 | 77 |
| Earth and Planetary Science | 196,673 | 31 |
| Agriculture, Food and Veterinary | 189,394 | 40 |
| Mathematical Engineering | 166,515 | 32 |
| Science (General) | 138,521 | 106 |
| Social Sciences (General) | 127,916 | 88 |
| Architecture | 112,978 | 13 |
| Civil Engineering | 107,865 | 13 |
| Language and Literature | 90,402 | 39 |
| Arts and Humanities (General) | 79,217 | 50 |
| Management and Planning | 65,341 | 35 |
| Philosophy and Religion | 63,981 | 44 |
| Electrical and Electronic Engineering | 62,378 | 21 |
| Library and Information Science | 61,557 | 59 |
| Education | 39,876 | 55 |
| Psychology | 35,675 | 23 |
| Total | 13,853,714 | 2,712 |

*Note:* Numbers of IAs and records may be placed in more than one subject category. As a result, total numbers exceed the real number of archives and records.

*Source*: Mukherjee & Nazim (2011). Reproduced with permission.

requirements because they were already motivated to embrace open archiving of their research. The study's author cautions the reader that the sample is comparatively small, with the results based on three UK higher education institutions (Davies, 2011).

Chemists and economists both commented on the multiple advantages of open access to their work. They were attracted to OA for public-spirited reasons and also viewed it as a personal benefit. Quality was considered an essential and perceived concern, as was the impetus to publish articles in high-impact journals. The subsequent negative attitude towards OA journal publishing was prevalent where the perception of quality takes time for a publication to acquire. In addition, abundant misconceptions towards the OA journals were focused on a lack of perceived quality in the peer-review process.

Both surveyed groups made their work available in an IR. The top three chemists' use of an IR equaled the number of colleagues that did not deposit in an open access venue. The next highest use location for publishing was in an OA journal, and thirdly, it was equivalent to posting articles on a department or personal website. The means for the top three economists to promote their research was chosen in this order: a personal website, a department website, and in an IR.

Another question focused on when the academics engage in OA and why. For both chemists and economists, the highest percentage of agreeing and strongly agreeing responses was how open access improves accessibility to their work. Both disciplines were in agreement that publicly funded research should be available to taxpayers. The economists had a high percentage of responses in favor of open access, as it increased: the amount of publicity for an author's work; the intellectual content expediently available; and there was greater opportunity for professional recognition.

Davies (2011) was further compelled to understand the philosophical reasons why chemists and economists held back in not making their scholarship open access. The primary reason for faculty from both disciplines not making their research openly available was the professional impetus to publish in high-impact journals. In addition, it was too expensive to publish work by pledging open access where article processing charges (APCs) were expected.

Academics who chose various publishing models in the survey were asked about methods for committing their work to be open in the future. Faculty in both disciplines stated they were more likely to deposit their research in an IR than in other locations, although the economists equally prefer a department website. The final survey question asked what might compel faculty to embrace OA in the future. The chemists and economists both acknowledged a high value for a community having a standard OA practice and would be encouraged to employ an open fee-based model if there was institutional support for paying the APCs.

A significant disparity in the pricing of online chemistry and economics journals was depicted in a *Library Journal* survey that focused on a merged Institute for Scientific Information (ISI) index charging structure comprising "print plus free online, online only, and the first tier of tiered pricing" (Bosch, Henderson, & Klusendorf, 2011: 2). The average annual expenditure for a chemistry title was $3,676, the most expensive of all the disciplines listed. The average cost per economics title (including business) was $754, creating a greater awareness of publishing cost disparities in academic journals. The researchers acknowledged the potential benefit of raising an IR's visibility by also adding a depth of access to their research.

As a side note, SUNY faculty took a stand on the continuation of their American Chemical Society (ACS) subscription. After five years of the Society raising its subscription fees by almost 50 percent, the State University of New York Potsdam faculty agreed with the Library Director that the ACS had gone too far: the pricing model was unsustainable. Instead of re-subscribing to the ACS in 2013, the Director cobbled together an acceptable chemistry research package (*http://www. arl.org/sparc/media/SUNY_Potsdam_Takes_Stand_Against_American_ Chemical_Society_Prices.shtml*).

The JISC survey confirms that economists make serious use of subject repositories; they think about the accessibility of their research and believe the open access dissemination model gets their work out more promptly. On a personal level, economists enjoy professional recognition and academic reward, and seem to have greater opportunities to engage with collaborators. Presented at the UK's Association of Research Managers and Administrators, a poster purveys the Hubbard, Hodgson, & Fuchs (2010) chemists and economists survey results from the University of Nottingham and is available at: *http://rcsproject.wordpress.com/*.

The Economists Online database, a social science repository based in Europe, is organized by how economists work and their personal and professional value system (*http://www.economistsonline.org/home*). The site offers features that corroborate the JISC survey results on how economists professionally maneuver in academia. It highlights bibliographic records, OA full-text documents, primary datasets, and more. Each represented author has a profile listing affiliation, an option for a photograph, and a list of publications. The motto of the Nereus service, *Economists Online*, is "SEE and BE SEEN." Open access is a priority with almost 40 percent of full-text content available. Nereus (*http://www.nereus4economics.info*) is "integrating access to the economics resources of key libraries, academic publications, and other online resources in Europe and beyond."

Another rich online source of economics research is the Research Papers in Economics (RePEc) (*http://repec.org/*), managed by hundreds of volunteers in 78 countries to "enhance the dissemination of research in economics." It supports institutional archives by providing links for readers to utilize full-text where available. If a working paper or a journal article full-text is not accessible from RePEc, readers are encouraged to contact an author or their own libraries. Incorporated into this site as of September 1, 2013 are 1.4 million research items and over 35,000 registered authors.

## Social and behavioral sciences studies and resources

The research and grey literature for the education discipline has been open to researchers and practitioners since 1966, by means of the Education Resources Information Center (ERIC), a tool created by the US Government to increase greater access to educational resources. These assets have set an open standard over time to pedagogic and additional useful course materials.

Commenced in 2012, the Institute of Education Sciences (IES) requires its grantees to submit their peer-reviewed research publications to ERIC. Investigators are to submit the e-version of their postprint manuscripts upon acceptance for publication in a peer-reviewed journal. Participating in open access to research through ERIC is strongly encouraged; the deadline to deposit is within 12 months of the official date of final publication. This requirement adheres to all scholarly activities supported through the IES research and training grant awards, cooperative agreements and contracts. It is also applied to peer-reviewed original research publications supported in whole or in part, with direct costs stemming from the IES. The mandate does not apply to book chapters, editorials, reviews, or conference proceedings. Articles resulting from IES contracts are already widely available through their website and ERIC. This policy requires grantees, beginning with those funded in fiscal year (FY) 2012 grant competitions, to submit their peer-reviewed research to ERIC (*http://ies.ed.gov/funding/researchaccess.asp*).

Coonin & Younce (2009) surveyed 918 authors who had published in the 2007–8 issues of OA education journals focused on the behavioral and social sciences, archived in the authoritative Directory of Open Access Journals (DOAJ). Subject areas were comprised of business management, psychology, women's studies, and music. The Directory's journals have specific compulsory inclusion policies, such as a registered ISSN and peer-reviewed content.

Survey respondents assigned the greatest significance to making a decision on where to publish based on peer-review. Second in importance was if the author's paper was a good match for a journal, and thirdly, the journal's reputation. The authors pointed out that a relatively low value was assigned to the importance of citation impact. Of the 306 responses to the self-archiving question, 37.3 percent stated they had deposited or posted one or more publications in an IR, on a personal website, or in an eprint archive. Retaining copyright for this group seemed unimportant overall, as the decision for authors to publish in a particular journal had a greater value.

The authors' survey questions concerning the acceptability of publishing in e-journals and/or OA journals may have been confusing to the survey participants. Online library journal subscriptions are typically referred to as e-journals; the term "OA journals" ordinarily refers to open online publications that are globally available. It was evident in the survey's general comments section that faculty misunderstood the terminology instead of "fully understanding open access as a publishing model, rather than as a format change" (Coonin & Younce, 2009: 88). Liaisons and other library staff who promote an IR need to be clear about the concept and the migration of print to a publisher's electronic article structure; they are not equivalent formats or models.

According to the 309 academics that responded to the survey question on the types of behavioral and social sciences publications that are considered essential to advance their discipline, the top three in order of preference were peer-reviewed articles, books/monographs, and presentations given at professional meetings.

These Education academics became aware of OA publishing through colleagues by searching the Internet for publishing possibilities and through professional societies. There was some awareness (16.5 percent) spread by institutions while libraries in particular offered 7.1 percent of the academics' knowledge of open access publishing.

With regard to article processing charges (APCs), 16.8 percent had published articles where fees were required. Approximately 27 percent of respondents stated they would publish with journals if a funding agency or university paid the APCs. More than 50 percent of the faculty stated if fees were required, they would not disseminate their research in those particular journals. This appears to be a discipline-specific motive and/or lack of a need to pay to publish because of other stable options that could include APCs paid by a university, library, or a grant.

Authors who responded to the above surveys remarked that overall, they would not pay for publishing an article in a journal unless the library or institution paid to distribute their research. Philosophically, some of the authors did not believe in "buying" their way into a journal.

# Open access journal article processing charges – who pays?

Multiple studies on open access APCs have revealed faculty reactions to the question of who is prepared to pay the journal article fees. The Study of Open Access Publishing (SOAP) (*http://project-soap.eu/*), a two-year (2009–11) European Commission-funded project, initiated a survey in May 2010 to assess researcher attitudes and experiences with OA publishing from developing and transition countries. Out of over 43,000 researchers from 11 countries with a sizeable participation, the top seven country responses were from China, Russia, Poland, Egypt, South Africa, Nigeria, and the Ukraine. There was also feedback from 34 other Electronic Information for Libraries (EIFL) partner countries, such as Ethiopia, Mozambique, and Estonia (Kuchma, 2011). EIFL is an international not-for-profit European organization with a global network of partners focused on increasing access to knowledge (*http://www.eifl.net*).

Of the SOAP survey respondents who replied to the employment question, 65 percent were working at a university or college and 23 percent worked in a research institute. The top seven discipline groupings for these faculty were: the biological sciences; medicine, dentistry and related subjects; physics and related sciences; engineering and technology; chemistry; the social sciences; and mathematical and computer sciences.

In response to the question that asked approximately how many OA articles the 3,544 researchers had published in the past five years, replies were distributed as follows: 51 percent had produced one to five articles; 7 percent six to ten articles; and nearly 5 percent had published more than ten articles. A query was then posed to these respondents concerning what the dollar amount of the APCs had been for their most recent open access article. Table 4.2 shows the results from the 2010 SOAP survey illustrating the percentage: of researchers who paid no APC; of researchers for whom a third-party organization clearly paid a fee; and of those who were unsure what the arrangement was for publication payment (in euros and US dollars).

Respondents answered a follow-up question with multiple-choice options. The majority of researchers used their allocated grant funding to pay the APCs. The next tier of responses stated that funds not specifically meant for OA publishing were used. Where it appeared there was no other financial support, institutions or the author paid the charges.

These same researchers responded to a "degree of ease" funding question that implicated either an author's institution or the organization's funder. The majority of those surveyed (59 percent) communicated that procuring funding was *difficult*, 27 percent found it *easy* to garner a subsidy, and 14 percent *had not exploited* these sources.

## Social sciences

**Table 4.2** Article processing charge results from the 2010 SOAP survey

| Publication fee for last OA article (n = 2,232) | | % of respondents |
|---|---|---|
| No charge: | 1,246 | 50.1 |
| Up to €250 ($350): | 259 | 7.2 |
| €251–€500 ($350–$700): | 159 | 6.0 |
| €501–€1,000 ($700–$1,350): | 230 | 12.6 |
| €1,001–€3000 ($1,350–$4,100): | 114 | 9.9 |
| More than €3,000 ($4,100): | 2 | 0.2 |
| I do not know: | 222 | 14.0 |

Source: http://creative commons.org/licenses/by/3.0/

As academic libraries are "leading the campus campaigns to transform the landscape of scholarly publishing" (Wirth & Chadwell, 2010), library faculty are simultaneously lacking a commitment to these goals with their own IR-depositing practices. In a 2009 study, Way (2010) distilled the top twenty library and information science journal articles from the year 2007 with the highest impact factor to determine OA availability. The author's findings were comprised of 922 located articles of which 27 percent (253 articles) were openly available in either repositories or on personal websites. The study's Google search results were found to be effective for locating articles only when the journal titles were already identified.

Few articles were archived in IRs or the library/information science subject repositories, such as E-LIS (E-prints in Library and Information Science) (*http://eprints.rclis.org/*) based in Europe or dLIST (Digital Library of Information Science and Technology) at the University of Arizona Libraries. Of further concern, Way noted that librarians and LIS (library and information studies) scholars were not practicing a leadership role in terms of aligning their values with their OA archiving rhetoric directed at faculty and administrators. For obvious reasons it is essential that library scholars and practitioners have credibility in terms of what they espouse. It is of interest to know if LIS faculty are promoting the benefits of open access to research in their classrooms.

The Social Sciences have a solid OA presence in the Social Science Research Network (SSRN) (*http://www.ssrn.com/*) that "has again been named the number one Open Access Repository in the World (for July 2012) by the Ranking Web of World Repositories (*http://repositories. webometrics.info/toprep.asp*), repeating their #1 Ranking from January, 2011." The SSRN is dedicated to expedient global dissemination of research throughout their specialized social science networks. As of September 1, 2013, the Research Network had 501,500 abstracts and 409,300 full-text papers. It also encourages and facilitates readers' communication with authors by noting detailed contact information that includes author email addresses for each paper. Also of note and upon request, a number of academic librarians mediate deposits in the SSRN for faculty in addition to archiving those same papers in their own IR.

Listed below are additional successful Social Science OA research repositories

- Political Research Online (PROL) (*http://convention3.allacademic. com/one/prol/prol01/index.php*) is "guided by" a consortium of US regional and UK associations. Preprints are the common currency for this resource that encourages researchers to submit their drafts for "early stages comment and potential partnering."

- The Open Folklore (*http://openfolklore.org/*) gateway, created by the American Folklore Society and the Indiana University Bloomington Libraries/Digital Library Program, facilitates OA to an expanding number of valuable books, websites, journals, and grey literature of interest to folklorists and ethnologists.

## *Humanities*

Through studies and action, the Humanities are known above all for their traditional publishing styles and networks. At present, humanities researchers, such as faculty in history, language/linguistics, literature, performing arts, philosophy, religion, and visual arts (Wikipedia, 2011), are engaging with IRs at a relatively low level in comparison to other disciplines.

Dartmouth College Library's 2008–9 eight-month study focused on determining what criteria humanities faculty would deem essential to embrace an IR. Seaman's study is based on the Humanities' scholars whose "information needs are rarely if ever considered during the design phase of an institutional repository" (2011: 2). In the world of IRs, it is common knowledge that the Humanities overall tend to lag behind in adopting OA behaviors, although that is evolving.

A 2009 Ithaka S+R survey examined faculty materials deposited in an IR by discipline, revealing classical studies and literature were at levels below 10 percent. In contrast, mathematics and statistics were at 20 percent, physics over 40 percent, and economics rising above 20 percent (Schonfeld & Housewright, 2010). In the "diffusion of innovation theory," there are groups of consumers who differ in their readiness and willingness to adopt or implement a new service, idea, product, or method (BusinessDictionary, *http://www.businessdictionary.com/*). Understanding how researchers in specific disciplines work may also aid in facilitating behaviors that encourage IR engagement.

By acknowledging Dartmouth's Humanities' faculty scholarly communication information needs, ownership and repurposing intellectual content, and assuring them that the repository model was a useful tool, there was a more likely chance the faculty would be interested in populating it. Library liaisons assisted in identifying the Arts and Humanities faculty who had shown an OA interest or had current needs that the IR could fulfill. Thirteen faculty participated and anecdotally responded by expressing their scholarly communication needs and preferences (Seaman, 2011):

- *Teaching*. Researchers conveyed less ability to manage and distribute their research data and publications on their own.

- *Research*. Storing sizable files such as music, video, and CAD (computer-aided design) programs on personal computers was a challenge. Other issues included a lack of institutional computer hard-drive backup, storage limitations that precluded adding materials to a college's web page, and networked drives were too slow for utilizing research content, while an overall lack of archiving assistance for scholarly works was also noted to be problematic.

- *Preferences*. These were focused overall on qualitative services to handle digital matter to enhance scholarship and teaching.
  - *Digitization*. Faculty interviewees articulated a need for digitizing their scholarship, such as research and assorted raw materials in a variety of formats – photos, slides, film/tape, and paper – for deposit in an IR. They envisioned physical objects being electronically findable in a repository.
  - *Data processing*. Format conversion to update file formats for use with current modalities would enable more items to be posted in an IR.
  - *Storage*. Large datasets, audio/video, 3D models, department records, and course material storage solutions were considered to be part of the infrastructure important to faculty.
  - *Copyright*. Interviewees believed that the process of retaining and negotiating rights would be valuable to enable them to showcase their work.
  - *Web 2.0 and collaboration features*. Social media interaction with the faculty's content by tagging, commenting, and editing using collaborative tools were seen as worthwhile.

The Dartmouth Humanities' Faculty Study is significant because it elucidates the faculty's requirements for integrating their unique scholarship in an IR. Communicating their work in this inclusive discipline may encompass a variety of material types, such as photos, slides, and 3D models. Marketing an IR to humanities scholars could resemble the basic formula of promotion to other disciplines whose common goals also include advancing their scholarship and teaching. Promoting an IR that incorporates a suite of library services targeting all disciplines across every nuance has the potential to increase faculty interest and deposit rate.

A quantitative Association of Research Libraries (ARL) study by Jantz & Wilson (2008) was conducted on selected subjects; pre and postprints and scholarly-related reports were set up to determine IR participation by disciplinary faculty. The authors' study, conducted in August/September 2006, could not locate an institutional repository for 50 of the ARL institutions. The remaining 49 IR websites were visited to review twelve disciplines with over 5,000 deposited items. Jantz & Wilson (2008: 192) found the following numbers of disciplinary repository objects (from the highest to the lowest quantities):

| | |
|---|---|
| Mathematics | 1,414 |
| Economics | 1,090 |
| BioScience | 1,081 |
| Engineering | 660 |
| Computer Science | 281 |
| Philosophy | 166 |
| Anthropology | 118 |
| Sociology | 104 |
| Political Science | 58 |
| English | 44 |
| History | 33 |
| Linguistics | 31 |

Over five years later, these IR subject demographics show an evolution from the ARL survey to current and prevalent disciplines. The Mukherjee & Nazim (2011: 321) study employing ROAR and *Open*DOAR "IR subject coverage" (see Table 4.1 not including the "multidisciplinary" subject heading) placed mathematics in the top six in terms of *the number of repository records*, with physical sciences, biology, and computer sciences ranked above and economics below. Philosophy also placed well in the Jantz & Wilson survey. History and archaeology/anthropology were listed after mathematics and statistics. Language and literature in both surveys scored low. Overall, the social sciences in both studies were in the bottom half of IR deposits.

## *arXiv: physics/astrophysics, mathematics, computer science, quantitative fields*

As Cornell University's arXiv reached its twentieth year of actively archiving research, accolades for its sustainable stance abound. ArXiv's creator, Paul Ginsparg, a professor of physics and information science, reflected on why he created the website to serve a variety of disciplines such as physics/astrophysics, mathematics, and computer science, that expanded to include quantitative biology and quantitative finance and statistics. Developing countries now have access to preprint and postprint papers. His initial rationale for creating arXiv was the concern that graduate students were further downstream from the supply chain of research materials. Ginsparg set up a scholarly system to eliminate the information hierarchy access in his field by creating arXiv (Steele, 2011).

Physicists Andre Geim and Konstantin Novoselov, regular contributors to arXiv, deposited their research on "graphene," a one atom-thick mesh of two-dimensional material, the strongest and thinnest substance known in the universe, that can be stretched like rubber and cannot be impregnated by liquid or gas. In 2010, these two scientists were awarded the Nobel Prize in Physics for their work on "graphene."

In the same year, arXiv experienced 65 million full-text article downloads, and as of October 2013, the database accrued in excess of 882,246 papers, with thousands of new papers added per month. Submissions are restricted to researchers with "scientific credentials" (Steele, 2011).

Recognized as a public good and also critical to scientists, it was awarded a Simons Foundation grant (2013–17) upwards to $300,000 per year based on matching funds generated by arXiv's membership fees. Cornell's Library is also the beneficiary of the same grant funds in recognition of their stewardship, an annual and unconditional gift of $50,000.

## SCOAP³: open access high-energy physics publishing

The Sponsoring Consortium for Open Access Publishing in Particle Physics (SCOAP³) (*http://scoap3.org/about.html*) is an innovative and cost-saving publishing model developed by high-energy physics (HEP) scientists, enabling them to produce their scholarship in an open publishing medium. Each SCOAP³ partner "will finance its contribution by cancelling journal subscriptions." As of 2010, the cost of OA as quoted from multiple publishers ranged from 1,000–2,000 euros per each published article. This translates to US $1,360–2,720 (conversion as of October 14, 2013). Monetary contributions are determined by a country's share of HEP publishing, of which there are six peer-reviewed journals from four publishers. This model is open to a burgeoning journal excellence of the future that fosters a commitment to a dynamic demand and vigorous competition.

Throughout the years 1991–2008, 90–100 percent of HEP pre and postprints have been deposited in arXiv. SCOAP[3]'s mission as the single financial funder is to engender unrestricted access to all HEP research in its final peer-reviewed format and "to contain the overall cost of journal publishing by increasing competition while assuring sustainability" (Vigen, 2009: 37). This is a global endeavor of high-energy physics funding organizations, research laboratories, libraries, and their consortia. Innovative OA publishing models exhibit a number of optimistic economic characteristics:

- Each SCOAP[3] partner will recoup its financial contribution by cancelling its journal subscriptions.

- Authors are not directly charged to publish an article; APCs are paid centrally from a mutually contributed common fund from libraries, consortia, research institutions, and funding agencies (*http://scoap3.org/news/news95.html*).

- Each country or consortia will contribute funds based on the number of its scientific publications (Vigen, 2009).

## Engineering

A 2008 study of five institutions with a high rate of IR submissions (University of Michigan, Ohio State University, Massachusetts Institute of Technology, Georgia Tech, University of Nebraska-Lincoln) commenced measuring engineering academics and their predisposition to engage in open access using their *five* most recent papers. These top-ranking IRs were located in the Registry of Open Access Repositories (ROAR) employing the Deposit Activity (*http://roar.eprints.org/*). The specific engineering fields common to all five universities were chemical, civil, and environmental engineering.

Baldwin (2010), the study's author, located faculty from university websites and subsequently used the *Web of Science* research database (Thomson-Reuters) to locate a faculty's five most current citations. To qualify for the study, an article had to be archived in an IR or subject repository, on a personal or author/co-author university website, or on an affiliated research group site. Open access journals or government websites that also tracked articles were used to discover the scholarship.

Author results show the percentage of chemical, civil, and mechanical engineering academics that archived at least one OA article. Chemical engineering papers from the five institutions ranged from 50 percent to over 90 percent with a minimum of one OA article per faculty archived in an IR. The deposit rate of civil engineering manuscripts varied from 34 per cent to 83 per cent, while the results for mechanical engineering articles were fewer at 38 percent to 67 percent archiving activity. Overall, this is a high proportion of engineering faculty who chose to embrace the open access publishing model for their work, especially with MIT as the only institution in the study with a deposit mandate.

The Institution of Engineering and Technology (IET) is one of the foremost global professional societies in the engineering and technology research community. In July 2011, IET signed an agreement with the International Network for the Availability of Scientific Publications (INASP) to afford specific regions in Africa, Asia, and Latin America access to IET journals, magazines, conference publications, and seminar digests (*bit.ly/13tf6iV*). These scientific materials were offered at no charge or at a considerably reduced cost. The vital research efforts in the Global South necessitate a supportive scientific community willing to build capacity, innovation, and networking, and to strengthen its focus on the scholarly needs of developing and emerging countries (LibLicense listserv communication, August 22, 2011).

## Agriculture

The efficient and healthful feeding of the global population is a public good that impacts everyone at a nutritional level to avoid starvation and famine. India's National Agricultural Research System (NARS) has established one of the world's largest publicly funded research networks with immense scholarly output from 97 Indian Council of Agricultural Research (ICAR) institutes and 58 agricultural universities, employing 26,178 full-time research staff. The barriers to access this goldmine of scholarship result from non-digitized grey literature, such as newsletters, research highlights, achievements, technical bulletins, annual reports, and research journals. Even when available online, materials may not be searchable (Gutam, 2011).

During the years 2004–8, Thomson-Reuters indexed an estimated 8 percent of the 126,000 agricultural, plant and animal sciences articles published in India. Consequently, the majority of the journals are in print only and in addition, websites may be inoperable or subscription paywalls may prevent entry to the scholarship produced in India and other countries. This lack of research dissemination precludes other scientists from accessing the intellectual content. In NARS, there are approximately 118 scientific/scholarly journals, of which only seven are OA and registered in the DOAJ (Gutam, Mishra, Pandey, Chandrasekharan, & Aneej, 2010).

Creating IRs for this vast cache of agricultural research is beneficial in multiple ways. As of September 1, 2013, there are 59 research repositories in India and the Open Journal Systems (open source) software is increasingly being employed for India's OA scholarly journals. Asian Journals Online (AsiaJOL) (*http://asiajol.info/index.php/about*) is a harvester that collects metadata and full-text information, searchable from the AsiaJOL database of journals published in Bangladesh, Nepal, the Philippines, Vietnam, Sri Lanka, and Indonesia.

By staying apprised of disciplinary research preferences and patterns, library liaisons and IR managers can be well informed and able to promote these resources to their faculty for potential OA scholarship that mirrors their needs.

## Academic library scholarship and the institutional repository

S.R. Ranganathan (1892–1972), an inventor, educator, librarian, philosopher, and mathematician (Elder, 2004), authored a book in 1963 on librarianship ideology that has remained a classic for understanding how libraries and librarians might optimally focus on a reader's advantage for an information need. His objectives and standards centered on the importance of organizing library materials and the impetus of access to enable use. Librarians still turn to the laws he set out for various situations, including the significance of easily discovering research resources that IRs provide so efficiently.

As librarians find themselves in a digital information environment, there is a benefit in extrapolating to current times from what Ranganathan might have philosophically considered in his five pragmatic laws:

1. Books are for use

2. Every reader his/her book

3. Every book, its reader

4. Save the time of the reader

5. A library is a growing organism.

These laws embody standards of practice and are the foundation of how librarians and researchers currently operate in a digital environment. It is a thought-provoking exercise to apply the five laws to contemporary library research activities.

The first two laws refer to the specific use of content. In Ranganathan's early years of librarianship, open stacks were not standard. The third law is situational whereby the vocation of librarians is to connect the library's resources to people who need and want them. The ability to browse and link to scholarly assets, engage with a useful library catalog, be exposed to related topics, and market intellectual materials is essential to satisfy a reader's research needs. A library's increased access to authoritative searchable and open resources enables readers to connect with scholarship. Cloonan & Dove (2005) explicate the current library culture and research options that relate to the third law, stating that the Google search engine helps satisfy the fourth law by "saving the time of the reader." The fifth law correlates with the other four laws by librarians ensuring that libraries continue the expansion of services and research resources to our information consumers.

Building campus relationships typically requires discussion both within the library and externally to dispel myths by demonstrating the advantages of a tool, such as an IR. Considering the years it may take for an author's article to reach its copyright limitations compared to the current option of sustainable scholarly communication options, it may be of interest to revisit and explore Ranganathan's laws in relation to open access to research and social media tools.

1. *Books are for use.* Books are essential to library users. There is an expanding trend in university presses and other publishers to provide a free or low-cost PDF and/or an HTML book or monograph version to download or save on an electronic device. A traditional hard copy option may be still available to purchase. Books and monographs deposited in repositories may offer a download or purchase copy.

2. *Every reader his/her book.* This is the "fundamental issue of tension between the cost of materials and the basic right of all persons to have access to the materials" (Elder, 2004). Readers do not pay a fee to obtain research in an IR. Patchwork and institutional mandates provide tremendous support for garnering scholarly articles to be globally available and read.

3. *Every book, its reader.* This is a basic tenet of open access research to be able to search, find, and read intellectual content. In engaging with

institutional repositories, researchers have the option to search or browse by collections.

4. *Save the time of the reader.* Ensure that librarians continue to lobby for increased open access in existing and new research venues, such as federally funded scholarly output generated by the US (*http://www.grants.gov/aboutgrants/agencies_that_provide_grants.jsp*) and other countries' funding mechanisms. Marketing content resources that are openly available is essential for findability, as well as – and peripherally – to also provide awareness of open research assets in a variety of formats. Web scale discovery services have vastly improved search capacity to encompass an academic library's IR and CONTENTdm™ materials in the array of possibilities.

5. *A library is a growing organism.* Libraries have enduring qualities and are continually subject to change. Budgets, collections, and technology evolve over time. The OAI protocol for meta-harvesting has facilitated research discovery in IRs. Repository scholarship is authoritative; data is "organized for self-directed and learner empowered inquiries" so that "the best qualities of well-arranged collections contribute to the search" (Cloonan & Dove, 2005).

# Summary

Regardless of disciplinary research habits, open access mandates play a significant role in capturing faculty postprints and journal articles, rapidly filling an IR with valued research. Opening the literature "to maximize research uptake, usage, and impact by making research journal articles accessible to all their potential users instead of just to those users whose institutions can afford subscriptions" (Harnad, 2010) promises that some day all scholarly works will be open access. New generations will experience a "right of use" and the rest will be history.

# 5

# Building internal and external campus institutional repository relationships

**Abstract.** Journal article access continues to be a simmering hot topic for authors, publishers, and readers in the twenty-first century. Research content is prolific; scientists and scholars, students, and the public have a need for access to satisfy their information and scholarly needs. The tension between green access and the gold article processing charge publishing models is omnipresent, and while publishers focus on profit, researchers and libraries strive for research access. Academic libraries continue to center on repository services, exercising record authority control, and garnering and archiving scholarly assets. By also collaborating with university presses, librarians can offer open access to additional erudite and special collections material.

**Keywords:** advisory committee, article processing charges, authority control, collection policies, e-theses/dissertations, gold access, green access, predatory practices, publishing models, repository staff, university presses

## Open access article publishing models (gold, green, gratis, libre)

Multiple open research options for the scientists and scholars who engage in toll-free access to scholarship embrace personal preferences that may include both the gold and green access models and their subsets. There are advantages to each type of publishing and each model complements the other.

The born-digital open access (OA) journal article (sans APCs) is considered the "pure" gold model. Its gold standard roots are embedded in the philosophy of open access to research, as in the Directory of Open Access Journals (DOAJ) content. Open access journal editors may be funded by academy monies, their departments, societies, and grants to create and maintain their publications. The gold OA article funder business model has variations on a theme of who pays the article processing charges (APCs). Funding of an APC gold article emanates from the author, the academic institution, the library, or grant funds. Article processing charges can typically be assigned from: an author's grant funding, especially if the funder requires an open access article; an academy's research funds; or authorized library reserves of partial or complete payment with a monetary cap, depending on the APC. As a funder example, the National Science Foundation (NSF) "builds" the APC into the grant-funding process. The larger question of payment depends on if and when capital is initiated or available on a first-come first-served basis until resources are depleted (see Table 4.2 in Chapter 4).

Multiple open access options to research by scientists and scholars who engage in toll-free access to scholarship provide personal or institutional (mandated) preferences that may include both the gold and green access models. There are advantages to each type of publishing; each model complements the other. Gold open access (OA) is conveyed by journals. Benefits of born-digital journal gold access over green include an absence of reader permission barriers and a lack of embargoes. The gold journal article model that requires an APC payment may be garnered from a variety of academic or other funding sources. Gold access to published research is immediate. These journals are self-sustaining and can be profitable, especially if the journal's business model is based on APCs. Their independent distribution mechanism is partially based on funded research grants that require an open access output venue. Researchers committed to the OA model value of disseminating their scholarship will pay for APCs from their available resources to ensure openness. Hybrid journals maintain both article types with a paywall and articles funded by APCs. Scientists and scholars who hesitate to publish with an open access journal due to a low or no impact factor might reconsider. Novice journals with a list of seasoned reviewers are worth investing in by submitting and publishing an article to build impact-worthy open access journals.

Journal policies and repositories convey green open access to postprints. The advantages of this model cover mandates without infringing upon academic freedom as stated by the American Association of University Professors: "the common good and not to further the interest of either the individual teacher or the institution as a whole" (*http://www.aaup. org/issues/academic-freedom*). Green access virtues over the gold access model include: university mandate policies cover the entire academy's open access scholarly article output, compatibility with toll access publication allows authors to retain their pre and postprint archiving rights and a time stamp registration establishing an author's completed research. Datasets, postprints, e-theses and e-dissertations, and other research item-types benefit from the green access model.

Green and gold access delivery relates respectively to venues or vehicles. Subsets of the gold and green OA models are referred to as gratis and libre. Gratis removes price barriers. Libre also removes price barriers and some permission obstructions. Every type of OA removes price barriers (Suber, 2012).

Open access journal article concerns reside with traditional journal subscriptions where approximately 80 percent of journals, including nearly all of the top-ranking journals, are tying up potential funds to pay for publishing gold open access articles. There is some apprehension that "paying to publish may inflate acceptance rates and lower quality standards" (Harnad, 2010: 1).

In Figure 5.1, Springer Publishing's gold open access growth curve S (20 percent per year) and Björk's simulated growth curve B (30 percent per year) (Laakso, Welling, Bulvovas Nyman, Björk, & Hedlund, 2011) were equalized for 2009. Note that the Björk curve would reach 100 percent gold OA for all journals (ISI + non-ISI) in 2022 at a time when the Springer curve would not yet have reached 40 percent for ISI journals. More importantly, either way, the Björk curve would reach 60 percent in 2019 and the Springer curve would reach 60 percent in 2025; the four sampled mandated repositories had already reached over 60 percent growth in 2004–6, within two years of having adopted their mandates.

A possible explanation for a greater open access growth rate among the non-ISI journals is perhaps the majority of gold OA today is not fee-based but comes from either born-digital open access journals or subsidized journals (APCs) simply by making their online version free to use. This form of gold open access predominates among the 15,000 non-ISI journals, but among the 10,000 ISI journals where there are much fewer gold OA journals, article processing fees are considerably more likely, especially for the "core" journals that institutions' readers find most desirable and need.

One of the green and sustainable open access deposit models provides for scientists and scholars to immediately archive their preprint or final, peer-reviewed postprint in a repository. (Check publisher websites for up-to-date publishing guidelines or the SHERPA/RoMEO tool that tracks green publisher policies (*http://www.sherpa.ac.uk/romeo/*).) The other, far more effective and challenging option is for institutions and grant funders to mandate green OA (Harnad, 2010). Once green open

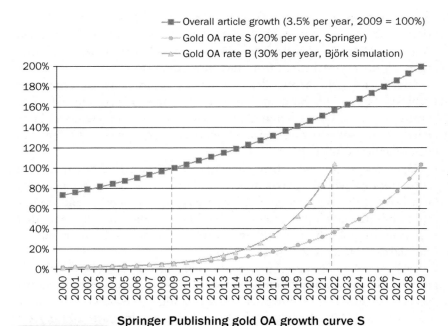

**Figure 5.1** Springer Publishing gold OA growth curve S (20% per year) and simulated Björk growth curve B (30% per year) equated for 2009 (Laakso et al., 2011)

*Source*: Poynder (2011a). This work is licensed under a Creative Commons Attribution-Noncommercial-No Derivative Works 2.0 UK: England & Wales License.

access reaches a critical mass and becomes more universal, print and electronic subscriptions become less sustainable and unnecessary; funds can be diverted to a less costly gold publishing model. Listed below are examples of gold open access "article processing charge model" publishers:

- BioMed Central is a science, technology, and medicine (STM) for-profit publisher of 243 peer-reviewed open access online journals. All content is published with a Creative Commons Attribution License CC BY to share, adapt, and use commercially. Standard article processing charges may be found at: *http://www.biomedcentral.com/about/apcfaq/howmuch*.

- The Public Library of Science (PLoS) (*http://www.plos.org/*) is a non-profit publisher of seven peer-reviewed open access journals whose mission is to lead a transformation in OA research communication. Their business model recovers expenses in part by charging APCs to authors or research sponsors for each article published. Complete or partial fee waivers are available. All content is published with a Creative Commons Attribution License CC BY to share, adapt, and use commercially.

- African Journals Online (AJOL) is the world's largest amassed peer-reviewed research "in support of quality African research and higher education." As of September 2013, AJOL has expanded to host over 462 African-published and peer-reviewed journals from 30 countries. The AJOL website is visited each month by an average of 150,000 researchers from all over the world: (*http://www.ajol.info/index.php/index/browse/alpha?letter=oa*). Subscription-based journal download charges are determined by the country location a reader is ordering from specified by the World Bank (*http://www.ajol.info/index.php/ajol/pages/view/FAQ#A3*).

- The Hindawi Publishing Corporation, based in Cairo, Egypt primarily focuses on science, technology, engineering, and mathematics (STEM), publishing 562 OA journals. Hindawi offers institutional memberships comprised of an annual or prepaid fee. The article processing charge model cost ranges from free to $2,395 as of September, 2013 (*http://www.hindawi.com/apc/*).

## Predatory journals

In the case of predatory journal articles that follow the APC model, faculty and graduate students need to take heed of predatory publishers resembling legitimate online publishing venues that take advantage of inexperienced and seasoned authors. By soliciting manuscripts offered by closely imitated journals resembling authentic online publishers, the predatory publisher misleads the author by not mentioning the requisite APC until after the paper is accepted. According to Beall, the typical billed fee is US $1,800. Authors who submit a manuscript and pay the APC expect to retain their copyright, not so with predatory journals.

Jeffrey Beall, a University of Colorado, Denver Librarian, has taken on the burden of tracking questionable open access journals that may have unethical scholarly communication practices (*http://scholarlyoa.com/about*). He has a growing and extensive list of potential, possible, or probable predatory open access publishers (*http://scholarlyoa.com/publishers/*) and also maintains a list of individual potential or probable scholarly open access predatory journals (*scholarlyoa.com/individual-journals/*).

# Engaging campus faculty to create gold open access journals

Academic libraries are currently in a prime position to support faculty who are financially struggling with journals they produce in-house. The recent downturn in the economy has filtered through to academy colleges and departments; subscription-based or print-copy journals may not be sustained without additional support. Faculty journal editors, once resourced with graduate students, office staff, and financial support, may lose these resources. Editors who produced and maintained a journal are now unsure of their publication's future. Moving from a subscription or paper-based model and creating a born-digital in-house gold journal by garnering library support can be a viable option for editors. Digital Commons® and Open Journal Systems offer viable software options.

# Collaborative library open access publishing strategies

## Open access journal publishing

Marketing open access scholarly add-on tools, such as the Open Journal Systems (*http://pkp.sfu.ca/ojs-journals*) or Digital Commons® software (*http://digitalcommons.bepress.com/online-journals/*) and a library's scholarly communication staff who support OA journals extend an effective collaboration to create new journals and revive those in decline or needing infrastructure support.

Academic library resources are finite, but can be robust, dependent on allocation. The IR manager or the scholarly communication librarian tend to have an interest in partnering with faculty who have a passion to create a new open access journal or transform or revive existing publications. Niche gaps in a specific subject area not covered in prevailing journals can utilize the OA advantage of visibility and impact, and satisfy the desire or need to create a no-fee journal are common factors that may inspire faculty to generate their own open access journal. One of the multiple benefits for scientists and scholars who embrace gold OA as a publishing model, authors automatically retain their article copyright and there are no article processing fees.

The library/faculty collaboration to build and maintain an OA journal is most successful with detailed guidelines stating who will be in charge of what aspects of the publication. Journal software determines what features are possible, appropriate, or are already embedded for use. Specified journal duties will logically fall to editors, IR managers or staff, while other responsibilities could be accomplished by creating (Buehler, 2010):

- a template for author manuscript submissions;
- documentation delineating the preprint (paper prior to peer-review) submission process;
- a digitization and OCR (optical character recognition) workflow of any scanned printed/graphical materials;
- an author's referral list of skilled graphic designers, copyeditors, etc.;
- a citation management plan;
- metadata;
- guidelines to intellectual property rights;
- an author copyright agreement or using a Creative Commons License; and
- a LOCKSS ("lots of copies keep stuff safe") account for archival purposes (*http://www.lockss.org/lockss/Home*).

External to the essentials of the journal content, further details are necessary that will increase journal visibility:

- software knowledge;
- an international referee board;
- an ISSN registration;
- marketing – displays, websites, listservs, call for papers;
- subject and citation indexing for information retrieval and to increase findability;
- print-on-demand *and/or* traditional publishing options.

Additional suggestions to achieve visibility and credibility for a journal originate from the Education & Behavioral Science ALA Discussion List (Mullen, 2011; Buehler, 2010):

- ensure the journal publishing system is crawled by Google and Google Scholar (such as OJS and Digital Commons®);
- maintain a scholarly web presence;
- once the first journal issue is published:

- add the journal to the library's online public access catalog (OPAC);
- announce the journal to listservs – providing an opportunity to be picked up by international blogs and newsletters;
- include in WorldCat;
- email the DOAJ administrator to be included in the journal database – check the new submission guidelines (9,919 journals as of October 2013);
- email Open J-Gate (14,950 journals as of October 2013);
- periodically review Ulrich's Serials Solutions to ascertain journal inclusion (in-depth information about journals);
- check journal information to ensure that the publication schedule lists as "regular" peer-reviewed and open access; they accept corrections;
- submit journal information to subject indexing services or electronic journal aggregators such as EBSCO or Thomson Reuters as a hallmark of excellence; publishers should be sending regular checks representing subscription journal article database download counts;
- follow the Scholarly Publishing and Academic Resources Coalition (SPARC) guide to indexing your journal (*http://www.arl.org/sparc/publications/papers/journal_indexing.shtml*).

Over time and with a journal track record, publication editors may invite a journal to be indexed. A publisher's indexing guidelines should be known and followed for the required time period to enhance the opportunity for journal inclusion.

SPARC has created an OA Journal Publishing Resource Index encompassing essential aspects of the journal creation process by providing business planning documents, governance and editorial issues, marketing, hosting and platform options, sustainable publishing models, and a resource guide (*http://www.arl.org/sparc/partnering/planning/index.shtml*).

Also listed in the SPARC resources are open access journal guidelines originating from the Open Society Institute (OSI). They have published three pragmatic business guides for developers and publishers of OA journals; authorship is by the SPARC Consulting Group (*http://www.soros.org/openaccess/resources/open-access-journal-business-guides*):

- *Guide to Business Planning for Launching a New Open Access Journal*;
- *Model Business Plan: A Supplemental Guide for Open Access Journal Developers & Publishers*;
- *Guide to Business Planning for Converting a Subscription-based Journal to Open Access.*

With editorial expertise shared among library staff and faculty, a carefully crafted OA journal has the potential to attract higher impact, new authors, and fresh campus relationships. It can be a worthwhile publishing journey to "spin a new journal into the gold publishing model" (Buehler, 2010).

## Open access journal publishing collaborations

Undertaking a major publishing project or a series of open access journals by collaborating with colleagues for a common goal can be efficient, more productive, and sustainable. By drawing on a variety of faculty and librarian expertise, a credible team can be formed that provides high value for the editors and the reader. In addition to ongoing operational activities, policies and possible funding will need consideration.

To assuage any seemingly daunting misgivings about supporting the creation of OA journals, an article titled "Establishing and publishing an online peer-reviewed journal: action plan, resourcing, and costs" by Lorna Shapiro, is a worthy step-by-step approach that takes a novice through the necessary procedures to success using Open Journal Systems (OJS). Bepress (formerly Berkeley Electronic Press) clients can deftly extrapolate the processes described in Shapiro's article to the Digital Commons® journal publishing platform. Editor publishing steps are described in an easy-to-understand format. Roles associated with the responsibility of publishing the journal, accompanying skill sets, and the estimated time to achieve the goals are clearly stated. The outline of the nine weekly guidelines describes the necessary tasks for the journal set-up to be prepared to accept articles (Shapiro, 2005).

A journal's administrative and design decisions are the backbone of an online publishing style, subscription philosophy, and revenue-garnering (advertising) based upon editor, author, and readership needs.

- *Online publishing style.* Online publishing offers the flexibility to publish one article at a time; additional articles are added as proof-ready building up to an issue. The most prevalent journal model publishes articles simultaneously in their entirety. The latter model offers a thematic approach to issues "which can improve readership" (Shapiro, 2005: 10).

- *Subscription philosophy.* Open access to journal article content is the optimum model for reader accessibility and to engender greater citation impact for the author(s). Other options may include paid subscriber or free access to back issues only; paying subscribers can only retrieve the current issue.

- *Revenue-garnering advertising.* Selling advertising space may be considered at the journal start-up time or at a later date. Advertiser contract fees are economically feasible to offset publishing costs.

According to the final draft of the "Library publishing services: strategies for success research report version 1.0" survey, the most prevalent journal publishing platforms disclosed were Open Journal Systems (OJS) (57 percent), DSpace (36 percent), and bepress's Digital Commons® (25 percent) (Mullins et al., 2011). An academic library may decide to select an online journal platform based on its resource management allocation, its technical capacity, the institution's size or needs, and the choice of repository software.

## University press and library-integrated open access publishing strategies: a survey of open access journal strategies

Advancing at a steady rate, academic libraries are motivated in a variety of ways to engage in open access publishing business models. Open access journals are currently supported on a larger scale than previously as complementary software to institutional repositories (IRs). To determine US publishing trends, Purdue University, Georgia Institute of Technology, and the University of Utah Libraries conducted a survey in October–November 2010, designed to employ a longitudinal comparison with a 2008 Association of Research Libraries (ARL) survey of their members on the topic of library publishing models and services. Each university focused on an aspect of publishing: open access journals, conference proceedings, and monographs, respectively.

Where applicable, a natural synergy was found to exist between a press's campus mission and the libraries, leading to more integrated alliances. Some partnerships assimilated the university press and the library into one unit. The November 2011 draft version was published by SPARC for comment. The Association of Research Libraries, the Oberlin Group, and the University Libraries Group directors participated in the survey (Mullins et al., 2011).

Key findings directed at open access journals showed 75 percent of the respondents had published one to six journals which were primarily electronic and had been published for less than three years. Fifty percent published conference proceedings, technical reports, and monographs, predominantly online with some print-on-demand services. Library support services included copyright consultation, digitization services, and peer-review management. Of the responding libraries, 32 published 211 journals; the majority, 158, were open access. Less than 50 percent charged subscription fees, and fewer had faculty or department charge-backs or collected article processing charges.

The three libraries testified that some journals were formally indexed by an abstracting and indexing service. The services of EBSCO Publishing were the most often employed, followed by ProQuest, PubMed, H.W. Wilson, and Scopus. Other references to the abstracting and indexing services were: OCLC, the DOAJ, Philosopher's Index, Project Muse, Westlaw, OAIster, Google Scholar, and GeoRef.

# University press publishing in the twenty-first century

Historically there are reasons why university presses are currently motivated to become more relevant, efficient, and viable. Once a necessary means of disseminating research, the university press was considered one of the university's key missions and, subsequently endowed with subsidies, was never expected to be lucrative. Current financial concerns related to institutional budgets and inflationary journal expenses have led to new expectations for the press in terms of publishing partnerships and OA frontiers. Lynch (2010: para. 34) forewarned that "any successful transition will clearly require active support – not only funding but also intellectual and political capital – from top-level academic leaders who have today become increasingly estranged from their university presses on too many campuses."

As of 2007, there are 88 US presses dating from 1860, a figure that reached a plateau in the mid-1970s to the present, and saw a mere eight new presses established in that period. The 2007 statistics represent a third of US research universities with presses and 189 research universities without presses (Clement, 2011). Many existing presses have proactively altered or are changing their publishing strategies to less expensive paperback editions, or are considering a smaller profit margin while simultaneously offering e-books and a print-on-demand model.

Currently, high-quality scholarly monographs are the primary product published by university presses, although to remain relevant and take advantage of new opportunities, journals and other publication types have been added to the repertoire of some presses.

## Cornell University Libraries and Duke University Press open access journal publishing partnership

Cornell Libraries' Project Euclid (*http://projecteuclid.org/DPubS?Service= UI&version=1.0&verb=Display&handle=euclid*) initially launched in 2000, and again in 2008, with Duke University Press as a collaborator and jointly managed partner. Their underlying purpose was to "address the unique needs of low-cost independent and society journals." Published subject areas were comprised of theoretical and applied mathematics and statistics. The dissemination model's framework encompassed a subscription model, a direct order from publishers, and open access. As of summer 2011, 64 journals were disseminated online with over 70 percent of the content open access.

The Cornell Libraries' publishing professionals remain committed to the backend infrastructure of ongoing technical maintenance, application development and support that is fulfilled by engaging their digital preservation knowledge. Duke University staff have experience in customer service applications that include order fulfillment, operations, journal recruitment and the incumbent sales/marketing and financial management proficiency (Walker, 2011).

## Purdue University Press and Libraries open access journal publishing

Purdue's e-pubs journal publishing program (*http://docs.lib.purdue.edu*) services and resources align well with the collaboration between the Libraries and the Press. Together they aspire to respond to the demand for new publishing venues, primarily in interdisciplinary fields. Mullins et al. (2011) revealed in their study that each partner had diverged into their respective value propositions, with the libraries focusing on the social value of open access and the press more closely aligned with Purdue's research, teaching, and outreach emphasis.

In addition to providing publishing services for university entities, the press aspires to offer open access dissemination as an alternative to relevant society commercial journals in agreement with Purdue's land grant mission, within subject areas such as technology or agriculture. As of September 2013, there are eight OA journals associated with academic departments, schools, or students; one is from the libraries and another is a legacy journal. The overall value of the press and libraries working together has resulted in:

- a central location for meeting potential authors that is integral to the libraries;
- sharing a business office;
- original charge-back services now covered by the libraries' services;
- transparent finances;
- migrating from print-only to all published products available online;
- moving from subscription-based journals to primarily open access journals;
- less than 20 percent of Purdue-authored works to more than 40 percent Purdue authors;
- a greater alignment in publishing within the university's signature areas;
- more regular meetings with stakeholders and an advisory board that includes senior university administrators and outside leaders in publishing (Mullins et al., 2011).

The Purdue Press and libraries identified value from the standpoint of the end customer by: optimizing the Press's location; increasing profits and lowering expenses; shifting from print to electronic access; and adjusting the focus to the university's recognized unique research areas. They eliminated the limitations of their operation that did not create value for their authors. The value-added steps were efficient so the end product flowed smoothly toward the customer accessing the desired online journal article. Extrapolating from the Lean Enterprise Institute's philosophy to the Purdue Press and libraries' collaboration, the authors pulled value from: each of the improved changes and processes; the end product of access to essential expert resources; and publishing and accessing online journal articles (Lean Enterprise Institute, 2009).

## Integrated university presses and library monographs

University presses have struggled financially largely due to the costs of scientific journal literature distributed by large publishers having increased their share of university library budgets. Subsequent shifting of purchasing funds has reduced monograph expenditures. The 2008 economic turndown exacerbated an already declining monograph market share. Willinsky's (2009) argument for maintaining a university press was to save the monograph as a "means to work out an argument in full, to marshal all the relevant evidence, to provide a complete account of consequences and implications, as well as counter-arguments and criticisms" (para. 4). His plea focused on maintaining the availability of the monograph and creating an open monograph press system (*http:// pkp.sfu.ca/omp*) to support publishing peer-reviewed scholarly publications.

## University of Utah monographs

University presses and libraries also partner to sustain the monograph. The University of Utah Press has become more closely aligned with the Libraries' strategy and enterprise through a joint investigation of publishing services of interest to the Utah community. Typically, academic library special collections are rich sources of rare and fascinating content begging to be showcased, used, and appreciated.

The Press and Libraries jointly considered publishing with service possibilities that encompassed: IR hosting of content complementary to the Press's scholarly monographs; supplementary Utah faculty research and publication content; and mining the libraries' Special Collections for press publication possibilities and utilizing open access to digital research materials or print-on-demand formats (Mullins et al., 2011). As a current trend to sustain press publishing, academic partnerships are expanding to integrate librarian skills, showcase compelling content, and think creatively about the collaborative possibilities.

The Mullins et al. (2011) report also found that approximately 65 percent of the libraries' publishing programs are in partnership with other campus units that may include academic faculty, the university press, and campus computing. The same percentage currently cooperates with off-campus individuals and organizations; there is a 50 percent expectation of expanded collaborations in the next year. Staff members who engage in publishing activities are often dedicated to a variety of tasks, averaging a 2.4 full-time equivalent (FTE) for ARLs and a 0.9 FTE for Oberlin Group institutions.

## Cornell University Library and Press collaboration

Cornell University Library's 2011–15 Strategic Plan, Goal 3, supports the full cycle of research and scholarly exchange by providing services to that end. Possessing multiple strategic advantages, the library has relationships with local scholars and a focus on scholarly communications in an e-publishing context.

Established in 1889, the Cornell University Press (*http://www. cornellpress.cornell.edu/aboutus/*) has a distinguished reputation. It employs traditional editorial and peer-review, carries out its own book design and production processes, and undertakes its own marketing. There is some opportunity for reading complete books online. Local scholars are deeply involved in the publishing which includes a division of effort among the library, press, and faculty. Library professionals proffer "high-level consultation services" and pay "particular attention to domains with limited dissemination options" (Walker, 2011).

The University Press and academic library staff collaboratively provide a quintessential example of academic libraries' commitment to model their services around a "goal of professionalizing their operations by introducing best practices in areas beyond their current expertise" (Mullins et al., 2011: 50).

# Institutional repository staff

Typically, the majority of institutional repository staff is comprised of library employees, such as: an IR manager/administrator or coordinator; technical services personnel; support staff; and students. To serve as many needs as possible, efficient employees are simultaneously: processing various materials for deposit; completing item deposits; creating community hierarchies, journal shells, and events; and assigning metadata. Additional library personnel may be engaged in special projects, broadening the academic library role to a wider range of staff that have integral skill sets and a committed enthusiasm to engage in new proficiencies and concepts to support the repository. Considering the variety of expertise and periodic academic library reorganizations, there are opportunities to expand the IR knowledge base infrastructure to form a larger repository team foundation that encompasses core routine work and special projects.

A variety of institutional repository efforts may be focused on a daily, weekly, monthly, or an as-needed basis. Every academic library's repository has various staffing nuances that offer possibilities for the organization to allocate resources. Employees on a broader scale may learn about repository opportunities and effectively contribute. An IR team typically consists of a trained workforce from technical services, systems, the liaison program, scholarly communication and copyright experts, visiting postdoctoral scholars, interns, and students. Regardless of whether an IR is hosted or not, a diversity of skill sets is necessary for success.

In the early stages of repository development, academic libraries invited liaisons to participate in the novel scholarly communication milieu. Interested and curious liaisons proffered their professional interests and experiences based on interactions with their colleges' faculty. Collection development librarians extended their knowledge by negotiating with publishers for added contractual rights to archive research database articles in institutional repositories.

## Institutional repository case study

The University of Illinois at Urbana-Champaign's (UIUC) one-year case study (Palmer, Teffeau, & Newton, 2008) explored IR triumphs and core challenges encompassing three research libraries with differing approaches to developing their repositories. In some of the libraries, intellectual property librarian positions were created to support the necessary copyright clearances and, in addition, to share the expertise in campus scholarly communication endeavors. Liaisons were part of the IR development teams.

Many of the UIUC liaisons expressed an interest in participating in policy and strategy decisions by taking part in taskforces and advisory boards charged to actualize preservation, collection development, and submission guidelines. They were also influential in analyzing and evaluating the IR's utility and interface design. A number of liaisons involved in the study exploited their existing robust faculty department relationships to conduct interviews. One interview example identified 90 faculty archiving requirements and the provision for supporting material types and formats. In another instance, a liaison assisted additional colleagues to recruit hard science and some social science early adopter faculty as repository study participants.

Collection development librarians who worked directly with publishers negotiated a "right to deposit" for the academy's faculty published papers. Direct publishing bargaining on behalf of the scientists and scholars was successful for one of the institutions, resulting in an "unprecedented bulk acquisition of the published versions of articles written by the university's faculty" (Palmer, Teffeau, & Newton, 2008: 14). A pivotal success might precipitate a future publisher's concession for IR deposit rights incorporated into the subscription contract. Negotiations require dedication, fortitude, and influence. Picture a scenario where academic libraries and consortia collaborated on each institution's identical or similar contract language – an interesting concept of solidarity to contemplate. Without a green postprint publisher agreement or deposit mandate, individual researchers cannot make the greater impact of garnering permissions by employing a contract addendum on a large scale.

# Technical services staff and authority control

Historically, the academic library technical services staff input metadata for all library catalog record items, check in new acquisitions, exert catalog quality control mechanisms for the researcher, and manage online finding tools, such as link resolvers and open URLs. An IR has multiple requirements for success – technical services staff intrinsically have congruent skill sets that nicely match a repository's needs. There is a definite role to be fulfilled for support staff and professionals to expand their expertise and knowledge in an essential area of individual proficiencies and their institution's repository.

One method of marketing the University of Oregon's IR content practiced by technical services was to catalog individual item records that linked to their Scholars' Bank (*https://scholarsbank.uoregon.edu/xmlui/*).

The library has also considered generating MARC records (*http://www.loc.gov/marc/umb/*) from the repository's metadata (Jenkins, Breakstone, & Hixson, 2005). Many academic libraries include the DOAJ and *Open*DOAR as research databases as well as adding their academy's open access journal records to their OPAC.

Ohio State University (OSU) Libraries' Technical Services personnel have a larger magnitude of responsibility for the processing end of the IR than other units in their library and on associated campuses. Reviewing publisher copyright policies, generating metadata, depositing scholarship, and exerting overall quality control are service fuctions and can be mirrored elsewhere. The libraries emailed a survey to the Association of Research Libraries' (ARL) directors' listserv to determine, based on organizational structure, if technical service's staff were integrating IR tasks into their workflow. Were there staff reorganizations to accommodate the new responsibilities, and what staff roles existed before and after the establishment of the repository (Connell & Cetwinski, 2010)?

Of the 22 libraries that responded to the question on repository staffing, the majority of responses, 20 out of 22, reported a high level of technical service engagement. Institutional repository personnel management and operational staff were situated across several library departments. A high percentage of technical services' positions were not new, but more than likely had taken on new IR responsibilities. Tasks such as cataloging, ordering, and receiving materials were replaced by IR assignments. Fifteen libraries created repository positions. Of the reported 12 new positions added to technical services, 11 were primarily focused on metadata and tasks within the librarian, coordinator, and technician roles (Connell & Cetwinski, 2010).

## Search engine optimization

At many university libraries, technical services staff add search engine optimization (SEO) text to the front and the back end of the IR to encourage the best possible opportunities for readers to find content. The SEO goal is to increase the reach of a repository's inventory by indexing digital objects in search engines, thereby intensifying visibility as a result of introducing robust and distinctive information. Metadata specialists may also add comprehensive FAST (Faceted Application of Subject Terminology) metadata to each item record, comprised of "eight distinct categories or facets: personal names, corporate names, geographic names, events, titles, time periods, topics, and form/genre" (*http://www.oclc.org/research/activities/fast.html*).

An OCLC/Harris Interactive (2010) study focused on "new insights into information consumers and their online habits, preferences, and perceptions" found that "84% of total respondents begin their search for information using a search engine; no respondents begin at the library website" (p. 43). The comScore US Search Engine Rankings (2011) corroborate the OCLC findings by confirming the importance of search engines, Google in particular. The monthly Explicit Core Search Share percentage shows the number of searches that occurred in major US search engines and the percentage of share each service has of the overall total. Google's share in January 2011 was 65.6 percent, Yahoo's 16.1 percent (*http://www. comscore.com/Press_Events/Press_Releases/2011/3/comScore_Releases_ February_2011_U.S._Search_Engine_Rankings*).

Metadata plays a significant role in increasing the number of digital collection pages in Google's search engine. The more uniquely and thoroughly described items, keywords, distinctive pages, relationships among concepts, taxonomies, and encoded archival description (EAD) finding aids, the more opportunity for findability. By leveraging strategic campus partnerships to create relevant outbound and inbound linking, Google sees these relationships as integral to scholarly content and worthy of a higher ranking (Arlitsch & O'Brien, 2011).

## Authority control

Authority control has characteristically been the provenance of a library's technical services department. Naming standards ensure consistency and research materials are reliably attributed to the correct person. Even with deposits mediated by library staff, an IR presents an additional challenge for author name uniformity, as publishers may utilize their own style of author name format that may not match an author's preferred or standard publishing name.

As an example, the author's full name that is consistently used in articles we will call James P. Morgan. A publisher may alter or abbreviate the author's favored publishing name to include initials and remove a first name: J.P. Morgan. These specific author's papers, archived in an IR, have the potential for inconsistent naming not obvious to readers or the library staff to correctly attribute the work. Common names can be particularly challenging.

Institutional repository staff that deposit papers and review the item records will see the array of author names and need to decide what is the author's preferred publishing name for the standardized IR record. If using a curriculum vitae to attribute a correct author naming convention, it may be obvious or not. In theory, library-mediated deposits should have improved this situation. Some IR software does feature "auto fill" fields to help achieve consistency in terminology and naming convention. This is an undeniable disadvantage to researchers who may miss an author's scholarship by searching for a full first name when only initials are listed or there is a misspelling. It is suspected that metadata may be applied inconsistently across many institutional repositories.

Subject repositories that typically employ author "self-serve" deposits rely on "amateur-created metadata … posing serious quality issues" (Salo, 2009). Few or no disciplinary archives undertake name authority control and their software may not offer "auto completion" as a tool. Authors who use DSpace and Fedora™ have feature access to "auto completion" if it has been coded in by their institution's technical support. EPrints has actualized auto completion into practice: the typed-in author name suggests an existing author in the repository system. This is also the case with Digital Commons® software.

Digital Commons® offers "auto completion" in conjunction with their author disambiguation tool; it is manually set up for each author's name versioning. Also implemented is batch author editing utilizing Excel spreadsheets to assist in managing authority control that operates in specific circumstances. On the JISC-Repositories listserv, an email post read: "CERN is recruiting two developers to help the INSPIRE digital library/subject repository effort in the areas of text mining and author disambiguation and management" (Mele, 2011). The posted staff employment skill sets suggest a necessary movement toward synchronizing author naming conventions to accommodate and benefit: an IR manager/administrator; library staff who deposit scholarship; authors who create amateur metadata; and especially the readers to locate specific and intended authors. Quality metadata is essential to all aspects of a repository and its institution.

Repository staff, knowledgeable student employees, and library interns have the aptitude to synchronize name authority control to disambiguate an IR's author list. In DSpace and Digital Commons®, it is obvious when scanning the author lists to see where there are naming discrepancies. Their disambiguation can be effectively performed periodically to keep author naming convention consistently up to date. EPrints has an "author cloud" feature that lists authors and their publications on one screen to avoid clicking numerous times on author names while cleaning up the list. If DSpace and EPrints' personnel can regularly maintain the author list, it may be adequate until new software is developed to automate dependable author indexing terms.

Expert author disambiguation is offered by ORCID (Open Researcher and Contributor ID) (*http://orcid.org/*), a tool "creating a central registry of unique identifiers for individual researchers and an open and transparent linking mechanism between ORCID and other current author ID schemes." Led by influential universities, publishers, and library representatives, authors can sign up with ORCID to receive their "personal digital object identifier."

An open source tool that offers IR authority control and other features is available for specific repository software: DSpace, Fedora™, and EPrints. "BibApp" was created and its ongoing design updates originate from the University of Illinois at Urbana-Champaign and the University of Wisconsin, Madison, to enable a "pen name" convention (*http://bibapp.org/features/*). It flags duplicate submissions and has additional sorting functions. Tools with the ability to sustain IRs by eliminating naming challenges can effectuate our goals for an accurate display of scholarship worth creating and exploiting.

# Hosted and non-hosted IR services and systems department support

Systems staff perform an essential role, especially in a non-commercial and locally hosted IR where open source software is utilized. Staff are responsible for the technical and server support. A systems' skill set is necessary to sustain the major repository open source software that includes both DSpace and FedoraCommons™, irplus, EPrints, Islandora, and Greenstone. Knowledge of standard web-based software systems, the ability to customize, deploy, and manage the back end of the repository, the ability to test the system and evaluate the results, the capability to design and develop the IR interface, and identify and create value-added services that may encompass community and collection pages, are all fundamental to maintaining a successful repository.

The MIT and Hewlett Packard DSpace collaborators assumed that each library would self-host the software and have sufficient hardware to run the UNIX operating system, including a systems administrator to install and configure the system. Systematic software upgrades are optimal, as are customizations that require the services of a Java programmer. DSpace can function as a turnkey repository operation with international service providers to maintain its IR system (*http://www.dspace.org/service-providers/*). BioMed Central hosts the Open Repository based on the DSpace software. FedoraCommons™ has a framework for building institutional repositories. DuraSpace is a partnership comprised of DSpace, FedoraCommons™, and DuraCloud.

Capturing ingenuity to customize and add functionality to the open source DSpace software repository applications, the Texas Center for Digital Knowledge submitted a proposal to design and implement value-added services to benefit developers and users. The outcome for global DSpace technology administrators was the ability to customize an engaging interface; the new applications require less technical effort and are visually appealing (Moen & Singh, 2007).

Engaging in hosted services can minimize the repository staff workload and financial impact on a library's direct expenditure on staff, servers, and space allotment. Low staffing levels may constrain the use of local personnel to manage equipment and upgrades, while hosting takes advantage of the service provider's employees and their efficient expertise. New IR content storage options are available for a price.

DuraCloud (*http://www.duracloud.org/*) offers management and storage solutions as a free open-source project and fee-based subscription services for researchers and working scientists. The use of DuraCloud is aimed at researchers who do not have IT support to archive and ensure access to their data. Institutions can operate and manage multiple cloud use from one dashboard interface with data distribution and streaming to any Internet-linked device (*http://www.duracloud.org/content/duraspace-launches-open-source-cloud-service*).

Amazon Web Services (AWS) (*http://aws.amazon.com/publicdatasets/*) hosts a repository of public datasets integrated into their cloud-based application at no cost. Users only pay for the computing and storage used for their own applications. A few universities have embraced Amazon for their IR information technology repository needs. AWS user groups reside in North and South America, Europe, Asia Pacific, and Japan are listed at their website (*http://aws.amazon.com/usergroups/*).

EPrints, based at the UK's University of Southampton, offers a range of options, from hosting to simply supporting the installation of a repository. EPrints Services provides the freedom for IR administrators to choose the appropriate mix of for-pay and for-free repository solutions (*http://www.eprints.org/*).

Digital Commons® (DC), a hosted visually appealing repository service from bepress is based in Berkeley, California. They support the back-end of an IR by creating series, communities, conferences, and journal frameworks that originate from IR staff who create the URLs and request the actual implementation. An institutional repository manager may engage university department heads or college deans in being aware of faculty scholarship and IR project download counts. These monthly emailed metrics have the potential to contribute to university or programmatic statistics, including accreditation reports. Authors receive monthly full-text item download numbers. Those who have scholarship in a DC repository have the option to view their Dashboard, an altmetrics display comprised of: search query keywords, download counts, reader institutions, and referrer URLs. Another value-add feature is a comprehensive hierarchy of sub-disciplines, recent articles, and popular institutions and their authors (*http://network. bepress.com/engineering/civil-and-environmental-engineering/civil-engineering/*), emailed monthly to IR managers.

The Digital Commons SelectedWorks™ feature showcases an institution's individual faculty research in a linked list format with a built-in email function in addition to a faculty's professional profile. Examples from Drexel University, Yale University, and Glasgow Caledonian University include: *http://works.bepress.com/terry_seligmann/*, *http://works.bepress.com/ian_ayres/*, and *http://works. bepress.com/david_edgar/*. Libraries that host DC software may create and pay for a university-branded Selected Works™ presence for their academy's authors. Faculty have the option through their repository to create a non-branded profile by using a straightforward WYSIWYG template process.

The University of Waikato, New Zealand, has created the Greenstone digital library software (*http://www.greenstone.org/*), a non-hosted open source system that supports English, French, Spanish, Russian, and Kazakh languages, enabling more countries to embrace creating IRs. Greenstone was developed and distributed in cooperation with UNESCO (United Nations Educational, Scientific, and Cultural Organization) and Human Info NGO (non-governmental organization). UNESCO's mission is to furnish an intercultural dialog focused on education, the sciences, culture, communication, information, and gender equality in Africa (*http://www.unesco.org/new/en/unesco/*). By producing the software to populate repositories with accessible scholarship in various languages catering to the Global South's research plan, there is an expectation that the quantity and quality of intellectual content will accelerate.

Located in Belgium and Romania, Human Info NGO's mission is to provide programmatic information that organizes and manipulates data to empower dissemination services to the United Nations and development organizations. Their charge is to also increase human potential through access to technology, open-source software, websites, and the resultant open access to research (*http://humaninfo.org/home_flash.html*). Institutional repositories and tangential scholarly communication tools, such as *Open*DOAR and DOAJ, also contribute to the distribution of scholarly assets on a global scale.

The University of Prince Edward Island's Robertson Library combined a set of open source tools, Fedora™ and Drupal™, to create a unique IR software product, named Islandora. The digital asset management system, in tandem with its software applications, has been designed to match the "collaborative requirements of digital data stewardship" and multiple other applications (*http://islandora.ca/about*).

## Systems department support

Web designers may guide and implement an institutional repository "interface look" where mandated university web standards actuate a cohesive academic web presence. A lack of a defined motif requirement permits the systems' designers, who may be loosely part of the IR team, to build a library-created IR site. They typically have the creative and technical expertise to also shape item cover pages that contribute to institutional branding.

It is customary for systems staff to set up a Google Analytics account for their libraries to track the nature of reader visits, including usage of the repository website, CONTENTdm® installations, and institutional repositories. As an informative statistical tool that identifies various aspects of web traffic and IR engagement during specific date ranges as determined by the repository manager's needs, Google Analytics provides:

- the number of visits and from what city, country, or subcontinental region;
- the numbers of viewed pages, unique page views, average page visits;
- the visit duration related to how many page views and percentage of total page views;
- the average time spent perusing the site;

- the percentage of new visits and return visits;
- keywords; and
- the bounce rate (how far readers drill into the IR site).

As shown in the above list, Google Analytics has the ability to provide broad and granular statistics, invaluable to highlight in a presentation to stakeholders, for annual repository reports, and for the IR manager to maintain a connection to the repository's various data as a value-added service option.

Large item files, such as mp4s and image-laden PowerPoint presentations, can be imported from an outside content source and sent via FTP (file transfer protocol) into a secure folder constructed by a systems department expert. The University of Nevada, Las Vegas, Libraries has an arrangement with the Black Mountain Institute (*http://digitalcommons.library.unlv. edu/blackmountain_lectures_events/*) for their systems staff to transmit large files for staff to capture and subsequently deposit the items. Libraries with a low threshold storage drive may find external drives are temporarily helpful, but not ideal for the long term. It is optimum for repository staff to have efficient access to IR content files.

# Institutional repository advisory committee/board

A multitude of IR considerations and decisions to address from its first moment of contemplation and subsequent creation may include: overall decision-making, staffing, choice of software, budget, equipment, storage, services, who contributes, appropriate content, management of materials, indexing and metadata creation, preservation, rights management/other legal aspects, marketing tactics, policies, and other essential responsibilities that can be shared within the library and the academy. From examining the literature, it appears there is no "one size fits all" advisory or committee-recommended approach to an institutional repository.

## Policies and responsibilities

It makes sense for qualified repository managers/administrators, library faculty and staff who participate as IR advisory committee members to be the people responsible for budgetary recommendations; research access decisions; scholarly communication tools; open technologies; and determining content.

The University of Maryland, Baltimore (UMB) IR Advisory Committee document, *An Institutional Repository for the UMB Campus: A White Paper* (*http://archive.hshsl.umaryland.edu/handle/10713/7*), outlines their repository guidelines and priorities, including admissible content, standards, and consideration of withdrawal requests. The structure of the UMB's IR advisory committee comprises the: Library Director, IR Project Manager, dean, or other representatives from each university school, the Library Advisory Committee chair, and library faculty member(s). The Repository Project Manager coordinates and facilitates the committee (Gresehover, Behles, Douglas, Fernández, & Pinho, 2008).

At North Carolina State University (NCSU), an advisory council was established for their Scholarly Publications Repository (SPR) (*http://www.lib.ncsu.edu/faq/faq.php?id=309*). The Council's role is to steer and generate policies and services, as well as to act in a consulting function to the Vice Provost, Dean of Libraries, and University Library Committee. Engagement from the Advisory Council ensures "that the SPR is developed in collaboration with the community that it serves."

The University of Utah Libraries' IR Advisory Board (*http://uspace.utah.edu/materials/utahIRcollectionpolicy.doc*) is comprised of librarians and staff from the health sciences, law, and the main libraries. The Advisory Board is responsible for the strategy, policy, and IR review process, and the evolution of the repository and its maintenance (includes library directors). Three coordinators that represent a library are accountable to the library directors for IR guidance. University staff may offer/suggest content for inclusion to their representative selector. Significant new or expanded projects need approval from the IR coordinators if additional staff or digitization resources are required.

The Scholars' Mine office (*http://scholarsmine.mst.edu/index.html*) established an advisory committee at the Missouri University of Science and Technology to propose new materials and updates to the IR. The varied committee membership allows faculty to "have a voice" on aspects of adding content. Members are recruited from teaching and library faculty, IT staff, and representatives from each school of engineering and mining/metallurgy. Less than a third of the committee are library staff; the chair is a librarian.

Another example of an IR advisory committee comprised of primarily academic affiliates is at the Singapore Management University (SMU). The repository chair is the Provost; collaborating office units include: research, strategic planning, legal, chief information officer, the Center for Teaching Excellence, the library policy committee (IT system specialists, metadata librarian, information specialist), and the IR manager, who is also the secretary. The SMU Advisory Committee has a responsibility to "champion the business case for the IR as a medium for scholarly communications" to: preserve the academy's research assets; contribute to repository strategies and insights; add synergy to initiatives; and endorse the use of the IR to their constituencies (Singapore Management University Institutional Repository, 2008).

# Institutional repository collection development policy

There is a host of intellectual and/or organizational matter that is appropriate and of value to include in an IR. Repository managers, library and university administrators, faculty, and students may have differing opinions on what research item types should be deposited. An IR collection development policy is an essential referral tool when a new item type is considered for archiving that should be updated regularly.

Basic elements of IR collection development is the selection, consideration, and acquisition of material to add to the repository. An IR manager/administrator and advisory board or equivalent take into account a repository's mission when considering the collection services that define the overall broad and exacting range of materials that might include exceptions. A shared understanding of an IR's purpose and its policies assist in defining the scope and building consensus. As an example, an item's file size may be a consideration for a local server or a hosted service, dependent on server size and the IR's policy.

Embargo options allow for protecting time-sensitive research for a specified period of time or date. A graduate school administration is typically an ally and collaborator in the creation of policies and procedures for graduate research in an OA repository, with defined embargo time periods. Graduate colleges also seek to showcase student scholarship that clearly reflects the university's breadth of research.

Without available full-text, additional feature benefits may encompass a built-in email "button" option to request a postprint from an author.

Discrete collections or documents may only be available to a department or another administrative body that could include various meeting minutes with different access levels. Entry to a collection or series level needs to be determined on a case-by-case basis. The innate OA nature of an IR specifies a tendency for the academic/administrative content to be available for use.

The sustainability and success of a repository relies on an overall commitment by an academy and/or its library to an IR's capacity to endure or persist. "In establishing institutional repositories, institutions are both accepting risks and making promises; they are creating new expectations" (Lynch, 2003: 5). Enduring institutional repository characteristics to consider are:

- the stewardship of an IR;
- utilizing archival file formats for continued access; and
- item types that contribute to the mission and academic environment.

In terms of responsible planning and the management of resources, an IR is an evolving organic environment that an academic library preserves, administers, distributes content from, and is progressive in offering the best technologies that champion the scholarly communication process.

## Specific collection and preservation policies

The breadth and wealth of an IR's assets may be one of the primary reasons that some scientists and scholars embrace open access, as it encompasses a vibrant and expanding erudite community. Collection policies establish "its identity, quality, and direction" (Mukherjee & Nazim, 2011). Institutional repository collection development may embrace a variety of materials that are scholarly, creative, educational, or are of a general university focus that documents campus life and other significant issues that concern the academy. Copyright and local custom policies may require permissions for items listed below:

- *Scholarly materials:*
  - Preprints
  - Postprints
  - Peer-reviewed articles: publisher copies
  - Conference proceedings, presentations, posters
  - University-produced journals

- Monographs
- Books, chapters
- Presentations (multimedia and/or transcribed, texts, slides)
- Grey literature
- Technical or research reports
- White papers
- Datasets (research and government): small
- Patents
- *E-theses/dissertations (ETDs):*
  - Dissertations – student and faculty
  - Theses – graduate, honors, and faculty
  - Capstones
  - Professional papers
- *Classroom resources:*
  - Lectures (filmed and/or transcribed)
  - Open access textbook materials
  - Learning objects
  - Syllabi
  - Supplementary course material, handouts
  - Photographs/images
- *Creative works* – select materials could encompass alternative expressions of a creative work:
  - Music scores
  - Music composition recordings
  - Dance recitals
  - Student music programs
  - Poetry
  - Fiction
  - Creative non-fiction
  - Art work
- *Campus life* – special collections and archives materials:
  - Student newspaper/magazine

- Alumni magazines, university produced magazines, newsletters
- Sports programs
- Oral histories
- Newspapers
- Photographs
- Academic senate, department, and student organization minutes
- Undergraduate and graduate course catalogs

Adding a "Source" field in an IR item template or individual item record allows pertinent "finding aid" information to be added, stating an item's archived location, such as Special Collections, and where more "like items" may be found.

By taking advantage of an institutional repository's archival formats, library repository staff can anticipate the future deposit and use of documents, presentations, data, audio/video, and other file types. Readers are not able to access proprietary software structures, such as Microsoft Office, once there are version upgrades unless software companies change their modus operandi. Current archival file types include: PDF/A, mp4, mp3, HTML, JPEG, GIF, TIFF, and Postscript. Ensuring long-term access to repository content is an essential factor for readers.

The International Organization for Standardization (ISO) has created a standard for a portable document format (PDF) that can be employed for word documents, presentations, or spreadsheet texts and their accompanying images. The PDF/A ISO version recognizes images in a file and makes the information about them obtainable by a researcher who is seeking open scholarship. It is also specialized for the long-term digital preservation of electronic media documents or as a printed item (Wikipedia, 2011).

# Students and open access opportunities

Students should have opportunities to deposit their research and other scholarly efforts wherever an IR has been established and the content fits the collection policy. Marketing open access advantages and archiving possibilities to campus students is typically not undertaken on a systematic scale by faculty or librarians. Libraries that build strong ties with their academy's student governing bodies have a greater chance of engaging the officers to consider a presentation possibility or other academic activity to spread the message of open access to student scholarship.

## SPARC-sponsored student open access participation

Impressing upon undergraduate and graduate students the importance of OA research while studying in higher education will benefit them as future scientists and scholars, including society as a whole. As the next generation of researchers, students will have various levels of scholarly access, dependent on university budgets and purchasing priorities. The ability to gain entry to high-cost scholarship beyond an abstract is necessary for students to successfully complete their school work and publishing demands. Research access will change for many graduates unless they are hired into academia or work for companies that conduct research. Once graduated, they leave their academic library card privileges behind. Open access to scholarly content provides the means to propel current and future research to where it is needed, increasing the breadth of knowledge. Student Scholarly Publishing and Academic Resources Coalition (SPARC) resources of value to be aware of include:

- The Rights to Research Coalition (*http://www.righttoresearch.org/*) – covers 71 student organizations with over 7,000,000 international members advocating for the adoption of open scholarly practices.

- The SPARKY Awards – an annual contest to create a video based on essential themes in OA scholarly communications: provides equal access to information for developing countries, the general public, taxpayers who fund research, and as a public good to advance knowledge (*http://sparkyawards.org/details/index.shtml*).

Graduate students immersed in higher education can take advantage of opportunities to reach out and embed the scholarly communication process in the classes they teach by learning from librarian-taught instruction. This is a culture shift for faculty and librarians to take a lead in educating for open access to intellectual materials through direct scholarly communication education and seminars. Students have a crucial role to play in ensuring open access to research now and for future generations. Open Access Week activities (*http://www. openaccessweek.org/*) and additional open events are ongoing and available in various settings.

# E-theses and dissertations (ETDs)

A university graduate school program wanting to employ an IR for archiving theses and dissertations requires collaboration with the library, including the IR manager, to create policies and procedures to deposit in the academy's institutional repository. It differs from the garnering of faculty and other research as the IR manager or liaisons do not routinely communicate with the graduate students about archiving their individual theses in the repository. This is an essential partnership that embraces the importance and value of graduate research and a university's strategic plan to showcase student scholarship.

An ETD is a born-digital departure from the written, carefully formatted, and hardbound document that represents the outcome of a student's graduate research, culminating in a thesis and/or a dissertation required for graduation. A scanned and digitized paper thesis or dissertation is also considered an ETD as the electronic version of the document transcends the paper format. As a final graduate student research project, they fare extremely well in an IR, generating high use volume shown by download counts.

## *ETD metadata*

Digital software has enabled ETDs to capture creative scholarly work, offering the optional ability to incorporate enhanced features that more fully represent the breadth of research or other work, such as datasets hypertext links, graphics, sound, and video. Software has been designed and built to support complex intellectual content in institutional repositories, including its dissemination and findability.

The Open Access Initiative Protocol for Metadata Harvesting (OAI-PMH) exposes ETD metadata to efficiently facilitate the dissemination of online research by collecting the metadata and full-text in a central location, such as in the Networked Digital Library of Theses and Dissertations (NDLTD) (*http://www.openarchives.org/*). Consequently, any erratic cataloging or misuse of metadata fields creates inconsistent information for the reader that originates from the item record, potentially making the ETD more difficult to locate. Park & Richard (2011) conducted an analysis focused on metadata where six Canadian universities furnished sample ETD catalog records. The study looked at the metadata element sets used to describe ETDs (after the year 2000), the metadata use patterns, and a consideration of the variations and inconsistencies of Canadian IR ETD cataloging. The six universities provided ten IR metadata records that described their ETDs.

The metadata standards background for this study was ETD-MS (*http://www.ndltd.org/standards/metadata/etd-ms-v1.00-rev2.html*), based on an unqualified Dublin Core with its 15 basic descriptive elements, including title, creator, subject, and the extra element, thesis. The unqualified Dublin Core enabled additional metadata sets to be added as predetermined subsets. The thesis facet had four varied qualifiers that functioned to further describe an ETD: degree name, level, discipline, and grantor (Park & Richard, 2011). Data and service contributors rely on this set of metadata elements; the relationship is symbiotic. According to Tennant (2004: 1): "Data providers decide which metadata formats to expose for harvesting beyond the one required data format of simple Dublin Core" (*http://dublincore.org/*) and "service providers harvest sets from data providers of interest and provide search services for the resulting collections of metadata."

Metadata created by amateur or professional staff in the Theses Canada portal did not reach a sufficient international descriptive standard, although most searches conducted had adequate information to be successful. In this study, there were a number of metadata ETD-MS guideline entry input issues based on six different treatments of the ETD type element, with no reference to the electronic format. Another record did not state that the item was a thesis or dissertation. In other instances, the description facet contained other information than the prescribed ETD's abstract. Other concerns were repetitive types of metadata using dissimilar elements and the incomplete recording of item record details.

The study's primary conclusion was that significant disparities existed in ETD metadata practice at the six institutions whose conventions were reviewed. The OAI-PMH is intended for low-barrier interoperability for broader data use, consequently "it gives opportunities for flexibility and inconsistency" (Park & Richard, 2011: 405). The authors' analysis of the metadata records suggests: "Some of the institutions studied appear to be simply disregarding the element descriptions provided by the ETD-MS standard" (Park & Richard, 2011: 405). A greater commitment to ETD metadata development, its standardization, and subsequent implementation will offer readers enhanced access to graduate research.

## Batch harvesting and IR ingestion of ETDs

Individually harvesting ProQuest Dissertation Publishing ETD content from the back end of a university's database can be tedious and time-consuming. Thousands of academy ETDs are ingested into ProQuest every semester. Many of the ETDs and their meta-content then proceed to institutional repositories to be manually archived.

To streamline this laborious process, the University of Iowa Libraries created a workflow procedure for utilizing ProQuest's ETD data through their FTP delivery. By taking advantage of the ProQuest metadata, the ETDs can be efficiently made accessible before creating the local MARC (machine-readable cataloging) records. Brief MARC records can be produced for the local catalog during a later manual review. The described workflow is for bepress's Digital Commons® software. According to the authors, the workflow can be easily adapted to DSpace and other IR platforms (Averkamp & Lee, 2009). To integrate a "lean approach," the librarians combined and simplified existing workflows and repurposed the existing metadata to circumvent labor-intensive procedures that did not create value for the user (Averkamp & Lee, 2009; Lean Enterprise Institute, 2009).

The primary benefit of using the ProQuest metadata is to deliver OA to ETDs more quickly than by harvesting OCLC metadata after cataloging. Institutional repository open access records with a ProQuest schema to transform the bepress™ plan take the place of a public document while catalogers create an OPAC record. A transformation was designed to automate part of the brief record process. After manual edits were made and using the ETD-MS metadata standards, the authors created a procedure to convert the bepress™ XML upload to the MARC2XML, capturing the majority of metadata. Libraries may choose to add other local fields that would require manual additions. MARCEdit, a free editing utility (*http://people.oregonstate.edu/~reeset/marcedit/html/index.php*), has the ability to convert the MARC2XML to a MARC file that can be imported into the OPAC system, automatically populating specific fields (Averkamp & Lee, 2009). The value-creating steps occurred in an exacting electronic and manual sequence so the ETDs could "flow smoothly toward the customer" (Averkamp Lee, 2009: 6; Lean Enterprise Institute, 2009).

A few manual text modifications were necessary to be addressed before and after a batch file was uploaded. As an example, some universities require all caps for a thesis/dissertation title; where "ProQuest inherits this convention" (Averkamp & Lee, 2009: 6) it may be necessary to reformat to a local cataloging style. Additional manual title editing is perhaps essential before transmitting if utilizing a batch file in lower or title case (all capital letters). A bepress™ batch-loading limitation that only supports the Latin-1 character set requires manual corrections to those letters external to the set, as do special characters such as ampersands that do not survive the processing. An additional opportunity for bepress™ upgrades includes the discipline field that is currently not visible to readers (Averkamp & Lee, 2009). The ProQuest ETDs to IR ingest workflow has removed wasted steps and in working with bepress™ continues the task to achieve the ideal where there is little or no waste of time in processing (Averkamp & Lee, 2009; Lean Enterprise Institute, 2009).

## *ETD history*

A brief history of ETDs may help increase awareness of OA and promote an understanding of how and why the important influence of graduate work has created a path of openness for other types of research. Open access visibility, impact, and cost factors have all been vastly enhanced. The need for entry to graduate student research was founded and developed by University Microfilms International (UMI) in the late 1930s and (much later) evolved into ProQuest Dissertation Publishing in 1997. Reader options were initially microfilm and print having matured to an online presence.

Major ETD milestones covered the development of the first document type definition and the subsequent Virginia Polytechnic Institute and State University (Virginia Tech) research in 1989–90, converting thesis and dissertation paper copies to disks into a standard electronic online format. A concerted effort among Virginia Tech, UMI, the American Council of Graduate Schools (ACGS), and the Coalition of Networked Information (CNI) converged in 1992 to develop ETD collections. By 1994, Virginia Tech had mandated students to submit their ETDs to the newly implemented online system. The 1995 precursor of the current NDLTD advanced its maturing collection focus in 1997 to encompass US and international ETDs. Standards were improved to embrace new software, systems, tools, and guidelines (Park & Richard, 2011).

## *ETD value*

The Networked Digital Library of Theses and Dissertations (NDLTD) and universities quickly realized the ETDs' scholarly market value and were subsequently persistent in garnering open access to graduate work, removing the invisibility research factor. Peter Suber (2006a), a significant leader in open access to research, has made meaningful observations of why ETDs are inherently worthy of dissemination and are of value to readers:

- They have extensive research content compared to journal articles and cover topics in greater detail.

- ETDs are more likely to contain in-depth retrospective scholarly literature than journal articles and are usually researched, refined, and amended over a longer period of time.

- They are not formally peer-reviewed but are studied with equal rigor and over time.

- The reputations of authors and committee reviewers are at stake, enforcing a high standard of thoroughness.

- Their originality can be verified in addition to their contribution to knowledge and mastery of the relevant literature.

University of Rochester graduate students were polled as part of an "Enhancing Repositories for the Next Generation of Academics" 2006–8 IMLS grant. The research premise was to examine ways for the libraries to support graduate students' work by understanding their scholarly behaviors. Interviews were designed to clarify the academic work practices of 25 students, nine from the physical sciences and eight from both the humanities and the social sciences (Randall, Clark, Smith, & Foster, 2008).

The focus was to create and support an authoring environment in which to integrate publishing tools, share scholarship online, publish dissertations in the IR, and increase the findability and readership of the research. The graduate students in the study perceived that their dissertations were equally a project and a key step in their "ongoing process of individual and career development" (Randall et al., 2008: 19).

The students were interested in highlighting their intellectual content where it would be seen and used. Engaging the use of an institutional repository as a tool was considered by some of the interviewees for their ETDs, as it included supporting and showcasing multimedia and other types of research. The students embraced innovation and aspired to be creative to garner support for visibility in their graduate endeavors.

From the Lippincott and Lynch ETD and Graduate Education Survey (2010) "we do know that less than a third of respondents noted that the ability to include non-text features was an important issue that encouraged implementation of an ETD program in their institution" (p. 13). There was a sense that graduate students would be more ambitious and incorporate multimedia in ETDs if there was library or institutional support.

## ETD mandates

Mandating the deposit of ETDs in an institutional repository is a natural progression since theses and dissertations have been electronically created on computers from the early-to-mid 1990s. The current practices of ETD preservation engage a variety of options. Some universities take up ProQuest Dissertation Publishing Archival Services and institutional repository ETD ingestion, while others prefer only IR preservation. In addition, bound theses/dissertations destined for an academy's archives may still be required for a student to graduate. Suber (2006a) delineates many of these ETD dissemination advantages through a repository that include the following:

- Intrinsically, ETDs are royalty-free research literature – by consenting to OA, no author revenue is lost, such as in book publishing.

- There is no formal ETD publishing; subsequently publishers are not involved to oppose OA and require permissions or negotiations.

- It is the "universal lesson" that OA mandates are *the* most effective method to garner close to 100 percent of available research.

- Theses and dissertations have been historically "invisible" to readers unless the researcher was physically on a campus where the graduate scholarship is housed, a factor adding to the inconvenience. Open access also solved the indexing issue, as NDLTD, OCLC, VTLS, and Scirus (a comprehensive science-specific search engine) have collaborated on an ETD search engine for those documents deposited in the NDLTD: *http://www.ndltd.org/find*. Interlibrary loaning a thesis/dissertation is economically unsustainable considering the cost of copying, postage, and staff processing time.

- ETD authors have enhanced visibility and impact. The OA citation advantage might be comparable to that of journal article citations (50–250 percent).

- Universities are in a unique position to make it a simple condition of graduation to mandate open access. Graduate students are more likely to acknowledge the OA benefits. There are multiple ETD open access avenues if an institution does not possess one: NDLTD and Proquest

UMI charge fees; there are also cost-free consortial and regional repositories.

- Mainstreamed open access is becoming a natural and familiar archiving method to upcoming young scholars and will be considered the norm.

- When students know their research audience is amplified, there are ingrained incentives to do excellent work to be proud of.

- If a university does not publicly disseminate a thesis or dissertation, it could send a subtle message to a student author that it is not a serious or recognized work of scholarship, but suitable only for internal circulation.

## Archiving ETDs

### The Networked Digital Library of e-Theses and e-Dissertations (NDLTD)

With more than 140 institutional and consortium members (*http://www. ndltd.org/about/members/ndltd-members*) the NDLTD continues to support local and worldwide access to ETDs. University members (*http://www.ndltd.org/join*) pay a $300 fee, the benefits of which include supporting the harvesting of an institution's ETDs into the NDLTD's union catalog and long-term preservation. Members are also eligible to serve on the board or working groups and there is the advantage of conference discounts. Developing nations pay one-third the standard membership; some organizations have a waived fee. As of September 2, 2013, the NDLTD has archived more than a million ETD records and full-text since 2006.

The NDLTD has a useful list of practical resources that are both directly applicable and tangential to an ETD: an ETD guide, a list of terms and definitions, advice on setting up a submission program, a mentoring network, symposia papers, information on copyright, an ETD university census interactive spreadsheet, preservation documentation (*http://www.ndltd.org/resources*), and a listserv (*etd-l@listserv.vt.edu*) to query colleagues on ETD dilemmas.

A significant value of graduate student membership and their institutions is the opportunity for aspiring students to apply for the annual NDLTD awards. Students and staff who are successful, showcase their research and work, simultaneously highlighting their academic institution. The details and full-text documents can be added to the winner's institutional repository. Awards have been given since 2004.

- The *Innovative ETD Award* recognizes a student's efforts to transform the genre of the print dissertation through the use of innovative software to create a cutting-edge ETD. Use of interpretation, photos, audio/video, and other multimedia objects or techniques included in the electronic document are considered part of the innovation and the work. (*http://www.ndltd. org/events_and_awards/awards/ndltd-etd-awards-2011-winners*)

  **Award example:** A Kansas State University PhD student wrote a 2010 dissertation on the worthy subject of pathogens that infect staple cereal crops such as rice, wheat, barley, and millet, a topic focused on the global impact of agriculture and hunger. Nine supplementary MP4 files were created to allow the reader to view images of fluorescent proteins and infection mechanisms, and the inoculation of the rice against disease. (*http://krex.k-state.edu/dspace/handle/2097/6761*)

- The *Innovative Learning Through ETD Award* recognizes a graduate whose professional life has been enhanced by the ETD process.

  **Award example:** A 2009 architecture master's thesis focused on the author's plans to revitalize a community development urban agriculture project that has since had an impact on the municipal center planners at the edge of Pretoria, South Africa. The strategists subsequently advocated for transforming the endemic poverty through micro-economic development. With a global viewpoint, the author wanted to provide a model for other city developers. Nine PDF files are included. (*http://upetd.up.ac.za/thesis/available/etd-02022010-163309/*)

- *ETD Leadership Awards* acknowledge university community members whose leadership and vision have facilitated awareness of ETD benefits and whose efforts have advanced graduate education through the ETD medium. The various leadership levels are:
  - national;
  - regional; and
  - individual institution.

How might an academy realize how essential ETD research is without IR download statistics or through using Google Analytics? In the past, the only records available were how many theses and dissertations were purchased from UMI or ProQuest Dissertation Publishing. Currently, IR managers have become aware, through download statistics, that graduate research is a significant part of a university's intellectual scholarship and "a vital element of a campus-wide distribution strategy" (bepress™, 2009). The demand for timely research is currently shown in the extremely high download counts that many ETDs experience. The University of Nebraska-Lincoln IR manager reported: "Open access theses and dissertations in the repository receive 60 times more downloads than closed access theses and dissertations. Additionally, these OA theses and dissertations were downloaded 35 times more on average than any other type of content within the repository" (Bankier & Smith, 2010).

Professional papers and capstones that address real-world and exemplary practice situations offer excellent scholarship that garners high-value use. Texas State, San Marco's Masters of Public Administration professional papers (*http://ecommons.txstate.edu/arp/*) address everyday dilemmas and suggest solutions that are practical and accessible (bepress™, 2009). Other diverse examples include:

- hospitality professional papers at the University of Nevada, Las Vegas (*http://digitalcommons.library.unlv.edu/thesesdissertations/476/*);
- nursing capstones at Simmons College (*http://dspace.nitle.org/handle/10090/23351*); and
- law capstones at New York Law School's Justice Law Center (*http://www.nyls.edu/user_files/1/3/4/30/59/65/68/Cap10Kleidman.pdf*).

## Global ETDs

The US' unique ETD model differs from other nations. Its physical size, population, and academic standards have shaped the decentralization of how and where ETDs are deposited. Individual institutions and geographical consortiums typically archive their ETDs, including by city and state. The US-based NDLTD is an early adopter exception, as they archive local and global ETDs. National and global ETD archives, such as in Canada, Brazil, the Czech Republic, and other countries, have achieved a great deal to overcome a variety of challenges, including the magnitude of their repository projects. Finland has a unique tradition of listing university theses and dissertations that authors will defend over the ten days following being listed on their IR homepage.

## Canada

Theses Canada (*http://www.collectionscanada.gc.ca/thesescanada/index-e.html*) is sponsored by Library and Archives Canada. Their mission is to "build a world-class national resource enabling Canadians to know their country and themselves through their documentary heritage and to provide an effective gateway to national and international sources of information." Canadian universities and their students have the option to submit ETDs to the national database.

Library and Archives Canada have acquired ETDs since 2003 from ProQuest Dissertation Publishing and by harvesting them from Canadian universities that have instituted online submissions. Sixty-five graduate schools are engaged in using Theses Canada. The once common barrier of faculty resistance to ETDs has diminished. In its place, there is an absence of an ETD advocate to advance the program that would benefit from senior-level administrative support (Reeves, 2010).

## Brazil

In late 2001, a proposal was put forward to build the nationally funded Brazilian Biblioteca Digital de Teses e Dissertações (BDTD). The system developers had to consider a uniform integration across the often incongruent scholarly university communities. Stakeholders that followed two early adopter ETD digital libraries (from 1993) that were already using metadata and technology standards, developed a feasibility study. The wide-ranging initiative encompassed integrating OAI-PMH, a meta-search engine, and the Z39.50 standard for local, national, and international ETD projects (Southwick, 2006).

Technical support was deemed essential for current and future disparate local communities. A toolkit was created and consisted of: an ETD publishing software package; a program to implement metadata harvesting; a training module; and the necessary equipment. The open source software satisfied project limitations, such as budget constraints, local integration of ETD software in a known programming language, and a pact to work in partnership for future improvements, including metadata standards. Argentina, Columbia, Uruguay, and Venezuela requested the toolkit, potentially expanding ETD repositories across additional South American countries (Southwick, 2006). The BDTD ranks a solid second place with 154,533 ETD records (2011 ROAR update) on the ROARMAP's archived ETD list (*http://roar.eprints.org/cgi/roar_search/*

*advanced?location_country=&software=&type=theses&order=-recordcount%2F-date).*

## Czech Republic

In 2008, the Czech Republic's Ministry of Education subsidized the Theses.cz portal (*https://theses.cz/?lang=en*) for archiving theses and dissertations and, additionally, to check for plagiarism. Masaryk University, Brno, in collaboration with 21 additional Czech Republic universities, hosts a nationwide registry of ETDs. The ETD Working Group set Czech XML and metadata standards that significantly contributed to retrospectively harvesting ETDs. Prague's Academy of Performing Arts is formulating a plan to integrate audio/visual and creative arts in their ETD portal (Horová & Mach, 2009).

## Finland

The University of Helsinki's IR homepage (*http://ethesis.helsinki.fi/en/*) lists dozens of dissertations that will be "publicly examined" over the ten days following the listing, acting as a notice to globally share the research in advance. The oral exam tradition has an extensive history in Finnish academic culture. The formal and democratic process, which could last up to four hours, allows the author to defend the ideas and research results presented in the dissertation. Anyone with a criticism has the opportunity to convey it to the author. A ceremonial dinner is held that evening at a restaurant in honor of the graduate with members of the examination panel and a few colleagues, supervisors, or friends. Formal and informal speeches are given related to the research and the graduate (*http://www.helsinki.fi/lehdet/uh/299f.htm*).

## United States

There is a myriad of diverse opportunities to deposit theses and dissertations in the US. Unless there is a patent pending or need for an embargo, the online graduate research is available to readers and authors, optimally having been deposited in an open access environment. Organized institutional repository consortia may archive ETDs at an individual university/college level, in a university consortium organized by state or city, and at the country/global level (NDLTD). ETD archiving examples utilizing university, state, and city consortia include the following:

- *Texas Digital Library (TDL).* The Texas ETD Repository uses a system, Vireo, as part of its TDL's solution for Texas universities and their graduate students that supports the ETD process, from submission to publication to preservation (*http://www.tdl.org/etds/*). Texas boasts 34 institutions granting PhDs; six Texas universities are members of the NDLTD. Three TDL universities (the University of Texas at Austin, the Texas A&M University, and Texas Tech University) have implemented ETD systems.

- *State University of New York (SUNY).* An example of a public university system's repository is the State University of New York. There are 64 university and college campuses with potential representation in the SUNY Digital Repository (*http://dspace. sunyconnect.suny.edu/*).

- *City University of New York (CUNY).* The City University of New York made a commitment in November 2011 to "educate the public by making knowledge accessible and affordable" when their faculty senate supported the creation of an IR (*http://openaccess.commons. gc.cuny.edu/2011/11/23/cuny-institutional-repository-coming-soon-ish/*). Faculty members are encouraged to contribute to the IR (*http:// dspace.nitle.org/handle/10090/894*). The CUNY repository includes the 23 university and college city campuses.

# Summary

In considering open access publishing model jargon, it is understandable that readers might glaze over and hope for just a plain and simple access to research. Some researchers feel the need for an interpreter (faculty or librarian colleague) to understand what current distribution options are available and what ramifications follow their choices. Within the scholarly communication author's publishing decision, color coded deposits have become part of the consideration. Recent graduate student theses and dissertations, with all of their reader benefits and less complicated research processes and mandates, are increasingly obtainable on a global scale.

# 6

# Institutional repository impact and value proposition

**Abstract.** Readers and authors who value the benefits of open access scholarship do so for a variety of reasons: it is convenient to access scholarly materials employing a Google search; there is the opportunity of being cited more frequently; and alternative metrics show added value. Traditional impact factors primarily focus on classic bibliometrics, typically not of value to the Humanities, open access journal articles, multiple-authored articles, or authors writing in a non-English language. New impact factors are under development to satisfy the need to exemplify the open access research advantage. Measuring institutional repository value stems from a variety of non-traditional processes, including faculty post-print and student ETD deposits, a process improvement approach, and value-chain/value-stream mapping.

**Keywords:** altmetrics, bibliometrics, citation impact, cost of an institutional repository, institutional repository value proposition, Journal Impact Factor, Journal Use Factor, open access citation advantage, open access value, predatory impact, process improvement

## Impact factors

### Journal Impact Factor

The Journal Impact Factor (JIF) is a powerful tool that can determine a researcher's reputation and career expectations. Within the science, technology, and medicine (STM) disciplines, impact is fundamentally defined by the frequency with which an author's journal article is cited within a journal publication. The JIF does not cover citations to books, book chapters, conference papers, ETDs, working papers, reports, or journals published in non-Thomson Scientific's Institute for Scientific Information (ISI) publications.

Eugene Garfield, one of the founders of bibliometrics (citation indexing and analysis) and the architect of the Institute for Scientific Information (ISI), established (in 1960) the first citation index for articles published in academic journals. Over time, Garfield created the Science, Social Sciences, and Arts and Humanities citation indexes. CiteSeer was the first (1997) computerized citation index (*http://citeseer.ist.psu.edu/index*) (Wikipedia, 2011).

Open access (OA) to articles has a distinct potential to raise a JIF. The more available scholarship is through a search engine or by browsing an institutional repository (IR), the greater the opportunity for an article or postprint to be found, used, and cited through increased visibility and accessibility.

The JIF formula follows a bi-annual computation. The JIF is calculated by averaging the number of citations to articles that were published in a journal during the two preceding years. The impact factor of a journal is intended to measure how often and on average authors cite moderately recent articles from a particular journal. The JIF's metric calculations have been under scrutiny; new assessment measures are under development.

The Journal Citation Report (JCR) derived from JIFs does not highlight an author, only the publication. In science this exclusivity is perpetuated as one "advantage begets further advantage" (*http://cup.columbia.edu/book/978-0-231-14948-8/the-matthew-effect*) and "the higher a journal's JIF, the more often it will be cited – these citations in turn will cause a higher JIF score" (Herb, 2010). Additionally, other disciplines, such as mathematics, social sciences, and the humanities, are at a disadvantage with the ISI impact factor equation as they tend to favor specific publication formats and the majority of citations have a propensity to occur after a two-year time period.

Arnold and Fowler have identified additional negative journal impact factors, the consequences of the JIF that "has been widely adopted as a proxy for journal quality" (2011: 434). The ISI impact factor has methodically embedded itself into tenure and promotion decisions, and the means to assess and advance Thomson Reuters journals. Academic libraries, tracking scholarly communication trends, have commonly employed the Journal Impact Factor as the basis on which to purchase and renew research databases and subscriptions. Researchers voice disapproval of the current impact factor method that encompasses aspects of publication that ignore "multiple authorship, self-citation, and language of publication" (2011: 434).

On no account did Garfield forecast that a JIF would replace the tool to measure scientific outcomes with the quality of publications (Herb, 2010). As the publisher, ISI determines which journals to incorporate into the research databases and which to index or not. Numerous authors, journal editors, and publishers aspire to add degrees of impact to their journal measures, which can diminish the purpose of the research in itself and "ceases to be a good measure" (Arnold & Fowler, 2011: 434). Exploiting the JIF occurs on various levels and in deleterious forms. Editors and journal authors who repeatedly cite their own and their colleague's journal articles within the two-year impact factor interval to increase and quantify a publication's worth are playing or gaming the system.

Are scientists truly benefiting from the JIF or are commercial interests engaging a model that focuses on competition and unfair practices? Scientists and scholars are at the mercy of complex and imperfect journal impact calculations, "based on hidden data" (Herb, 2010: 3). Another consideration of the current JIF is the task of the researcher, the journal editor, and librarian to ground their respective decisions on objective calculations of appraising journal excellence. Over the last half-century, "these measures of assessing journal quality, also known as bibliometric indicators, have emerged as the chief quantitative assessment of the quality research papers published, the authors, and that of the institution with which these researchers are associated" (Mathur & Sharma, 2009: 81).

In comparison to the JIF, the Journal Citation Report (JCR) is also an imperfect journal impact tool, although generally accepted, has a simple quantitative measure, is global, has comparable data over decades, and its shortcomings are generally known. Used because there is a lack of accepted alternatives, it is most favorable towards the biomedical sciences, and does not cover all scholarly disciplines (Shepherd, 2011). The Hirsch Index (h-index) and JIF are calculated primarily by citation measures, but the h-index is based on a performance index of the frequency a scientist is cited.

## Hirsch Index (h-index)

Like all citation measures, the h-index is not an ideal tool and has its own advantages and imperfections. It is linked to and based on the distribution of citation frequencies received by a scientist's articles. As an alternative to the JIF, it measures a researcher's impact and not the comparative impact of journal citations. The h-index is computed using the following formula: "A scientist has index h if h of N papers have at least h citations each, and the other (N – h) papers have less than h citations each" (Herb, 2010). University of Southhampton's Library has created a tool for finding an h-index in Google Scholar (*http://www. soton.ac.uk/library/research/bibliometrics/factsheet03-hindex-gs.pdf*). The h-index shares some of the faults found with the JIF, such as multiple-authored articles are not taken into consideration, nor are papers written in languages other than English.

## *Journal Usage Factor*

One of the reasons the journal Usage Factor (UF) has gained traction is the dominant JIF measure has multiple and significant shortcomings. Alternative metrics are needed to measure all scholarly disciplines' impact. Current methods to quantify use often discriminate against open access (OA) journal articles. The standardization of download count technologies would benefit from ensuring that it is reader-centered and involves a trustworthy process. The Digital Commons® repository software employs reliable COUNTER technologies that libraries have used for years to tally download statistics for research subscription database article download statistics that filter out automated robots and crawlers (*http://www.bepress.com/download_counts.html*).

The Counter Project (Shepherd, 2011) has developed a journal Usage Factor (UF) that parallels a "usage-based measure of journal performance becoming a viable additional metric" (Shepherd, 2011: 6). As an improvement to the JIF, the UF embraces open access journals:

- in all disciplines;
- with a greater accessibility to a larger number of periodicals;
- with usage statistics for practitioner-oriented publications;
- to expediently record and report usage;
- to potentially moderate the over-emphasis of impact factors;
- for authors who would appreciate a usage-based metric for OA publications.

In 2007–8, Counter conducted market research to garner an initial assessment of the viability of advancing and applying UFs. Authors, editors, librarians, and publishers participated in thorough telephone interviews and a web-based survey. There was broad support that substantiated its implementation.

Key findings and conclusions of the study included the impact factor. The participants had a keen desire to develop a credible substitute for the JIF and replace it with a "more universal, quantitative, and comparable measure of journal value" (Shepherd, 2011: 16). All web survey author and librarian interviewees believed the usage factor would be worthwhile in evaluating journal value, status, and relevance. Publishers indicated that support would be contingent on their "confidence in the basis of the JUF calculation" (Shepherd, 2011: 13).

A large majority of authors were in support of using the JUF to rank journals; there was less accord among the publishers who were inclined to qualify their positive and negative responses. However, the publishers appreciated the benefits they could accrue and appeared to be agreeable, in theory, to compute JUFs for their journals.

In the 2011 CIBER Research Limited study outcome report (see *http:// www.projectcounter.org/documents/CIBER_final_report_July.pdf*), journal article "patterns of use and citation" in 2008 were quantified by ISI's measures. The use of 148 journals in five broad subject areas – engineering, humanities, medical and life sciences, physical sciences, and social sciences – plotted against the ISI impact factor, illustrated that "usage and ISI impact factors are statistically independent," a vital finding from which it could be extrapolated that the knowledge of one variable does not enable someone to predict the value of the other variable, as "citation and reading behaviors are different" (2011: 35).

According to Davis (2011), the JUF is misleading and should actually be referred to as a journal download factor (JDF), due to an uncertainty with regard to "*who* downloaded an article and for *what purpose*" (2011: 2); it may imply greater popularity for a journal and/or an author. A more expansive viewpoint focused on download factors suggests an article of interest used in garnering ideas, as background knowledge, exhibits some value to the reader, as a future collaboration, or as an inspiration for further research or a paper. Article downloads or visits display some curiosity or importance, whether formally employed in the future or not.

# Open access journal citations: disadvantages and advantages

## Disadvantages

Open access journal article funding using a publisher's article processing charges' gold model such as the PLoS, BioMed Central, and SAGE Open, suffer from a lack of impact factors unless they are indexed by relevant research databases, such as Scopus, the Web of Science, Journal Citation Reports, Elsevier, and others. This is one of the reasons that OA journals are perhaps initially or perpetually at a disadvantage to gain JIFs. There is also a need to take into account:

- nascent publications lack the citation history that is required to be indexed by Journal Citation Reports (JCR) and to attain a sufficient JIF score;
- the plethora of non-English language journals from developing countries that typically achieve minor JIF scores or are not indexed at all (Herb, 2010).

There is a substantial body of open access research article publications that are often met with prejudice because of lacking impact metrics. Self-archived postprints (papers approved by peer-review) and journal articles in an IR are excluded from these indices where they would profit from alternative and multiple aspects of impact measurements. In addition, scientists and scholars could be incentivized to engage with OA scholarship if, as a minimum, it communicated current and added alternative metric value, such as author reputation, journal and article impact, download counts, and the maximized advancement of individual and collective research.

## Advantages

It is common knowledge that globally open access research is available on the Internet, either in an IR, open access journal, or through other trusted sources that may be pressed into service and cited. The value of research can be "defined as the degree to which one's ideas have freely contributed to knowledge and impacted the thinking of others," and where "authors use citations to indicate which publications influenced their work, scientific impact can be measured as a function of the citations that a publication receives" (Bollen, Van de Sompel, Hagberg,

& Chute, 2009). Citation data can provide reliable quantitative measures of scientific impact for relevant and applicable OA scholarly materials as "citability rests upon the quality, relevance, originality, and influence of a piece of work" (Swan, 2010: 1).

The outcome of Swan's 2010 study was the complexity and multiplicity of the citation variables that differed by discipline, dependent on the magnitude of citation and publishing timeframe, also differing with the percentage of open access documents. A number of OA articles would have more utility, as would subsequent citations, than the counterpart of the subscription literature that is financially locked up behind a subscription. Potential advantages to open access citations were found to include:

- *a general open access advantage* – citable articles became available to those researchers who had no previous access and found articles worthy of citing;
- *an early advantage* – the earlier an article has global access may affect ensuing citation patterns;
- *a self-selection bias* – authors are more willing to showcase their higher-quality articles;
- *a quality advantage* – high-quality articles profited from the general open access advantage, as they were more citable than articles of lesser quality.

Elements of the 31 studies spanning 2001–10 focused on: the area of discipline; samples that ranged from a few hundred to millions of articles; a variety of basic analytical methods; whether self-citations were filtered out; if there was a citation advantage; and if there was an attribution of advantage to a particular aspect of open access.

To summarize the survey measurements, a positive OA citation advantage was found in 27 of the studies, while four of the studies found no OA citation advantage or an OA citation disadvantage. Table 6.1 portrays the size of the OA citation advantage when found in the study and where specifically stated by discipline.

Authors who self-archive their green OA postprints in an institutional repository (IR) to supplement publisher versions under subscription-based access are cited considerably more than other articles in the same journal publication year that were not open access. Some have expressed that the OA advantage may be indicative of a self-selection bias under which authors only favor depositing their higher-valued scholarship.

A 2010 study by Gargouri et al. was designed to compare the self-selective and self-archiving behaviors with mandatory self-archiving. The

| Table 6.1 | The size of the OA citation advantage when found and where specifically affirmed by discipline |
|---|---|

| Disciplines | % increase of citations in OA |
|---|---|
| Agricultural Sciences | 200–600 |
| Physics and Astronomy | 170–580 |
| Medicine | 300–450 |
| Communication Studies (IT) | 200 |
| Computer Science | 157 |
| Mathematics | 35–91 |
| Political Science | 86 |
| Electrical Engineering | 51 |
| Philosophy | 45 |
| Biology | –5–36 |

Source: Creative Commons License Attribution 2.5 Generic (Swan, 2010).

sample was comprised of 27,197 articles in 1,984 journals published from 2002 to 2006. The principal findings confirmed that the OA advantage was high for both self-selective and mandatory self-archiving.

# Additional bibliometrics

## Ranked journal list

As a ranked journal list alternative to the JIF, the Australian Research Council (ARC) (*http://www.arc.gov.au/era/journal_list_dev.htm*) conducted its first complete Excellence in Research for Australia (ERA) evaluation across eight discipline areas (ARC, 2010). Journal quality ratings were founded on the overall value of the publication and defined in terms of how one research periodical compared with other journals, regardless of subject area. The overall criteria for journal tier ranking was based on the quality of the papers:

A*   one of the best in its field or subfield;

A   very high quality;

B   solid though not outstanding reputation;

C   does not meet the criteria of the higher tiers.

The ERA website information was designed with transparency in mind to enable researchers and editorial staff to remain apprised of the process. The Ranked Journal List was developed on the basis of expert review, public consultation, and learned academies/discipline bodies drafting journal rankings for their pertinent disciplines. Over 700 expert reviewers in relevant subject areas engaged in final consultations that were used to develop the ERA 2012 Journal List. The evaluated quality ratings of over 22,413 unique peer-reviewed journals are listed on their website (see *http://www.arc.gov.au/era/era_2012/era_journal_list.htm*).

## Eigenfactor™

A journal's Eigenfactor™ (*http://www.eigenfactor.org/*) score is the measure of the journal's total importance to the scientific community. The Article Influence score measures the average impact of each journal article over the first five years after publication by visually mapping the structure of science (*http://www.eigenfactor.org/map/maps.php*). Journal price information and a cost-benefit search tool ranks journals according to the value-per-dollar afforded the academic community. An interesting example of a publication's cost value, journal subscription price, and its Eigenfactor™ ranking in terms of Article Influence score can be found at the following website: *http://www.eigenfactor.org/cost.php?search=AZ &year=2009&searchby=isicat*.

## Predatory impact factors

Jeffrey Beall, librarian at the University of Colorado, Denver, has become an expert in exposing numerous predatory journals and impact factor websites. He noticed an increased number of imitation journal metric sites appearing, such as CiteFactor (*http://www.citefactor.org/*). With its initial website debut, the base of its homepage had numerous academic library logos. Within days, the logos had disappeared. Impact factor "companies" have emerged basing their criteria on qualitative journal features that might include editorial, presentation, publishing, and manuscript value, typically unrelated to standard and alternative impact factors. One of the websites states, "We are charging a nominal fee for processing your journal to get Journal Impact Factor" (see *http:// scholarlyoa.com/2013/08/06/bogus-impact-factor-companies/*).

# Measuring the value of an institutional repository

Citation impact is a principal value that authors naturally strive for. Research that is archived in an open access repository has the ultimate advantage of being available to readers. Measuring and assessing an IR's value, its sustainable practices, and its success factors are imperative for efficiency and accountability to stakeholders.

## Institutional repository value proposition

The uptake of IRs has been steady since the early years of the twenty-first century, with a continuous flow of noteworthy tools necessary for their operation and complementing open access processes. In the garnering and depositing of IR content, the literature suggests "a failure to engage with the full potential impact of OA" and the cause is manifest in the message not getting through to "provosts and to vice chancellors in significant numbers" (Hubbard, Hodgson, & Fuchs, 2010: 5). The medium (open access) is the message. To profit from open access research technologies and to place "an open access archive at the heart of the university ... that can add real value not only to researchers at the institutions but also to society as a whole" is a viewpoint endorsed by Wim Leibrand, chief executive of the Netherlands' SURF Foundation (Hubbard, Hodgson, & Fuchs, 2010: 6).

## Institutional repository value study: Victoria University, New Zealand

Cullen & Chawner (2010), Victoria University of Wellington's School of Information Management faculty conducted a study on OA adoption factors and success from the perspective of IR managers and the academic community. These researchers suggest that a long-term sustainability of IRs depends on "gaining a stronger commitment from the academic community" (2010: 1).

Faculty answering (134 responses) the question of why they would archive in an institutional repository saw positive value in:

- making their research available to their students and colleagues;
- increasing exposure to their work;
- providing a method of maintaining copies and listing research output;

- using new technologies in research and publishing activities;
- deposited research attracting students and other academics to their institution;
- the benefits that colleagues were accruing;
- the recognition of archived research; and
- assisting with career advancement.

The institutional repository benefits were calculated from 522 respondents that noted:

- a greater exposure to the institution's scholarship;
- the IR makes it easier to organize academic research output and preserve it long term;
- the individual researcher's work attracts more discovery;
- a reduced dependence on universities for the rising costs of scholarly publishing.

There were also the common concerns or barriers to archiving in an IR, such as a: lack of repository knowledge or being unable to perceive the value; shortage of comfort with a new technology; insufficient time to deposit an article; and no invitation to archive. In the realm of repositories, these basic "barriers" can be overcome with support and, preferably, a deposit mandate.

## Measuring institutional repository value

Studies conducted by Swan (2010) and Gargouri et al. (2010) suggest that "conventional wisdom" has prevailed with scientists and scholars who typically showcase their more satisfactory articles as they aspire to highlight their best research. A study measured OA repository value centered on the quality of deposited materials and whether it was representative of an institution's academic reputation, and if the repository's value was dependent on institution type (defined by the Carnegie Classification System (*http://classifications.carnegie foundation.org*)), and what materials were archived.

In place of focusing on the characteristic measure of an IR's quantity of items, Wacha & Wisner (2011) attempted to ascertain content quality that an institution perceives as possessing the highest impact to assess the repository's value. The study's sample of 48 US colleges and universities, all non-profit, were located in *Open*DOAR, sorted by institution type and basic Carnegie Classification. Five institutions were randomly selected from each category, and groupings with less than five institutions were all included. The Scopus citation index was employed, as it remains the largest science abstract database with a number of arts and sciences citations.

Results of the study showed only three IRs had deposits of the highest impact papers authored by faculty at their institution. A number of scholarly items deposited by the same researchers in 16 repositories provided 36 percent of the sample. Private colleges and universities archived a notable number of more high-impact articles and authors than their public equivalent. Master-level institutions had the highest number of high-impact articles in their institutional repositories.

Universities with very high research activity (RU/VH), high research activity (RU/H), and doctoral/research university (DRU) classifications all included high-impact authors in their respective institutional repositories, but very few high-impact articles were deposited. Academies with the RU/H and the DRU classification possess IRs with greater overall impact value than other research activity categories.

In general, public institutions are inclined to deposit a diverse selection of intellectual content, while private institutions primarily archived articles and ETDs. Both public and private shared their top five item types that mirror their missions: articles, ETDs, multimedia works, conference papers, and unpublished materials.

Lacking high-impact articles deposited with an author's best work may lead someone to believe there might be a conscious or unconscious reason for not archiving in an IR. High-impact authors are depositing research other than their high-impact articles, leading to low-value institutional repositories. The authors consider this an indication of "a lack of commitment on the part of faculty to deposit their best work and the failure of their institutions to collect it" (Wacha & Wisner, 2011: 384). In the case of IR staff garnering CVs and requesting or depositing postprints, high-impact articles or their metadata are potentially accessible. The authors suggest adding interactive features, such as a customizable interface and editorial commentary that includes Web 2.0-style options to entice researchers to connect more deeply with their institution's repository.

## Institutional repositories: funding and staff contributions

At a time when academic fiscal responsibility is essential and record low budget challenges are not far behind, an institutional repository offers opportunities to sustainably showcase and reflect an institution's research. An IR is relatively inexpensive when we consider what it offers to the academy, its stakeholders, and the global scholarly marketplace. Repository expenses for hosted services typically include initial and annual maintenance charges and library staff salaries. Open source software requires technical staff, servers, and staff salaries.

In *The Survey of Institutional Digital Repositories* (Primary Research Group, 2011) sample, the mean institutional repository budget was $75,413 in a span of $0 to $260,102 in expenses, with research universities deploying larger financial allotments. US annual allocations were by far the highest, averaging more than $110,000. Developing nations' yearly institutional repository budgets averaged closer to $22,000.

In 2010–11, the proportion of increased expenditures for an institutional repository was 5.76 percent and the expected rate of increase for 2011–12 was 11.31 percent. The median of expenses was zero for both. Anticipated increased spending was lowest in the US at 2.36 percent and highest in developing countries at 28 percent. Private colleges presumed the highest rate of spending.

In the sample of institutions, repository employees spent a mean of 2,597 annual academy staff-hours to operate and promote IRs, averaging to 1⅓ full-time equivalent positions. Canada and Australia used approximately half of the US' staff hours.

Table 6.2 outlines what percentage of IR support is given from budgeted funds or donated staff-hours of service to provide for a repository's needs (Primary Research Group, 2011: 221). The library, information technology administrative division, or an academic department may furnish monetary and/or personnel resources.

**Table 6.2** Percentage of support for IRs from budgeted funds and/or donated staff-hours of service

| Country | Academic library | IT-related administrative divisions | Academic departments |
|---|---|---|---|
| US | 86.36% | 4.55% | 9.09% |
| Europe | 83.33% | 8.33% | 8.33% |
| Canada/ Australia | 100.00% | 0.00% | 0.00% |
| Developing countries | 57.14% | 28.57% | 14.29% |

It is of interest to note that developing countries' academic libraries do not have exclusive management or primary technical responsibilities to maintain their IRs. It could be a blessing or a hindrance, dependent on circumstances, to have multiple information technology administration and academic departments involved.

Creating an awareness of an institutional repository's strategic influence becomes a critical issue in a period of economic instability. It has the potential to endanger the enduring sustainability of a repository that scientists, scholars, faculty senate, and administrations have not fully embraced. This is an opportune time to boost morale and value with research performance metrics and encouragement to deposit scholarship.

# The cost of an institutional repository

According to Cassella, when determining an IR's cost structure, "all possible outcomes, benefits, and consequences deriving from the broad dissemination of scholarly institutional output should be taken into account and promoted to stakeholders when assessing the repository's costs" (2010: 218). It is not an easy task to place a price tag on the advantages of an institutional repository, although there are other ways to show value to those not already on board, such as administrators, faculty, and students.

## Cost and value per item deposit

Various and disparate institutional repository calculations have been offered to determine the cost and/or value structure of an IR. A University of Southampton faculty timed an item deposit at approximately ten minutes. There is growing evidence that OA in all disciplines suggests a gain in time investment, reaping a minimum of a 200 percent increase in citations and as a consequence, an increase in downloads. The enhanced research impact that requires little time renders large returns that scientists and scholars value: research progress and funding, prestige, career advancement, and salary. The yearly archiving time "cost" for articles was estimated to be "as little as 40 minutes per year for a highly active researcher" (Carr & Harnad, 2005: 1).

Interactive journals, such as the *PLoS ONE*, additionally create value by showcasing "hubs" that import and enrich OA articles with enhanced data that solicit comment and potential discussion. Inspired by online literature that can be reused, reorganized, and filtered, empowers an exchange of research, analysis, and data among its community members (Hubbard, Hodgson, & Fuchs, 2010).

# Value of institutional repositories from an internal and external perspective

A multitude of studies have focused on institutional repository qualitative assessment, as "author attitudes towards self-archiving were [and are] regarded as key factors of IR success" (Cassella, 2010: 212). A variety of performance measures that originated from a lean business point of view creates value for the customer with fewer resources. In this context the researchers who engaged with an IR (Cassella, 2010) put to use the balanced scorecard (BSC) approach (*http://www.balancedscorecard.org/ BSCResources/AboutheBalancedScorecard/tabid/55/Default.aspx*) as "a management system (not only a measurement system) that enables organizations to clarify their vision and strategy and translate them into action." The BSC can be recruited as a library performance measurement for an internal IR value proposition from the perspective of: its users; internal processes; finances; learning; and growth. This model has the potential to align IR managers' mission "to align their repository strategies to the institutional mission and goals and to identify priorities in performance measurement by focusing on a core set of meaningful PIs [performance indicators]" (Cassella, 2010: 214).

Institutional repository users, as scientists and scholars in the role of authors and readers, are the primary researchers using the repository, indicating their level of commitment by their deposits, downloads, and scholarly impact. The author has adapted Casella's first ten internal IR touchstones and BSC principles' framework, combining them with diverse stakeholder and repository value-added perspectives.

*User frame of reference:*

1. A measurement of researcher commitment to the IR.
2. The average number of items archived per scientist or scholar calculates IR growth and acceptance of depositing practices.

3. Disciplines vary in their open access uptake; a diverse list of subject communities is a benchmark of an IR's success.

4. Item downloads or visits measure, at a minimum, an interest in the intellectual content. Projects are underway to define and establish a set of standards for calculating and reporting scholarly item usage, as an example, interoperable repository statistics: *http://irs.eprints.org/about.html*.

*Internal frame of reference (library practices).* An IR manager employs a range of meaningful material types, ideally encompassing all faculty needs. In addition, "value-added services developed for authors are strategic components of a successful repository" (Cassella, 2010: 216).

5. Item deposit statistics encompass IR records: bibliographic metadata only or full-text records. There is a disparity in value for the reader with only metadata, unless there is library access or an ability to request a copy, another step in the research process.

6. A daily number of deposits are essential to sustain the flow of research into an IR to encourage community engagement, amplifying scholarship. A well-embedded institutional repository is "shared out across *all* the individuals and departments in an institution, and hence all the communities and collections in the repository" (Carr & Brody, 2007: 6).

7. An ideal research community will encompass full-text scholarly content locally obtainable, dependent on fair use or fair dealing/copyright constraints. Viable author deposit options include retaining rights by maximizing addendums/contracts, archiving postprints, or taking advantage of depositing publisher copies where legally possible. It is inevitable that embargoes and copyright will prevail.

8. Full-text open access scholarship is "one of the most meaningful measures of a successful repository" (Carr & Brody, 2007: 17). It is optimum to deposit all interpretations of an article: the preprints, postprints, and the publishers' copy, where possible. Versioning has the inherent possibility of adding confusion. Implementing the Version Identification Framework (*http://www2.lse.ac.uk/library/vif/index.html*) assists authors, content creators, and IR managers with improved version archiving techniques.

9. Active IR collections incorporating a diverse range of quality and high-impact scholarship appeal to scientists and scholars as depositors and readers.

10. Researchers' value-added services for faculty and students position their work in an institutional repository to include significant worth to readers that could include: repository statistics, Google Analytics data, copyright policies' review, metadata and citation creation, Web 2.0 features, alerts, and RSS/Atom feeds (*http://en.wikipedia. org/wiki/Web_2.0*).

# Lean Six Sigma Process Improvement approach

An institutional repository is laden with processes, specifically in archiving various item-types and what steps are necessary to make the deposit, from garnering the scholarly research to its final collection destination and adding the metadata. Lean Six Sigma, a quality improvement method coupled with process speed and low cost-efficiency, uses employee and customer data to identify and remove procedural issues. Among its key themes are customer-defined quality and expedient delivery of promised services at a minimal cost. Institutional repository staff can be more effective through teamwork, sharing ideas, utilizing data, and subsequently enabling an understanding of each item-type process (George, Rowlands, & Kastle, 2003).

## *The University of Arizona experience*

The University of Arizona (UA) Library has profited from Lean Six Sigma principles that brought about a cost-saving and resulted in service quality refinements. Their process improvement teams discovered strategies to decrease staff numbers on a task and also to enhance quality by eliminating low and non-value-added steps, reformulating actions, establishing more effective technologies, and upgrading staff training (Phipps, 2001).

Repository staffing is typically acquired by utilizing "dedicated blocks" of staff time and hiring students, other than for the IR manager's position. This is an opportunity to consider lean and sustainable IR personnel practices to improve operational procedures. The UA Library staff engaged in a process improvement for a different project than an institutional repository. The basic formula may be extrapolated to other quality-related procedural needs of the library.

Best practices that lead to efficiency and satisfaction start with learning about the scholarly communication expectations of faculty and administrators and what qualities of the repository service they value most. By mapping the current workflow of an IR and by specifying the associated steps to achieve the complete process, there is a greater understanding of how staff might work on each part of a project. This activity often discloses a "duplication of effort, lack of clarity as to who does what, [and] differing methodologies used by each staff member for completing a step in the process, and the identification of 'non-value-added' checking or approval of work that is 98% correct to begin with" (Phipps, 2001: 651).

Staff might be surprised to learn that their perceptions of how a process functions are sometimes incorrect, especially as they pertain to the variability or predictability of the detailed IR process and customer expectations. A basic knowledge of the scholarly communication process is useful to understand faculty and graduate student needs. The Lean Six Sigma approach emphasizes documenting the procedural workflow steps by reviewing and redesigning the "flow of work," in this case repository staff, ensuring their knowledge and training to continually improve their work (George, Rowlands, & Kastle, 2003). Assisting staff to adjust to change is accomplished by finding out what part of the process they are interested in, cross-training to preserve IR procedural knowledge maintained during staff changes, and helping all to see the larger picture the personnel are part of.

An institutional repository is laden with a variety of statistics based on staff efforts and process outcomes. The more knowledgeable and accurate personnel are in their work, the greater the likelihood that staff will produce needed facts and figures. Data information sharing, as it reflects staff endeavors, is useful feedback to "help staff learn, grow, and increase performance that relates to customers' changing expectations" (Phipps, 2001: 646).

"Value-stream mapping," as seen in Figure 6.1, is a technique for visually identifying potential process improvements by drawing a map of the process or, as in this illustration, using portable sticky notes to examine and re-examine each procedural step to determine efficiency and added value to the final product or action steps. The linear sequences depicted are five different IR item types, with a few sticky notes on end, denoting a decision needs to be made in the value stream's process. The convenience of using sticky notes enables a visual and ongoing physical manipulation of the action steps that are necessary to understand the manual tactics entailed for each item-type from the receipt of an object to deposit.

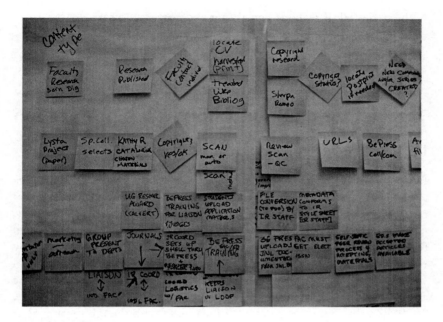

**Figure 6.1**    Mapping the value stream

*Source: Author.*

# Institutional repository value chain approach

In addition to the Balanced Scorecard (BSC) and Lean Six Sigma approaches previously mentioned, there are a number of other applicable business methodologies that focus on value to the IR customer (faculty, administrators, library staff, students). A value chain is a series of activities that an organization performs in order to deliver a valuable product by promoting its service. According to Swan (2008: 20), the business model definitions proffered by Chesbrough & Rosenbloom (2002) are among the most conventional and have proven to be practical in universal professional contexts. The authors established six business model factors comprised of:

- articulating the value proposition;
- identifying a market segment (users for whom the contribution is useful and for what purpose and value);
- defining the business value chain structure;

- the potential of revenue-generating and cost structure;
- a specification of business position within the value network; and
- the conception of a business's competitive strategies.

# The institutional repository value proposition

## *Value stream and value chain*

Business activity determines where an enterprise stands in the value chain. The direct value proposition for the business of institutional repositories is achieved to benefit the academy's scholarly community, including the library. The impact of online technologies has transformed the research information system, allowing and encouraging new communication capabilities and economic realities.

The value stream and value chain are business concepts that can be extrapolated to an institutional repository's set of processes (Whittle, 2009). A value stream is a process of activities with the foremost goal of satisfying a customer; in this context it is primarily faculty and student researchers. An example is the accumulation of scholarly assets such as articles and the step-by-step procedure required to deposit them in a repository. The researcher is "delighted" (Whittle, 2009: para. 9) because the article is openly accessible. The item depositing process will engage IR staff at varying levels that intersect with other library staff, external faculty, administrators, and students.

In relation to an institutional repository, each link of the value chain represents a relevant activity that adds value to the process. An example to clarify the concept is the scholarly communication workflow that includes depositing a postprint or publisher article copy where legally possible, in addition to the metadata. For those who support the concept of OA and rely on the availability of intellectual content, the increased worth of open full-text research is a global good and establishes the possibility of new value each time a reader downloads or cites a paper.

Transforming the scholarly communication process promotes the selection of scientific research by readers as of foremost importance, whereas its exposure is an author's paramount goal. These actions and the author–reader relationship principally establish the value chain within the realm of scientific information. Any persuasive alteration to the traditional scholarly communication process, such as open access research archiving disrupts the status quo of publishing paywalls and alters the value chain in a positive direction (Roosendaal, Huibers, Geurts, & van der Vet, 2003).

The compelling catalyst for modification in the current model of scholarly information in the value chain as it transitions from a "low volume/high margin business to a high volume/low margin business" (Roosendaal, Huibers, Geurts, & van der Vet, 2003: 121) is changing the publishing and research access environment. Academic libraries, (some) publishers, authors, and readers are all circumspect, for each of their respective best interests lay in the "rapidly moving target" landscape of open access.

The scholarly communication value chain can be experienced as a series of steps with added value from each stakeholder, on the continuum from intellectual material creation to delivery to an intended audience. The primary actors in the chain are content creators, editors, reviewers, and publishers, with potential input from libraries, document delivery, and rights management services. The increased worth of the scientific value chain can be mapped to the four primary elements of scholarly communication (Roosendaal, Huibers, Geurts, & van der Vet, 2003):

- *Registration.* An author submits a paper to a journal to establish scholarly findings or concepts.

- *Certification.* The paper is emailed for a peer-review of research quality validation. This stage is most critical to the authors and readers, and subsequently for the value chain as a whole.

- *Awareness.* A guarantee is given to disseminate the research and to ensure accessibility for readers to build upon.

- *Archiving.* Storage and preservation of research is an intellectual heritage for future readers.

In addition to the four primary scholarly communication elements in the value chain, Swan (2008) proposes to compare the reader's merit offered by commercial academic publishers with the current and potential advantages afforded by open access to research. The author augmented attributes to the list of reader value-add features to complement those of Swan (2008) (see Figure 6.2):

- *Cost to reader.* What is the monetary or time outlay to gain access to available research outputs?

- *Navigability.* How efficient is the interface for searching, finding, and retrieving intellectual content?

- *Presentation (as a graphical user interface).* The reader's engagement in the quality and utility of the site.
- *Additional functionality.* Extra value added – citation linking, rich metadata, linking to supporting data.
- *Editorial value.* Copyediting, reproduction, and translations from original work.
- *Usage feedback.* Author's data and download statistics depict how the output is being read, cited, and used by its incorporation into the progress of science.
- *Archiving/preservation.* How well is the scholarship being stored or preserved for future use.

Social media features are evolving to facilitate additional transparency, including commenting and following authors on publishers' websites, in repositories, and blogs.

Figure 6.2 lists scholarly communication elements in the value chain on the left. On the right are three components related to what provides

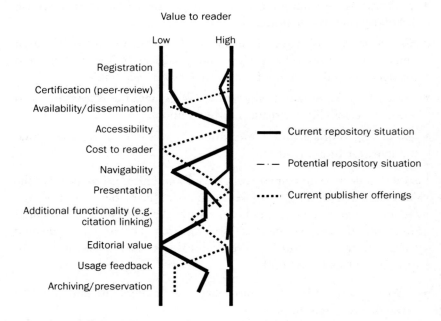

| **Figure 6.2** | Value chain curve for scholarly research communication |

*Source:* Swan (2008).

value to the reader, comprising the current and potential repository situation, and current publisher offerings. The figure graphically demonstrates that repositories and publishers participate in a number of disparate activities.

As the technical aspects of the scholarly communication process and institutional repository software evolve, potential opportunities and specific goals for the IR of the future may capture more that is of high value to the actors in registration, certification, availability/dissemination, navigability, additional functionality, and editorial value.

## The repository value chain and proposition

Several frames of reference analyze the scholarly communication value chain and articulate a value proposition on behalf of the research community. This is an opportunity to combine Swan's (2008) digital repository and Porter's (1985) primary value chain activities and perspectives to summarize the benefits.

The five primary activity terms described in a value chain (listed below) when combined with value proposition attributes, appear applicable to an IR value model that equates to a repository value proposition:

- *inbound logistics* – enable discoverability (of research) and increased functionality (of scholarly communication systems);
- *operations* – enable long-term storage and curation;
- *outbound logistics* – maximize the accessibility and availability of research, and enable discoverability;
- *marketing and sales* – scholarly research outputs at no cost to the reader; and
- *service* – maximize the accessibility and availability of scholarship, enable discoverability, increase functionality, provide long-term storage and curation.

The global research community is the central recipient of the shared knowledge repository value proposition. Academic institutions, as well as publicly financed research funders, are the primary stakeholders archiving their scholarly content. Open access repositories have other potential benefits that suggest "enabling the transfer of knowledge between sectors in the 'knowledge triangle' (research, education, industry) and maximizing the efficacy of technology transfer" (Swan, 2008: 25).

## Business sector value and open access to research

To be more efficient and cost-savvy, the private business sector might make use of publicly funded research and grey literature. Studies have furnished evidence of economic benefit to business by achieving product innovations and time efficiencies accelerated by readily available scholarly content. Organizations operating in multi-disciplinary and innovative environments are offered significant benefits by their approach to employing open access research to eliminate paywall barriers (Parsons, Willis, & Holland, 2011).

## Summary

Journal Impact Factor metrics have existed for decades, surviving rampant criticisms and few revisions. A recent impact factor model, altmetrics, has garnered attention by its filters that exploit social media tools, showing promise to be integrated into the open access influencer mainstream. Predatory impact, the latest service from predatory open-access publishers, is a prime example of taking advantage of the open access scholarly communication process. Collectively, there is a need to expose these imposters to faculty, graduate, and undergraduate students. Institutional repository staff, always laden with a plethora of details, might consider engaging in tracking new developments that support the scholarly communication repository environment with its expansive set of inherent value proposition opportunities.

# 7

# Looking ahead to open access data and textbook opportunities

**Abstract.** Legislation as a driver to oppose open access to data and journal article dissemination is not focused on the public good of accelerating research if it means sliding profits. US Federal Government legislation has mandated open access to data and its scholarly article output when the public has funded the research. Supporters of open research include scientists and scholars, librarians, students, and citizens, advocating for policies that encourage global dissemination. Academic liaisons have embraced data curation and management plans in conjunction with faculty and the IR administrator to chart complementary partnerships to handle multi-size datasets. Deposited scholarly materials comprised of research and data in an institutional repository can be embedded in web scale discovery services, affording the ability for readers to search and find using their library's search box. Faculty are taking advantage of open research resources to develop their own teaching scholarship, taking the place of expensive textbooks and saving students the need to purchase them.

**Keywords:** data curation, data definitions, data management, datasets, liaison and faculty collaboration, open access research legislation, open education resources, repository tools, web scale discovery services

## Data and research management legislation

Academic open access (OA) data sharing management is a concept that met with new legislative rigor on January 18, 2011, affecting two major US grant-funding agencies, the National Science Foundation (NSF) (*http://www.nsf.gov/eng/general/dmp.jsp*) and the National Institutes of Health (NIH) (*http://publicaccess.nih.gov/*). The agencies' new and more stringent mandates for transparency and open access data plan (NSF) and journal literature (NIH) have initiated many questions and concerns regarding implementation and sustainable action for data management plans and the datasets they describe.

The May 2013 US Office of Science and Technology Policy (OSTP) data policy memorandum stated the need for the direct results of federally funded scientific research to be made available and useful for the public, industry, and the scientific community. Results may include peer-reviewed publications and scientific data widely accessible to the American people through a comprehensive government-wide strategy (*http://www.whitehouse.gov/sites/default/files/omb/memoranda/2013/m-13-13.pdf*).

# Data curation and management

Data curation and its accompanying literature has accelerated over the past few years, consequently eScience librarians are in place at many research institutions. Data curation models are integrating with research libraries as they support the management of data. Academic libraries are poised and prepared with a wealth of data support website resources and engaging in individual consultations. Data curation has the potential to become a monumental task, as the multiplicity of data across science disciplines requires corralling the researcher's and supporting content created in various formats and amounts.

Libraries are considering collaborative data intersections with their institutional repositories (IRs) to highlight grant research projects, potentially archiving small and medium datasets. The magnitude of the big data would typically be inappropriate for an institutional repository. Supercomputers with mega-power processing and space have recently become capable of partitioning publicly accessible research through a URL. By establishing an alliance with researchers, liaisons, an IR manager, and the supercomputer center director, big data resources have the prospect of being positioned in a more accessible environment. By creating a repository item record with rich metadata and a URL that links to the supercomputer's archived data, readers will have a novel and sustainable capability to view and reuse the datasets.

The expertise of library subject liaisons is a value-added service for any size of data researchers; STEM and STM librarians are engaged in the research process and are training to align with the data management milieu.

Sponsored Research (SR) staff in partnership with an IR manager has possibilities to reinforce the existing open access repository option for grant scholarship output, especially given the February 14, 2013 bipartisan FASTR open access legislation and the White House OSTP Directive requiring federal grant agencies to develop open-access policies within six months, due in August 2013. The research community is waiting to hear.

# Data curation definitions

Consistent definitions relative to data curation and management are useful to maintain researchers' and librarians' understanding of the same terminology. The National Science Board and Cornell University Library Data Working Group (2008) and additional resources have provided definitions for the following terms:

- *Digital research data*. The National Science Board (2011) characterizes data as digitized information stored in a digital format and its associated digital metadata. This encompasses predominantly digital data collected or generated in the course of conducting science and engineering research (known as eScience). It can be classified as observational, experimental, or computational, enabling other researchers to reproduce studies, validate outcomes, and build upon previous work to further advance science (*http://www.nsf.gov/nsb/publications/2011/nsb01211.pdf*).

- *Data collections*. The National Science Board report defined the infrastructure and staff necessary to maintain and provide related access to data collections. From the Northern Illinois University's Responsible Conduct in Data Management website, data collection is described as the process of garnering and measuring information on variables in an established systematic fashion that enables scientists to answer their research questions, test hypotheses, and evaluate the outcomes. The data collection is common to all fields of study that include: physical and social sciences, humanities, business, etc. Data collection methods vary by discipline; the emphasis on verifying accurate and principled collection processes persists (*http://www.niu.edu/rcrportal/datamanagement/dctopic.html*).

  While defining data as quantitative or qualitative regardless of discipline, accurate data collection is essential to preserving the integrity of research. Both the selection of appropriate data collection instruments (existing, modified, or newly developed) and unmistakably outlined instructions for their correct use reduce the likelihood of errors occurring.

- *Data curation.* The Digital Curation Centre (*http://www.dcc.ac.uk/about/what/*) defines data curation as the "activity of managing the use of data from its point of creation to ensure its availability for discovery and re-use in the future." Data curation is a broad term and may also be integrated with digital preservation and archiving terms. Preservation and archiving could be considered as subsets of data curation, research, and professional practice. In some contexts, curators annotate or link to data to add interpretation. Data curation terms may have different connotations in contrasting communities.

- *Data-driven research.* Comprehensively encompasses data-driven science and scholarship, eScience, e-research, and e-scholarship. This set of terms refers to emerging research practices made possible by a cyber-infrastructure and includes data/text mining, data visualization, advanced simulation modeling, and remote collaboration.

- *Datasets:* factual, structured, or unstructured.

  - *Big data.* "Data sets so large and complex that it becomes difficult to process using on-hand database management tools or traditional data processing applications" (*http://en.wikipedia.org/wiki/Big_data*). Big data creates multiple challenges in its capture, curation, storage, sharing, interpretation, and conceptualization; there is a considerable amount of information to process.

  - *Medium-size data.* Databases of moderate size where a correlated database structure is vital to access and make use of the data.

  - *Small science.* Research endeavors undertaken by individuals or small to medium-sized groups. Data files tend to be small enough to utilize on personal computers. A single file may comprise one entire dataset, as opposed to storing large amounts of content in a database.

- *Data management.* As an excellent example of data support, the Massachusetts Institute of Technology (MIT) Libraries created a comprehensive data management plan subject guide covering aspects of: a description of the project and data; standards; storage; legal/ethical issues; access policies; and means for archiving. In addition, there is support for data planning utilizing a checklist or exploring other plan resources (*http://libraries.mit.edu/guides/subjects/data-management/plans.html*).

  Academic libraries have been compelled to embrace creating data management plan resources for their institutions, engaging in a new leadership role. The Association of Research Libraries (ARL) has aggregated a comprehensive list of institutional resources for data management planning, NSF guidance on specific plans, data and digital curation, archival resources, and tools for assessing research data needs (*http://www.arl.org/rtl/eresearch/escien/nsf/nsfresources.shtml*).

- *Additional data definitions* (HM Government, 2011):
    - *Open data.* Data that can be freely used, re-used, and redistributed.
    - *Data information.* Interpretation and analysis of data represents added value, meaning, or a message when presented in context.
    - *Flat data.* Each record is part of a larger list of records. An example would be a spreadsheet of names and affiliations with one record per row of the table. A flat data structure allows for the reuse of information.

## Library support for data curation

Data curation involves faculty, library liaisons, IR administrators, and archival resources that could include an institutional repository (IR). Many faculty are in a continuous spiral of regularly creating and manipulating datasets. The Johnston (2010) survey shows 64 percent of faculty researchers or graduate students access their data on a daily basis and 25 percent interact weekly with their data. Liaisons, familiar with their faculty's disciplinary research typically have existing working and trust relationships to engage collaboratively in a data review.

## Library roles in data management plans

### University of Minnesota

The University of Minnesota (U of M) Library has established a program called "Managing Your Data," providing standards for the sharing and discovery of data, preservation and archiving, copyright, and ethics. Part of the Library's program success was attributed to the collaboration with the Office of the Vice President of Research, requiring the attendance of all principal investigators and offering continuing education credit. Further marketing to alert researchers to available data support encompassed online videos/slideshows, training opportunities, and a compilation of resources related to a data management plan, metadata standards, and storage (*http://www.lib.umn.edu/datamanagement*). U of M liaisons have consulted with over 250 faculty and have multiple department invitations pending (Kelley, 2011).

## University of Minnesota Library data curation study

To understand the eScience needs at the U of M campus and identify computing resources and support for research, a 2009 assessment of user-needs was conducted by Johnston (2010) and her library colleagues. Out of 8,403 faculty and graduate students solicited, 780 participated at a 9.3 percent response rate. The top three participating research roles were represented by: 37 percent faculty; 31 percent graduate students; and 21 percent staff. The research discipline responses were greatest in the health sciences (22 percent), biological sciences (21 percent), social sciences (20 percent), and engineering, mathematics, and technology (13 percent).

In the majority of research projects cited in the survey, the number of people involved in the small projects was a principal investigator (PI) or an individual faculty with fewer than five scientists or graduate students (59 percent). Centers, large projects with multiple PIs, or a large laboratory with more than five people were the next largest combined segment (35 percent) of research project models.

As the academic environment rapidly evolves, a faculty's advantage may be dependent on technology storage and back-up support. Respondents showed a preference for "low tech" storage for their research data; the prevalent means were on a desktop computer (63 percent), department server (40 percent), and a work laptop computer (39 percent).

A system's back-up used as security for data is particularly essential with regard to losing content that cannot be recovered or easily recreated. There was a differing opinion among the survey respondents about who would optimally secure their data; it was likely related to their personal work style. In the majority of research groups, a second hard drive (43 percent) was a first choice and 29 percent preferred a CD/DVD or other media storage. Scientists, scholars, and graduate students opted for a central department (26 percent) or academic server system (23 percent).

The primary contact for additional data support in providing services for data storage, security, space, support, compliancy, bandwith, and access to outside data, was forwarded to the local information technology unit. Outside data services were not seen as necessary for many researchers.

## *Purdue University Library data curation study*

The evolution of open access to research has created a wealth of intellectual content and data in the scholarly communication landscape, engaging library liaisons and IR managers. Liaison collection development activities have tapered off with the economic realities of inflationary serial costs overtaking the collection management and purchasing of library materials due to semi-flat budgets, providing librarians time to collaborate on data projects.

With Purdue faculty in need of library liaison expertise in additional areas of research, the cultural shift to data curation was a natural progression. For liaisons, the notion of the enterprise of building and archiving datasets in institutional repositories or other venues raises issues of organizational challenges, technological requirements, understanding disciplinary data compilation, and applications of its use.

In the midst of their project, Purdue liaisons became aware that the collection of datasets "resists automation" and the familiar vendor tools to identify eligible data were not that helpful. Instead, data selectors found "interpreting faculty research profile databases, scouring research news feeds, monitoring funding awards, and announcements that come out of research offices and departments" (Newton, Miller & Bracke, 2010: 13) are of value. Utilizing third-party high-level-rated information registries and data discovery references are valuable for providing data. Examples include the following resources:

- National Space Science Data Center: *http://nssdc.gsfc.nasa.gov/*
- Global Change Master Directory: *http://www.apple.com/*
- Humanities Resource Center Online: *http://www.humanitiesindicators. org/humanitiesData.aspx*
- North Carolina University Social Sciences and Humanities: *http:// www.lib.ncsu.edu/data/socialscienceandhumsets.html*
- Emory University Libraries: Economic and Financial Data Resources: *http://einstein.library.emory.edu/econlinks.html*

As libraries and liaisons participate in more "upstream" content (where the work is being done) with provider and collaborator roles in data curation, an embedded research partnership with faculty early in the process is an ideal opportunity for liaisons to participate as consultants or co-investigators, becoming familiar with the data from the outset. The data curation product outcomes also have the potential for creating documentation prototypes, best practices, or benchmarks that will "assure the longevity of the data downstream," where the content is available (Gold, 2007: 6) benefiting scientists, scholars, and readers. The pressing requirements of data curation matched with liaison and IR managerial skill sets will become more evident to researchers, potentially creating incentives to work in partnership and share their scholarly output, where possible, in their local institutional repository.

A further perspective from the Purdue data project was articulated in a case study published by two members of the Purdue chemistry faculty who collaborated on an eScience project. Garritano & Carlson (2009) expressed the value of liaison librarian attributes, such as current awareness and reference skills relevant to locating necessary information, although subject expertise was thought to enhance a liaison's skill set. Internal/external outreach and partnerships, sponsored research participation, and the ability to balance a workload were also deemed to be expected or cultivated as a skill set. Leadership from institutional repository managers/administrators was considered important in areas of expertise, including open access, open data, digital scholarship, digital stewardship, and online preservation. The subject domain librarian was considered the appropriate liaison between the IR manager and the faculty.

It has been suggested that repositories "might bridge the downstream/upstream divide" (Gold, 2007: 6) by supporting pre-publication and data collection workflows in an IR, an approach especially suited to small and medium datasets. Centralized subject-based repositories may be more appropriate for larger data project outputs and long-term curation. The "downstream" output of published articles, research artifacts, and associations with linked datasets can create synergy among all of the project's facets. Researchers, in collaboration with liaisons and the IR manager, have the ability to contribute to a more valuable body of information of their multi-faceted research components by making it globally available. Commercial publishers are increasingly interested in garnering data to repackage and market, "publishing the datasets in peer-reviewed data journals, and in both creating tools for data management and discovery" (Gold, 2007: 4).

Building the capacity to embrace data management concepts and opportunities commences with a willingness, a skill set, and the knowledge to perform the new roles that are needed. The actions involved in liaison data curation must occur with a consideration for quality, usefulness, and subject suitability. How relevant the datasets are to other disciplines beyond the faculty collaborators is less predictable and begs the question of worth beyond the local institution. The library's value proposition in data curation partnerships is predominantly with the domain liaison and the IR manager to assess the viability of archiving, sharing datasets, and related research outputs.

Scientists and scholars are not always willing to share data before publishing their research findings – someone else might assert ownership of their discoveries. They may hoard their data by adhering to the notion that there is the possibility of more to be discovered and published. As scientists and scholars use their data and findings to establish their research reputations, there may be little motivation to openly share their work (Marcus, 2010).

Domain expertise may not be imperative to work effectively with researchers in the upstream phases of the data management groundwork, although the Purdue's task force experience suggests that an "awareness of faculty research ranks among the most important aspects of the data collection process" (Newton, Miller, & Bracke, 2010: 63).

## University of Wollongong institutional repository data collection

An example of how one institution used their institutional repository for multiple data management projects may be found at the University of Wollongong Library in Wollongong, Australia. The Library has archived: a variety of research data covering rich metadata records; information on accessing a dataset; full-text guides; and data, where available. Usage statistics for a specific six-week period showed that, on average, the data collections with full-text descriptive materials had twice as many visitors assisted by search engine queries compared to the metadata-only item records in the collection, an evidence-based transaction (*http://ro.uow.edu.au/data/*).

# Data management tools

Data management tools facilitate the data curation process and may be employed by scientists, scholars, and librarians. There is an escalating variety of in-development options available for institutional and data repositories.

OCLC's Faceted Application of Subject Terminology (FAST) keywords are currently used in IR keyword fields where a decision has been made to effect the retrieval of a more detailed item record by delineating "eight distinct categories or facets: personal names, corporate names, geographic names, events, titles, time periods, topics, and form/genre" (*http://www. oclc.org/research/activities/fast/default.htm*). OCLC's mission is to further access to global information. To that end, they released a linked data service, designed to enhance published data by making more detailed references linkable across domains (*http://www.oclc.org/ research/news/2011-12-14.htm*).

The Digital Curation Centre (*http://www.dcc.ac.uk/*), based in Edinburgh, Scotland, is a world-leading institution with expertise in digital information curation. It focuses on building capacity, capability, and skills for research data management across the UK's higher education research community. Their Curation Lifecycle Model offers a graphical and granular overview of the requisite stages for the successful curation and preservation of data from the initial conceptualization (*http://www. dcc.ac.uk/resources/curation-lifecycle-model*).

The scientific production of Europe's OA research has begun cross-linking publications to data and their funding schemes through OpenAIRE and its second-generation of OpenAIREplus (Open Access Infrastructure for Research in Europe). Scientific domain-specific fields will be integrated into the current repository networks, engendering 41 pan-European partners that include three interdisciplinary research communities (*http://www.openaire.eu/en/home*).

The Microsoft Excel spreadsheet has been transformed by the University of California Digital Curation Center and the California Digital Library to facilitate data management, sharing, and archiving for scientists. The Digital Curation for Excel (DCXL) project was initially focused on earth, environmental, and ecological domains, and project it will be useful for a wide range of scientists who wish to generate collections based on Excel spreadsheet data. The team, in conversation with scientists, is learning about how Excel is used in the course of their research, data sharing practices, familiarity with data archiving, and foreseen barriers to good data stewardship (*http://dcxl.cdlib.org/?page_id=11*).

With the January 18, 2011 NSF mandate for a data management plan (*http://www.nsf.gov/bfa/dias/policy/dmp.jsp*) supplement to accompany all grant proposals, academic libraries have moved quickly to produce funding documentation to support faculty researchers. Each of the following institutions lists library service options for data management planning obligations:

- *University of Massachusetts, Amherst* – data management planning, guidance, and a template: *http://www.library.umass.edu/services/ services-for-faculty/data-management/*

- *Massachusetts Institute of Technology* – resources for creating plans, a data planning checklist, data integration, organizing files: *http:// libraries.mit.edu/guides/subjects/data-management/plans.html*

- *Colorado State University* – templates for all sizes of datasets, data sharing information, IR information, copyright FAQs: *http://lib. colostate.edu/repository/nsf*

- *University of Michigan* – templates, tools, funder guidance, best practices, data preparation guide, natural science examples and global resources: *http://www.icpsr.umich.edu/icpsrweb/ICPSR/dmp/ resources.jsp*

Academic librarians are embracing new digital data curation and management skill opportunities. Librarians are attending data workshops and classes to prepare to partner with faculty in their data-rich research projects. In addition, eScience librarians have created in-depth online data resource guides. Library Information Studies' programs are keeping apace with the Library Science field and are offering a variety of data-related programmatic opportunities:

- LIS programs for continuing education – not inclusive:
  - University of Illinois at Urbana-Champaign, Graduate School of Library and Information Science, Center for Informatics Research in Science and Scholarship: *http://cirss.lis.illinois.edu/index.html*
  - University of Arizona Dig-in Program: *http://digin.arizona.edu/ instructors.html*
- The creation of or using existing eScience portals for academic use and beyond – not inclusive:
  - eScience Portal for New England Librarians: *http://esciencelibrary. umassmed.edu/data_curation*
  - Science and Technology Digital Research Data Curation Resources: *http://www.istl.org/10-fall/internet2.html*

# Web scale discovery services

Google is known for its simplicity, its aggregated content, and its subsequent searching from a unified index of accessible web content. Library catalog search tools have aspired to Google's ability to return results from a single query based on the Internet's information sphere.

Library web scale discovery services are the newest search tools that hold great promise to streamline a search and improve the relevance ranking of results, while simultaneously querying commercial research databases and locally held digital content, which could include a library's OPAC, archived IR materials, and CONTENTdm® digital collection projects (Luther & Kelly, 2011; Vaughan, 2011).

Before web scale discovery services were created, researchers using the library had to search each commercial database separately. Institutional repositories and digital collections generally fare well with Google locating digitized items from a query. Scientists, scholars, and students, using a web scale discovery system from their academic library, will have the convenience of a one-stop search directed to reliable and carefully selected online special collections and research resources. Including IR content in a discovery platform increases the possibility of greater visibility, value, and the expanded use of an academy's repository.

## Open education resources and open access textbooks

In the same year (2001) that Massachusetts Institute of Technology (MIT) Libraries embraced open access to research by co-creating an IR with Hewlett-Packard, MIT embarked upon another unique and "open" concept, open courseware. According to the MIT website (*http://ocw. mit.edu/about/*), the university's OpenCourseWare is the online publication of "virtually all MIT course content, globally available," and is a "permanent MIT activity" that "reflects most undergraduate and graduate subjects taught at MIT." Open access course materials are a forerunner to expanding education-related content.

Open access to research and course content is the precursor of the next major education movement and development, OA textbooks. The rising cost of textbooks and student dissatisfaction with purchasing a required textbook to read only a chapter or minimally updated text has driven students, faculty, and institutions to consider and act on alternatives. Massive open online courses (MOOCs) are free education opportunities provided through various platforms and embraced by notable research universities: edX (Duke, Princeton, and Stanford Universities), Coursera (MIT, Harvard, U of Texas system), and Udacity (San Jose) (*http://ucsd.libguides.com/content.php?pid=403885&sid=330 6405*).

*The Chronicle Review* (March, 2013) featured a thought-provoking article with reference to the free MOOC opportunities abounding primarily in non-public universities with a greater revenue stream that could interfere with the existing traditional college income flow. The students who attend MOOCs may not have "the bulk of scholarly research freely available [that] could transform the possibilities of education advancement, scientific discovery, and public engagement with academic work" (Mittell, 2013: para. 6). University policies that support open research broaden the reach and impact of scholarly materials having the ability to reduce or eliminate the "disconnect between the rhetoric of MOOCs and open-access policies" (Mittell, 2013: para. 7) (*http://chronicle.com/article/ The-Real-Digital-Change-Agent/137589/*).

## Open textbook content

The Open Access Textbooks Project (OATP) (*http://www. openaccesstextbooks.org/*) funded by a grant from the Fund for the Improvement of Postsecondary Education (FIPSE) (*http://www. openaccesstextbooks.org/*), is a two-year project building on lessons learned in open textbook endeavors across the US and "seeks to create a collaborative community to further sustainable implementation of open textbooks." The Orange Grove repository, listed on the OATP site among other resources, is Florida's Digital Repository focused on open and global educational resources, including open textbooks (*http:// florida.theorangegrove.org/og/access/home.do*). Since 1997, MERLOT (Multimedia Educational Resource for Learning Online Teaching) has offered peer-reviewed online teaching and learning materials, encouraging sharing advice and expertise about education with expert colleagues and recognition for contributions to quality education (*http://www.merlot. org/merlot/index.htm*). Library IR collection policies may encompass highlighting teaching modules, textbooks, chapters, experiments, exercises, labs, and other types of faculty teaching materials that can be deposited in an academy's repository, benefiting local students and incorporated into the global sharing of open resources.

The University of Massachusetts, Amherst's Provost's Office and University Libraries jointly launched the Open Education Initiative program, initially awarding eight faculty members a total of ten grants, $1,000 per course, to engage in innovative and sustainable "curricular research strategy" in spring 2011. Instructors created a variety of materials, such as streaming media from the Libraries' research databases and an open access lab manual to e-books. Another faculty took his own scholarship and published it as an open access course pack. Students can view the course pack online at no cost or purchase a printed copy for $13. It is estimated that 700 students will save a minimum of $72,000 in the 2011–12 academic year (*http://scholarworks.umass.edu/cgi/viewcontent.cgi?article=1030&context=libraries_news*) (Schaler, 2011). Current U Mass Amherst open education initiatives may be found here: *http://guides.library.umass.edu/content.php?pid=87648&sid=1714807*.

Open access to a variety of intellectual and scientific materials, course content, and textbooks, is raising expectations integral to the growth of education and scholarly content for further basic and applied research, stimulating innovation, and subsequently enriching students' academic lives, saving them money in the process.

# Summary

The recent US Open Data Policy has the potential to ensure that agencies "must adopt effective data asset portfolio management approaches" within six months of this memorandum, dated May 9, 2013 (*http://www.whitehouse.gov/sites/default/files/omb/memoranda/2013/m-13-13.pdf*). In addition, awarded public research funds will share the results to discover new findings and continually build upon existing knowledge. Archiving small and medium datasets, where possible in an institutional repository, is an advantageous step toward further use and additional discoveries. Librarians and faculty with their unique and complementary skill sets have the opportunity to collaborate in the data curation and management process. Additionally, open textbook scholarship is evolving to engage faculty in creating open educational resources (OERs) to save students having to purchase expensive textbooks.

# References

Arlitsch, K. & O'Brien, P. (2011). *Search engine optimization (SEO) for digital repositories*. Presented at the Coalition for Networked Information, Spring Forum, San Diego, CA. Retrieved from *http://content.lib.utah.edu/cdm4/item_viewer.php?CISOROOT=/ir-main& CISOPTR=60502*

Arnold, D. & Fowler, K. (2011). Nefarious numbers. *American Mathematical Society. Notices of the AMS, 58*(3), 434–7. Retrieved from *http://www.ams.org/notices/201103/rtx110300434p.pdf*

Association of American Universities (2011). About AAU. Retrieved from *http://www.aau.edu/about/default.aspx?id=58*

Association of Research Libraries (2009). ARL statement to scholarly publishers on the global economic crisis. Retrieved from *http://www.arl.org/bm~doc/economic-statement-2009.pdf*

Averkamp, S. & Lee, J. (2009). Repurposing ProQuest metadata for batch ingesting ETDs into an institutional repository. *Code{4}Lib Journal, 7*. Retrieved from *http://ir.uiowa.edu/lib_pubs/38/*

Baldwin, V. (2010). Open access availability of publications of faculty in three engineering disciplines. ASEE Annual Conference and Exposition, Conference Proceedings. Retrieved from *http://digitalcommons.unl.edu/cgi/viewcontent.cgi?article=1068&context=library_talks*

Bankier, J.G. & Smith, C. (2010). Repository collection policies: Is a liberal and inclusive policy helpful or harmful? *Australian Academic and Research Libraries, 41*(4), 245–59. Retrieved from *http://works.bepress.com/courtney_a_smith/7/*

Baudoin, P. & Branschofsky, M. (2004). Implementing an institutional repository: The DSpace experience at MIT. *Science and Technology Libraries, 24*(1/2), 31–45. Retrieved from *http://dspace.mit.edu/handle/1721.1/26699*

bepress™ (2009). Open access grad scholarship draws wide readership. *Digital Commons Subscriber Newsletter*, 1–4. Retrieved from *http://digitalcommons.bepress.com/newsletters/2/*

Blythe, E. & Chachra, V. (2005, September/October). The value proposition in institutional repositories. *Educause Review: New Horizons*, 76–7. Retrieved from *http://net.educause.edu/ir/library/pdf/ERM0559.pdf*

Bollen, J., Van de Sompel, H., Hagberg, A., & Chute, R. (2009). A principal component analysis of 39 scientific impact measures. *PLoS ONE*, 4(6). Retrieved from *http://www.plosone.org/article/info:doi/10.1371/journal.pone.0006022*

Bonn, M. (2010). Experimenting with the open access monograph. *College & Research Libraries News*, 71(8). Retrieved from *http://crln.acrl.org/content/71/8/436.full*

Bosch, S., Henderson, K., & Klusendorf, H. (2011). Periodicals price survey 2011: Under pressure, times are changing. *Library Journal*. Retrieved from *http://www.libraryjournal.com/lj/ljinprintcurrentissue/890009-403/periodicals_price_survey_2011_.html.csp*

Bourg, C., Coleman, R., & Erway, R. (2009). *Support for the research process: An academic library manifesto*. Report produced by OCLC Research. Retrieved from *http://www.oclc.org/research/publications/library/2009/2009-07.pdf*

Branin, J. (2011). Editorial: *College & Research Libraries* goes fully open access. *College & Research Libraries*, 72(2), 108–9. Retrieved from *http://crl.acrl.org/content/72/2/108.short*

Brown, J. & Sadler, K. (2010). Vision, impact, success: Mandating electronic theses. Case studies of e-theses mandates in practice in the UK higher education sector, *UCL Discovery*, 1–16. Retrieved from *http://eprints.ucl.ac.uk/116947/*

Buehler, M. (2010a). Collaborating with faculty to "start up" an open access journal. Poster session presented at the annual meeting of the American Library Association, Washington, DC. Retrieved from *http://digitalcommons.library.unlv.edu/libfacpresentation/16/*

Buehler, M. (2010b). Developing repository collections – the benefits matter most [presentation slides], Digital Commons® webinar presentation. Retrieved from *http://digitalcommons.bepress.com/repositoryresearch/8/*

Buehler, M. (2011). Engaging your campus in utilizing institutional repositories [presentation slides], ALCTS webinar presentation. Retrieved from *http://digitalcommons.library.unlv.edu/libfacpresentation/40/*

Buehler, M. & Boateng, A. (2005). The evolving impact of institutional repositories on reference librarians. *Reference Services Review*, 33(3), 291–300. Retrieved from *http://digitalcommons.library.unlv.edu/lib_articles/7/*

BusinessDictionary.com, Diffusion of innovation – see *http://www.businessdictionary.com/definition/diffusion-of-innovation.html*

Canadian Association of Research Libraries (2012). Retrieved December 4, 2012, from *http://carl-abrc.ca/en/scholarly-communications/resources-for-authors.html*

Carr, L. (2006, March 9). Use of navigational tools in a repository. American Scientist Open Access Forum listserv. Message posted to *http://listserver.sigmaxi.org/sc/wa.exe?A2=ind06&L=american-scientist-open-access-forum&D=1&F=Pl&P=16792*

Carr, L. & Brody, T. (2007). Size isn't everything: Sustainable repositories as evidenced by sustainable deposit profiles. *D-Lib Magazine*, 13(7/8). Retrieved from *http://www.dlib.org/dlib/july07/carr/07carr.html*

Carr, L. & Harnad, S. (2005). *Keystroke economy: A study of the time and effort involved in self-archiving*, Technical Report, ECS, University of Southampton. Retrieved from *http://eprints.ecs.soton.ac.uk/10688*

Cassella, M. (2010). Institutional repositories: An internal and external perspective on the value of IRs for researchers' communities. *Liber Quarterly*, 20(2), 210–23. Retrieved from *http://liber.library.uu.nl/index.php/lq/article/view/7989*

Chesbrough, H. & Rosenbloom, R. (2002). The role of the business model in capturing value from innovation: Evidence from Xerox Corporation's technology spin-off companies. *Industrial and Corporate Change*, 11(3), 529–55.

Chronicle of Higher Education (2011, December). HathiTrust defendants respond to authors guild lawsuit, *The Ticker*. Retrieved from *http://chronicle.com/blogs/ticker/hathitrust-defendants-respond-to-authors-guild-lawsuit/38805*

CIBER Research Ltd (2011). *Stage 2 Final Report. The Journal Usage Factor: Exploratory Data Analysis*, 35. Retrieved from *http://www.ciber-research.eu/download/20110527-The_Journal_Usage_Factor.pdf*

Clement, R. (2011). Library and university press integration: A new vision for university publishing. *Journal of Library Administration*, 51(5–6), 507–28. Retrieved from *http://digitalcommons.usu.edu/lib_pubs/104*

Cloonan, M. & Dove, J. (2005). Do digital libraries violate the third law? *Library Journal*, 6(1), 58. Retrieved from *http://www.libraryjournal.com/article/CA512179.html*

Coonin, B. & Younce. L. (2009). *Publishing in open access journals in the social sciences and humanities: who's doing it and why.* Presented at the ACRL Fourteenth National Conference, Seattle, WA.

Connell, T. & Cetwinski, T. (2010). The impact of institutional repositories on technical services. *Technical Services Quarterly*, 27(4), 331–46. Retrieved from *https://kb.osu.edu/dspace/bitstream/handle/1811/38978/Impact_of_IRs_on_TS_KB_Preprint20090127.pdf?sequence=1*

Cornell University Library, Project Euclid (2011). Retrieved from *http://projecteuclid.org/DPubS?Service=UI&version=1.0&verb=Display&handle=euclid&page=about&aboutPage=about_subscriptionPlans&aboutArea=librarians*

Cornell University Library, Data Working Group (2008). Digital research data curation: Overview of issues, current activities, and opportunities for the Cornell University Library. *A Report of the CUL Data Working Group.* Retrieved from *http://ecommons.cornell.edu/handle/1813/10903*

Covey, D. (2013, June). Publishers and universities respond to the OSTP mandate. Retrieved from *http://works.bepress.com/cgi/viewcontent.cgi?article=1088&context=denise_troll_covey*

Crow, R. (2002). The case for institutional repositories: A SPARC position paper. *ARL Bimonthly Report*, 223(2). Retrieved from *http://works.bepress.com/ir_research/7*

Cullen, R. & Chawner, B. (2010). Institutional repositories: Assessing their value to the academic community. *Performance Measurement and Metrics*, 11(2), 131–47.

Davidson, M., Dove, L., & Weltz, J. (1999). Mental models and usability. *Cognitive Psychology*, 404(1). Retrieved from *http://www.lauradove.info/reports/mental%20models.htm*

Davies, S. (2011). *Analysis of chemists' and economists' survey on open access.* Commissioned by the JISC Research Communications Strategy Project at the Centre for Research Communications, University of Nottingham, pp. 1–10. Retrieved from *http://crc.nottingham.ac.uk/projects/rcs/Chemists&Economists_Analysis-Steve_Davies.pdf*

Davis, P. (2011, September). The journal usage factor – think locally, act locally. Message posted to the Scholarly Kitchen *http://wp.me/pcvbl-5Hl*

Devakos, R. & Toth-Waddell, A. (2007). Ontario government documents repository D-Space pilot project. *OCLC Systems and Services*, 24(1), 40–7.

Diab, P. (2011, September, 28). Transitioning project managers. Message posted to *http://philipdiab.com/2011/09/pmtransition/*

Digital scholarship.org. (2011). *Weblogs.* Retrieved October 24, 2011, from *http://digital-scholarship.org/irb/irb.html*

Directory of Open Access Repositories (2011). *Open access repository types – worldwide.* Retrieved from *http://www.opendoar.org/onechart. php?cID=&ctID=&rtID=&clID=&lID=&potID=&rSoftWareName =&search=&groupby=rt.rtHeading&orderby=Tally%20DESC&char ttype=pie&width=600&height=300&caption=Open%20Access%20 Repository%20Types%20-%20Worldwide*

Elder, C. (2004). Shiyali Ramamrita Ranganathan. Retrieved from Library, Archival and Information Studies at the University of British Columbia website *http://www.slais.ubc.ca/courses/libr517/03-04-wt2/ projects/ranganathan/contri.htm#five*

Farley, L. (2011). University of California (UC) Libraries expand access to orphan works. UC Newsroom, Retrieved August 21, 2011, from *http://www.universityofcalifornia.edu/news/article/26172*

Fernandez, L., Nariani, R., & Salmon, M. (2010). Promoting public access policies: A new role for librarians. *Sci-Tech News*, 64(3), 1–15. Retrieved from *http://jdc.jefferson.edu/scitechnews/vol64/iss3/5/*

Foster, N. & Gibbons, S. (2005). Understanding faculty to improve content recruitment for institutional repositories. *D-Lib Magazine*, 11(1). Retrieved from *http://www.dlib.org/dlib/january05/foster/ 01foster.html*

Galayda, J. & Yudelson, J. (2010). Benchmarking campus sustainability. *Campus Sustainability: Peer Selection and Benchmarking.* Retrieved from *http://www.greenbuildconsult.com/pdfs/benchmarking.pdf*

Gargouri, Y., Hajjem, C., Larivière, V., Gingras, Y., Carr, L., Brody, T., & Harnad, S. (2010). Self-selected or mandated, open access increases citation impact for higher quality research. *PLoS ONE*, 5(10): e13636. Retrieved from *http://www.plosone.org/article/info:doi/10.1371/ journal.pone.0013636*

Garritano, J. & Carlson, J. (2009). A subject librarian's guide to collaboration on e-science projects. *Issues in Science and Technology Librarianship*, 57. Retrieved from *http://www.istl.org/09-Spring/ refereed2.html*

George, M., Rowlands, D., & Kastle, B. (2003). *What Is Lean Six Sigma.* New York: McGraw-Hill Professional Series.

Gierveld, H. (2006). Considering a marketing and communications approach for an institutional repository. *Ariadne*, 49. Retrieved from *http://www.ariadne.ac.uk/issue49/gierveld/*

Gilman, I. & Kunkel, M. (2010). From passive to pervasive: Changing perceptions of the library's role through intra-campus partnerships. *Collaborative Librarianship*, 2(1), 20–30. Retrieved from *http://commons.pacificu.edu/cgi/viewcontent.cgi?article=1006&context=libfac*

Gold, A. (2007). Cyber-infrastructure, data, and libraries, Part 2: Libraries and the data challenge: Roles and actions for libraries. *D-Lib Magazine*, 13(9/10), 1–13. Retrieved from *http://www.dlib.org/dlib/september07/gold/09gold-pt2.html*

Gresehover, B., Behles, R., Douglas, M., Fernández, P., & Pinho, T. (2008). An institutional repository for the UMB [University of Maryland, Baltimore] campus: A white paper. Retrieved from *http://archive.hshsl.umaryland.edu/handle/10713/7*

Gutam, S. (2011, June 20). India's NARS should accelerate open access movement in agriculture research for development. Message posted to *http://aims.fao.org/community/open-access/blogs/indias-nars-should-accelerate-open-access-movement-agriculture-research-*

Gutam, S., Mishra, A., Pandey, P., Chandrasekharan, H., & Aneej, G. (2010). Need of open access repositories for NARS in India. *Current Science*, 98(12). Retrieved from *http://www.ias.ac.in/currsci/25jun2010/1564.pdf*

Hahn, K. (2009). Introduction: Positioning liaison librarians for the 21st century. *Research Library Issues: A Bimonthly Report from ARL, CNI, and SPARC*, RLI 265(1–2). Retrieved from *http://www.arl.org/resources/pubs/rli/archive/rli265.shtml*

Harle, J. (2011). Breaking down the barriers: Building an African working group on research information. *INASP Newsletter*, 46, Winter, 1–2.

Harnad, S. (2006, August 5). Open access archivangelism. The immediate-deposit/optional-access (ID/OA) mandate: Rationale and model. Retrieved from *http://openaccess.eprints.org/index.php?/archives/71-guid.html*

Harnad, S. (2010). No-fault peer-review charges: The price of selectivity need not be access denied or delayed. *D-Lib Magazine*, 16(7/8). Retrieved from *http://www.dlib.org/dlib/july10/harnad/07harnad.html*

Harnad, S. (2011a). Open access is a research community matter, not a publishing community matter. *Lifelong Learning in Europe*, XVI(2), 117–18. Retrieved from *http://eprints.ecs.soton.ac.uk/22403*

Harnad, S. (2011b). Open access to research: Changing researcher behavior through university and funder mandates. *JEDEM Journal of Democracy and Open Government*, 3(1), 33–41. Retrieved from *http://eprints.ecs.soton.ac.uk/22401/*

Hatcher, A. (2002). *Algebraic topology*. Cambridge: Cambridge University Press. Retrieved from *http://www.math.cornell.edu/~hatcher/AT/ATpage.html*

Herb, U. (2010). Alternative impact measures for open access documents? An examination of how to generate interoperable usage information from distributed open access services. Presented at the World Library and Information Congress: 76TH IFLA General Conference and Assembly. Retrieved from *http://conference.ifla.org/past/2010/72-herb-en.pdf*

Hitchcock, S., Brody, T., Hey, J., & Carr, L. (2007). Digital preservation service provider models for institutional repositories towards distributed services. *D-Lib Magazine*, 13(5/6). Retrieved from *http://www.dlib.org/dlib/may07/hitchcock/05hitchcock.html*

Hitchcock, S., Bergmark, D., Brody, T., Gutteridge, C., Carr, L., Hall, W., & Harnad, S. (2002). Open citation linking: The way forward. *D-Lib Magazine*, 8(10). Retrieved from *http://www.dlib.org/dlib/october02/hitchcock/10hitchcock.html*

HM Government (2011). Making open data real: A public consultation. 1–57. Retrieved from *http://data.gov.uk/sites/default/files/Open%20Data%20consultation%20August%202011.pdf*

Honn, J. (2011, March 6). Open peer review. Message posted to *http://www.michaeljkramer.net/issuesindigitalhistory/blog/?p=70*

Horová, I. & Mach, J. (2009). National repositories of ETDs and grey literature in the Czech Republic. CASLIN 2009: 16th International Seminar on Institutional Online Repositories and Open Access. Retrieved from *http://www.knihovna.zcu.cz/Caslin/Caslin09.pdf*

Horwood, L., Sullivan, S., Young, E., & Garner, J. (2004). OAI-compliant institutional repositories and the role of library staff. *Library Management*, 25(4/5), 170–6. Retrieved from *http://dtl.unimelb.edu.au/R/8SY29T5B6NS983XKN73KP2AXMQJNHJ177PEAH26EI6V5EEQ7-00262?func=dbin-jump-full&object_id=65912&local_base=GEN01&pds_handle=GUEST*

Howard, J. (2011). Universities join together to support open access policies. *Chronicle of Higher Education: Wired Campus*. Retrieved from *http://chronicle.com/blogs/wiredcampus/universities-join-together-to-support-open-access-policies/32632*

Hubbard, B., Hodgson, A., & Fuchs, W. (2010). Current issues in research communications: Adding value and sharing research. *Research Communications Strategy: 3rd Report to JISC*, 1–16. Retrieved from *http://eprints.nottingham.ac.uk/1456/1/RCS_December_2010.pdf*

Huffine, R. (2010). Value of grey literature to scholarly research in the digital age [PowerPoint slides]. Retrieved from *http://www.elsevier. com/framework_librarians/Docs/2010RichardHuffine.pdf*

Jantz, R. & Wilson, M. (2008). Institutional repositories: Faculty deposits, marketing, and the reform of scholarly communication. *Journal of Academic Librarianship*, 34(3), 186–95.

Jaschik, S. (2011, June 2). Rejecting double blind. *Inside Higher Ed News*. Message posted to *http://www.insidehighered.com/ news/2011/05/31/american_economic_association_abandons_double_ blind_journal_reviewing*

Jenkins, B., Breakstone, E., & Hixson, C. (2005). Content in, content out: The dual roles of the reference librarian in institutional repositories. *Reference Services Review*, 3(3), 1–16. Retrieved from *https:// scholarsbank.uoregon.edu/xmlui/handle/1794/704*

Jensen, M. (2007). The new metrics of scholarly authority. *Chronicle of Higher Education: The Chronicle Review*. Retrieved from *http:// chronicle.com/article/The-New-Metrics-of-Scholarly/5449*

JIME (2011). Peer-review process. *Journal of Interactive Media in Education*. Retrieved from *http://jime.open.ac.uk/jime/about/editorial Policies#peerReviewProcess*

Jinha, A. (2010). Article 50 million: An estimate of the number of scholarly articles in existence. *Learned Publishing*, 23(3), 258–63. Retrieved from *http://www.ingentaconnect.com/content/alpsp/lp/2010/ 00000023/00000003/art00008*

Johnston, L. (2010). User-needs assessment of the research cyber-infrastructure for the 21st century. Presented at the International Association of Scientific and Technological University Libraries, 31st Annual Conference, 1–16. Retrieved from *http://docs.lib.purdue.edu/ iatul2010/conf/day1/5*

Jones, R. & Nixon, W. (2004). A report to JISC of the DSpace Users Group meeting, March 10–11, 2004. Retrieved from *https://dspace. gla.ac.uk/bitstream/1905/194/1/dugmarch04final.pdf*

Joseph, H. (2012). SPARC: Sponsors and supporters back away from Research Works Act. Retrieved from *http://www.arl.org/sparc/media/ sponsors-and-supporters-back-away-from-research-wo.shtml*

Kar, A. (2011). Marketing mix – the 4 P's of social marketing. Retrieved June 9, 2013, from *http://www.social-marketing.com/Whatis.html*

Kelley, M. (2011). Librarians at University of Minnesota make an impact with data management program. *LibraryJournal.com*. Retrieved from *http://www.libraryjournal.com/lj/home/891540-264/librarians_at_ university_of_minnesota.html.csp*

Kirchner, J. (2009). Scholarly Communications: Planning for the integration of liaison librarian roles. *Association of Research Libraries, RLI 265*, 22. Retrieved from *http://publications.arl.org/rli265/23*.

Kotler, P., Armstrong, G., Saunders, J., & Wong, V. (1999). *Principles of marketing* (2nd European edn). Harlow: Prentice Hall.

Kuchma, I. (2011). Results of the SOAP Survey: A preliminary overview of the situation in EIFL partner countries (EIFL: knowledge without boundaries). Retrieved July 31, 2011, from *http://www.eifl.net/system/files/201102/soap_survey_results_eifl.pdf*

Laakso, M., Welling, P., Bukvova, H., Nyman, L., Björk, B., & Hedlund, T. (2011). The development of open access journal publishing from 1993 to 2009, *PLoS ONE*, 6(6). Retrieved from *http://www.plosone.org/article/info:doi/10.1371/journal.pone.0020961*

Lean Enterprise Institute (2009). Principles of lean. Retrieved from *http://www.lean.org/WhatsLean/Principles.cfm*

Lewis, D. (2008). Library budgets, open access, and the future of scholarly communication: Transformations in academic publishing. *C&RL News*, 69(5), 271–3. Retrieved from: *http://crln.acrl.org/content/69/5/271.full.pdf*

Lippincott, J. & Lynch, C. (2010). ETDs and graduate education: Programs and prospects. *Research Library Issues: A Bimonthly Report from ARL, CNI, and SPARC*, 270, 6–15. Retrieved from *http://www.arl.org/resources/pubs/rli/archive/rli270.shtml*

Luther, J. & Kelly, M. (2011). The next generation of DISCO. *Library Journal*, LJ Series: The Big Tools, pp. 66–71. Retrieved from *http://ce.uoregon.edu/aim/ElecInfoU11/LutherKellyNextGenDiscovery.pdf*

Lynch, C. (2003). Institutional repositories: Essential infrastructure for scholarship in the digital age. *Association of Research Libraries*, 61(7). Retrieved from *http://www.arl.org/resources/pubs/br/br226/br226ir.shtml*

Lynch, C. (2010). Imagining a university press system to support scholarship in the digital age. *Journal of Electronic Publishing*, 13(2). Retrieved from *http://quod.lib.umich.edu/j/jep/3336451. 0013.207?rgn=main;view=fulltext*

McMillen, P. & Tucker, C. (2010). Advocating for scholarship: Why open access? *Journal for International Counselor Education*, 2(1), 19–41. Retrieved from *http://digitalcommons.library.unlv.edu/jice/vol2/iss1/2/*

Malenfant, K. (2010). Leading change in the system of scholarly communication: A case study of engaging liaison librarians for outreach to faculty. *C&RL News*, 71(64). Retrieved from *http://crl.acrl.org/content/71/1/63.full.pdf*

Marcus, A. (2010). My data, your data, our data. *Wall Street Journal*. Retrieved from *http://online.wsj.com/article/SB100014240527487036 25304575116512173339800.html*

Mathur, V. & Sharma, A. (2009). Impact factor and other standardized measures of journal citation: A perspective. *Indian Journal of Dental Research*, 20(1), 81–5. Retrieved from *http://www.ijdr.in/text.asp?2009/20/1/81/49072*

Mee, N., Clewes, D., & Read, A. (2004). Effective implementation of a marketing communications strategy for kerbside recycling: A case study from Rushcliffe, UK. *Resources, Conservation & Recycling*, 42(1), 1–26.

Mele, S. (2011, June 30). Job opportunities at CERN – two developers for the INSPIRE digital library/subject repository. Message posted to JISC-REPOSITORIES Archives electronic mailing list. Archived at *https://www.jiscmail.ac.uk/cgi-bin/webadmin?A2=JISC-EPOSITORI ES;4a7e2e93.1107*

Meloni, J. (2011). Libra: An unmediated, self-deposit, institutional repository at the University of Virginia. Presented at Open Repositories 2011 Conference, Austin, Texas. Retrieved from *http://www.slideshare.net/jcmeloni/libra*

Mittell, J. (2013, March). The real digital change agent. *Chronicle Review*. Retreived from: *http://chronicle.com/article/The-Real-Digital-Change-Agent/137589/*

Moen, W. & Singh, V. (2007, June). The Texas course redesign learning object repository. University of North Texas. Retrieved from: *http://thecblor.unt.edu/files/THECB_Phase2Proposal_wem__PUBLIC_29June2007.pdf*

Morris, C. (2010). Open access to Nobel physicists' articles through arXiv. Nobelprize.org. Retrieved August 19, 2011, from *http://www.nobelprize.org/nobel_prizes/physics/laureates/2010/*

Mukherjee, B. & Nazim, M. (2011). Open access institutional archives: A quantitative study. *DESIDOC Journal of Library and Information Technology*, 31(4), 317–24. Retrieved from *http://publications.drdo.gov.in/ojs/index.php/djlit/article/view/1112*

Mullen, L. (2011). Getting a journal indexed/cataloged in libraries. Message posted to EBSS Education and Behavior Science ALA Discussion List electronic mailing list. No archive.

Mullins, J. (2011). Integration of the press and libraries collaboration to promote scholarly communication. Presented at the ALCTS Scholarly Communication Interest Group – ALA conference, New Orleans, LA.

Retrieved from *http://connect.ala.org/files/25884/mullins_integrating_ and_managing_a_press_pdf_71969.pdf*

Mullins, J., Murray-Rust, C., Ogburn, J., Crow, R., Ivins, O., Mower, A., et al. (2011). Library publishing services: Strategies for success research report version 1.0. Scholarly Publishing and Academic Resources Coalition (SPARC), draft version for comment, 1–82. Retrieved from *http://docs.lib.purdue.edu/lib_research/136/*

Murphy, J. (2008/09). New entry tries new publishing model. *Research Information*. Retrieved from *http://www.researchinformation.info/ features/feature.php?feature_id=197*

National Science Board (2011, December). Task force on data policies committee on strategy and budget, pp. 1–13.

National Science Foundation, National Science Board (2005). Long-lived digital data collections enabling research and education in the 21st century, No. NSB-05-40. Washington, DC: National Science Board. Retrieved from *http://www.nsf.gov/pubs/2005/nsb0540/*

Netherlands National Commission for UNESCO (2011). *A global perspective on open access*. Netherlands, Amsterdam, pp. 1–3. Retrieved from *http://www.unesco.org/new/fileadmin/MULTIMEDIA/ HQ/CI/CI/pdf/themes/access_to_knowledge_societies/open_access/ en%20-%20UNESCO%20expert%20meeting%20Open%20Access %20conclusions.pdf*

Newton, M., Miller, C., & Bracke, M. (2010). Librarian roles in institutional repository data set collecting: Outcomes of a research library task force. *Collection Management*, 36(1). Retrieved from *http://docs.lib.purdue. edu/cgi/viewcontent.cgi?article=1153&context=lib_research*

OASIS (n.d.). Open access can increase sales. *Open Access Scholarly Information Sourcebook*, para. 1. Retrieved from *http://www. openoasis.org/index.php?option=com_content&view=article&id=348 &Itemid=381*

Ober, J. (2002). CDL opens online repository for working papers, *UCLA Library Staff Newsweb*, 960(1). Retrieved from *http://staff.library. ucla.edu/newsweb/news960.htm#6aOCLC (2010).*

OCLC (2010). Perceptions of libraries, 2010: Context and community. *A Report to the OCLC Membership*, 1–108. Retrieved June 10, 2011, from *http://www.oclc.org/reports/2010perceptions.htm*

OCLC (2011). FAST (Faceted Application of Subject Terminology). Retrieved from *http://www.oclc.org/research/activities/fast/default.htm*

OpenDOAR (2011). Retrieved from *http://www.opendoar.org/onechart. php?cID=&ctID=&rtID=&clID=&llID=&potID=&rSoftWareName*

*=&search=&groupby=c.cContinent&tallyby=DISTINCT%28o.oID*
*%29&orderby=Tally%20DESC&charttype=pie&width=600&height*
*=300&caption=Proportion%20of%20Repository%20Organisations*
*%20by%20Continent%20-%20Worldwide*

ORBi repository, University of Liège – see *http://orbi.ulg.ac.be/*

Palmer, C., Teffeau, L., & Newton, M. (2008). Identifying factors of success in CIC institutional repository development – Final report. Urbana-Champaign, IL. Retrieved from *http://www.ideals.illinois.edu/handle/2142/8981*

Park, E. & Richard, M. (2011). Metadata assessment in e-theses and dissertations of Canadian institutional repositories. *Electronic Library*, 29(3): 394–407.

Parsons, D., Willis, D., & Holland, J. (2011). Benefits to the private sector of open access to higher education and scholarly research. *Research Report to JISC*, 1–52. Retrieved from *http://apo.org.au/research/benefits-private-sector-open-access-higher-education-and-scholarly-research*

Phipps, S. (2001). Beyond measuring service quality: Learning from the voices of the customers, the staff, the processes, and the organization, *Library Trends*, 49(4), 635–61. Retrieved from *https://www.ideals.illinois.edu/handle/2142/8365*

Porter, M. (1985). *Competitive advantage: Creating and sustaining superior performance.* New York: Free Press.

Poynder, R. (2011a). Open access by numbers. Retrieved from *http://www.richardpoynder.co.uk/Open_Access_By_Numbers.pdf*

Poynder, R. (2011b). The OA interviews: Bernard Rentier, Rector of the University of Liège. Retrieved from *http://poynder.blogspot.com/2011/06/oa-interviews-bernard-rentier-rector-of.html*

Poynder, R. (2012). The Finch Report and its implications for the developing world. Retrieved from *http://poynder.blogspot.com/2012/07/the-finch-report-and-its-implications.html*

Primary Research Group (2011). *The survey of institutional digital repositories.* New York.

Randall, R., Clark, K., Smith, J., & Foster, N. (2008). *The next generation of academics: A report on a study conducted at the University of Rochester.* Rochester, NY: University of Rochester Libraries. Retrieved from *http://hdl.handle.net/1802/6053*

Rausing, L. (2010, March 12). Toward a new Alexandria: Imagining the future of libraries. *The New Republic*, 1–4. Retrieved from *http://www.tnr.com/article/books-and-arts/toward-new-alexandria*

Reeves, S. (2010). What's going on with ETDs in Canada and at Library and Archives Canada. Ontario University Registrar's Association Conference, 2010. Retrieved from *http://www.oura.ca/conf2010/papers/G3_Reeves_2.pdf*

Research and Graduate Education Implementation Team (UNLV) (2010). FOCUS 50–100: Research and graduate education implementation team: Progress on action plan items. Retrieved from *http://planning.unlv.edu/updates/2010/50-100-Research-Implementation-Team%20Update-Fall-2010.pdf*

Research Councils UK (2013, April). RCUK Policy on Open Access and Supporting Guidance. Retrieved from *http://www.rcuk.ac.uk/documents/documents/RCUKOpenAccessPolicy.pdf*

ROARMAP (Registry of Open Access Repositories Mandatory Archiving Policies) – see *http://roarmap.eprints.org/*

Robinson, M. (2007). Institutional repositories: Staff and skills requirements. SHERPA document. Retrieved from *http://www.sherpa.ac.uk/documents/sherpaplusdocs/notts-Repository%20Staff%20and%20Skills.pdf*

Roosendaal, H., Huibers, T., Geurts, P., & van der Vet, P. (2003). Changes in the value chain of scientific information: Economic consequences for academic institutions. *Online Information Review*, 27(2), 120–8.

Sale, A. (2007). The patchwork mandate. *D-Lib Magazine*, 13(1/2). Retrieved from *http://www.dlib.org/dlib/january07/sale/01sale.html*

Salo, D. (2009). Name authority control in institutional repositories. *Cataloging and Classification Quarterly*, 47(3/4), 249–61.

Schaler, L., (2011, Fall/Winter). Taking a bite out of textbook costs. *UMass Amherst Friends of the Library Newsletter*, 42(4), 1–15. Retrieved from *http://scholarworks.umass.edu/cgi/viewcontent.cgi?article=1030&context=libraries_news*

Schonfeld, R. & Housewright, R. (2010). Faculty survey 2009: Key strategic insights for libraries, publishers, and societies, April 7. Ithaka S+R. Retrieved from *http://www.ithaka.org/ithaka-s-r/research/faculty-surveys-2000-2009/Faculty%20Study%202009.pdf*

Schreiner, A. & Friedman, H. (1985). Introduction to compiler construction with UNIX. Retrieved from *https://ritdml.rit.edu/handle/1850/8122*

Seaman, D. (2011). Discovering the information needs of humanists when planning an institutional repository. *D-Lib Magazine*, 17(3/4). Retrieved from *http://www.dlib.org/dlib/march11/seaman/03seaman.html*

Senge, P. (1994). *The fifth discipline fieldbook: Strategies and tools for building a learning organization* (1st edn). New York: Currency, Doubleday.

Shapiro, L. (2005). *Establishing and publishing an online peer-reviewed journal: Action plan, resourcing, and costs.* Public Knowledge Project: University of British Columbia. Retrieved from *http://pkp.sfu.ca/files/OJS_Project_Report_Shapiro.pdf*

Shepherd, P. (2011). The journal usage factor project: Results, recommendations and next steps. COUNTER Online Project. Retrieved from *http://www.projectcounter.org/documents/Journal_Usage_Factor_extended_report_July.pdf*

SHERPA/RoMEO: Summary of copyright permissions – see *http://www.sherpa.ac.uk/romeo/statistics.php?la=en*.

Schulenberger, D. (2007, October). University research publishing or distribution strategies? Presented at the 151st ARL Membership Meeting, Washington, DC. Retrieved from *http://www.arl.org/bm~doc/mm-f07-shulenburger.pdf*

Shulenburger, D. (2008, November). Presented at the SPARC Digital Repositories Meeting 2008: Closing keynote for the Association of Research Libraries (ARL). Retrieved from *http://www.arl.org/sparc/bm~doc/shulen_trans.pdf*

Singapore Management University Institutional Repository (2008). Presentation by the Li Ka Shing Library, Singapore Management University, for the Library Policy Committee. Retrieved from *http://library.smu.edu.sg/aboutus/IR_Concept_Approach_LPC_Sep29.pdf*

Smith, R. (2011, August 3). KU establishes first coalition of institutions practicing open access. KU (University of Kansas) news release. Retrieved from *http://www.news.ku.edu/2011/august/3/openaccess.shtml*

Southwick, S. (2006). The Brazilian electronic theses and dissertations digital library: Providing open access for scholarly information, *Ciência da Informação, 35*(2), 103–10. Retrieved from *http://dx.doi.org/10.1590/S0100-19652006000200011*

SPARC (2011a). Retrieved from *http://www.arl.org/sparc/advocacy/frpaa/index.shtml*

SPARC (2011b). Retrieved from *http://www.arl.org/sparc/advocacy/frpaa/highered.shtml*

Starratt, J. (2010). WSU Libraries collection development decisions: Calendar 2010. Retrieved from Washington State University Libraries, Collection Development and Scholarly Communication website *http://www.wsulibs.wsu.edu/collections/cancelcover.html*

Steele, B. (2011, September). The arXiv at 20: A global resource. *ChronicleOnline* (Cornell University). Retrieved from *http://www. news.cornell.edu/stories/Sept11/arXiv20th.html*

Suber, P. (2006a). *SPARC Open Access Newsletter*, Issue No. 99. Retrieved from *http://www.earlham.edu/~peters/fos/newsletter/07-02-06.htm#etds*

Suber, P. (2006b). *SPARC Open Access Newsletter*, Issue No. 100. Retrieved from *http://www.earlham.edu/~peters/fos/newsletter/08-02-06.htm#dual*

Suber, P. (2007). *Open Access News*. Retrieved from *http://www.earlham. edu/~peters/fos/2007/09/nsf-jisc-workshop-report-endorses-oa.html*

Suber, P. (2009a). *Open Access News*. Retrieved from *http://www. earlham.edu/~peters/fos/2009/10/oa-mandate-at-us-national-lab.html*

Suber, P. (2009b). Timeline of the open access movement. Retrieved from *http://www.earlham.edu/~peters/fos/timeline.htm*

Suber, P. (2010). *Open access overview*. Retrieved from *http://www. earlham.edu/%7Epeters/fos/overview.htm*

Suber, P. (2011). Networked Digital Library of Theses and Dissertations: Open access for ETDs. Retrieved from *http://www.ndltd.org/resources/ publishers/open-access-for-etds*

Suber, P. (2013). *Open Access*. Cambridge, MA: MIT Press.

Swan, A. (2006). The culture of open access: Researchers' views and responses. In Neil Jacobs (ed.), *Open access: Key strategic, technical and economic aspects*. Oxford: Chandos Information Professional Series. Retrieved from *http://eprints.ecs.soton.ac.uk/12428/1/asj7.pdf*

Swan, A. (2008). The business of digital repositories. In K. Weenink, L. Waaijers, & K. van Godtsenhoven (eds), *In a driver's guide to European repositories* (pp. 15–43). Netherlands: Amsterdam University Press. Retrieved from *http://eprints.ecs.soton.ac.uk/14455/*

Swan, A. (2010). The open access citation advantage: Studies and results to date. Truro, UK: Key Perspectives Ltd. Retrieved from *http://eprints. ecs.soton.ac.uk/18516/*

Taylor, M. (2012). Academic publishers have become the enemies of science. *theguardian*. Retrieved from *http://www.guardian.co.uk/ science/2012/jan/16/academic-publishers-enemies-science*

Tennant, R. (2004). Bitter harvest: Problems and suggested solutions for OAI-PMH data and service providers. Retrieved from *http://roytennant. com/bitter_harvest.html*

Ulrich's Serials Analysis System™ – see *http://www.ulrichsweb.com/ ulrichsweb/usasfaq.asp* and *http://www.istl.org/03-summer/databases. html*

University of Nevada, Las Vegas (2010). UNLV–NSHE planning report (2011–2014). Retrieved from *http://planning.unlv.edu/updates/UNLV-NSHE-Planning-Report.2011-2014.pdf*

University of Nevada, Las Vegas (2010, October). FOCUS 50 100 Research and Graduate Education Implementation Plan: Progress on action plan items. Retrieved from *http://planning.unlv.edu/updates/2010/50-100-Research-Implementation-Team%20Update-Fall-2010.pdf.*

Van Orsdel, L. (2007). Faculty activism in scholarly communications opportunity assessment instrument. Sponsored by the Institute on Scholarly Communication: Association of Research Libraries and the Association of College & Research Libraries. Retrieved from *http://www.arl.org/bm~doc/opp.pdf*

van Wesenbeeck, A. (2011, February). Bridging the gap: OAPEN and SPARC Europe; three initiatives to promote open access monograph publishing. Presentation at the First OAPEN Conference, Berlin, Germany. Retrieved from *http://188.40.186.170/wp-content/uploads/2011/05/2011.SPARC_Eu_OAPEN_Berlin.pdf*

Vaughan, J. (2011, January). *Investigations into library web scale discovery services.* Information Technology and Libraries Preprint, pp. 1–61. Retrieved from *http://digitalscholarship.unlv.edu/cgi/view content.cgi?article=1043&context=lib_articles*

Vigen, J. (2009). Open access and repositories: A status report from the world of high-energy physics. Presentation at CASLIN: Institutional Online Repositories and Open Access Conference, pp. 381–5. Retrieved from *http://crl.du.ac.in/ical09/papers/index_files/ical-64_224_479_1_RV.pdf*

Wacha, M. & Wisner, M. (2011). Measuring value in open access repositories. *Serials Librarian,* 61(3–4), 377–88. Retrieved from *http://www.tandfonline.com/doi/pdf/*

Walker, K. (2011, June). Library–press collaboration: Partnering across and within institutional lines. Presented on the ALCTS Panel for Library–Press Collaborations, ALA Annual Meeting, New Orleans, LA. Retrieved from *http://connect.ala.org/files/25884/walker_working_with_a_press_pdf_27357.pdf*

Walters, T. (2007). Reinventing the library – how repositories are causing librarians to rethink their professional roles. *portal: Libraries and the Academy,* 7(2), 213–25. Retrieved from *http://smartech.gatech.edu/handle/1853/14421*

Way, D. (2010). The open access availability of library and information science literature. *College & Research Libraries*, 71(4), 302–9. Retrieved from *http://works.bepress.com/doug_way/2/*

Wellcome Trust – see *http://www.wellcome.ac.uk/About-us/Policy/Spotlight-issues/Open-access/index.htm*

Whittle, B. (2009). The business architecture, value streams and value chains. BPM-Institute.org. Retrieved from *http://www.bpminstitute.org/articles/article/article/the-business-architecture-value-streams-and-value-chains.html*

Wikipedia (2011a). Institute for Scientific Information. Retrieved from *http://en.wikipedia.org/wiki/Institute_for_Scientific_Information*

Wikipedia (2011b). List of academic disciplines. Retrieved from *http://en.wikipedia.org/wiki/List_of_academic_disciplines*

Wikipedia (2011c). PDF/A. Retrieved from: *http://en.wikipedia.org/wiki/PDF/A*

Wikipedia (n.d.). Data management definition. Retrieved from *http://en.wikipedia.org/wiki/Data_management*

Williams, K. (2009). A framework for articulating new library roles. *Research Library Issues: A Bimonthly Report from ARL, CNI, and SPARC*, 265(7), 3–8. Retrieved from *http://www.arl.org/resources/pubs/rli/archive/rli265.shtml*

Willinsky, J. (2009). Toward the design of an open monograph press. *Journal of Electronic Publishing*, 12(1). Retrieved from *http://quod.lib.umich.edu/cgi/t/text/text-idx?c=jep;cc=jep;rgn=main;view=text;idno=3336451.0012.103*

Wireman, B. (1998). Characteristics of change agents. *Vital Speeches of the Day*, 65(5), 152–5.

Wirth, A. (2010, June). OA policy panel: Oregon State University Libraries' policy. Presented at ALA Annual, Washington, DC. Retrieved from *http://connect.ala.org/files/25884/andrea_wirth_oapolicynotes062710_pdf_18762.pdf*

Wirth, A. & Chadwell, F. (2010). Rights well: An authors' rights workshop for librarians. *portal: Libraries and the Academy*, 10(3), 337–54. Retrieved from *http://ir.library.oregonstate.edu/xmlui/handle/1957/17099?show=full*

Yakel, E., Rieh, S., Markey, K., St Jean, B. & Yao, X. (2009, May). Secrets of success: Identifying success factors in institutional repositories, extended abstract presentation. Fourth International Conference on Open Repositories, Atlanta, Georgia. Retrieved from *http://smartech.gatech.edu/bitstream/handle/1853/28419/118-449-1-PB.pdf?sequence=2*

Ziontz, M. (2011). University of Wollongong increases discovery of data collections on ResearchOnline. Digital Commons® Subscriber Newsletter. Retrieved from *http://digitalcommons.bepress.com/newsletters/6/*

Zuber, P. (2008). A study of institutional repository holdings by academic discipline, *D-Lib Magazine*, 14(11/12). Retrieved from *http://www.dlib.org/dlib/november08/zuber/11zuber.html*

# Index